Denison150

Celebrating Untold and Under-Told Stories from Denison's First 150 Years

Authors

Dr. Mavis Anne Bryant
Donna Hord Hunt
James K. Sears
Jim Matthews
Natalie Bauman
Brian Hander

Reviewed & Edited By

Elsie McMurray Russell

Aerial views at front and back of book are from 1958 and 2022 showcasing downtown Denison and surrounding neighborhoods looking west from the Katy Depot. Photographer of the 2022 photo is Mel Hander.

Dedication

Dedicated to those past, present, and future who call Denison "home." May our city continue to move forward towards a brighter future, together.

****

To Nash Harrison Hander and Magnolia Anne Truxal, the Main Street babies, who can't read just yet but will be 50 years old when Denison celebrates her Bicentennial in 2072. May you both continue to serve your community as your parents and grandparents have. Be proud of who you are and where you come from for you are both from Denison, and Denison is a place where legends are born.

Figure 1 Nash Harrison Hander (18 mos. at left) and Magnolia Anne Truxal (15 mos. at right) proudly wearing their Denison150 shirts, 2022. Nash is the son of Brian and Erin Hander, and Magnolia is the daughter of Matt and Melanie Truxal.

Contents

Figure 2 Students from the carpentry class at Terrell High School begin construction of a picket fence around the birthplace of Dwight David Eisenhower in 1946. At this time, he was known as General Eisenhower but soon would be President of the United States. From the 1946 Terrell High School Yearbook.

Figure 3 Postcard glimpses of Denison.

Foreword

"You have for to have something in which you believe. You have got to have leaders, organization, friendships, and contacts that help you to believe that, and help you to put out your best."

-*President Dwight D. Eisenhower*

Denison, Texas is my hometown, how lucky am I!! As with any city, we have had ebbs and flows.........but have always been a city with a community spirit, like none other, and we face each circumstance, each part of our history, and do what needs to be done to move us forward! Here we are.......in our sesquicentennial year, the very best of times in our community's history and yet, the best is still to come! Our future has NEVER been brighter!

Our community is so very fortunate to have had so many dedicated historians that have captured and preserved our history! We have been blessed by Donna Hunt and Mavis Bryant who have passionately researched and penned all those things that make us unique, special, and maybe even a little quirky! These two gifted authors have served us well, and for that we are grateful! And now, as fate would have it, they are joined by a new generation historian, Brian Hander, who has an old soul when it comes to our history, but a young heart that loves our community.......almost to a fault!

In this very special edition of our community's history, Donna, Mavis and Brian are joined by contributing authors Jim Sears and Natalie Bauman as they tell newly revealed stories. These 300 pages are filled with, never before written, "firsts" in the history of our community. "Firsts" you have never heard, treasured stories about those who have made a difference, and pictures you have never seen! It is full of events and people that have made us who we are! Some of them will surprise you, amaze you, make you laugh, and others will cause you to say, "what took so long!"

This sesquicentennial edition is intended to be passed from generation to generation so we never forget those who came before us and desire that it will inspire those who are yet to come!

As for my tiny place in our history, serving as the mayor of my hometown has been among the greatest honors of my life, and I will always be grateful that I got to live my life, in Denison, Texas, my community of choice........hope it is yours!

Happy Birthday Denison......150 years young!!

Janet Gott, Mayor
City of Denison

THE LITTLE WHITE HOUSE ON THE CORNER

In the State of Texas
Down where the Bluebonnets grow,
In a little white house on the corner,
A babe was born long ago.

A babe whom was destined for greatness
Both here and over the sea,
And now has achieved highest honors
As President of our Country.

From the little white house on the corner
Where his life begun,
He has rose to be the Nation's leader
In the White House in Washington.

And the little white house on the corner
Still stands in all its pride,
Of the birth that made it famous
Throughout the countryside.

There, visitors are always welcome,
So travel down Texas way
Stop in Denison and visit Ike's birthplace
At the corner of Lamar and Day.

-Bertha Lebrecht

Figure 4 The birth-place of President Dwight David Ei-senhower in Denison, Texas.

Acknowledgements

This volume spans a great deal of Denison's rich history covering 150 years of changes that occurred throughout our community and nation during that time. This required a wealth of historical documents and references, and none of that would have been possible without the help of many individuals who donated their time, images, expertise, and stories about the rich history of our community.

Several different authors have contributed to this work and have helped publish stories that help tell the full Denison story. Many of the topics covered in this book would have never seen the light of day had it not been for the diligent research of my co-authors. I would like to recognize Natalie Bauman, Dr. Mavis Anne Bryant, Donna Hord Hunt, Jim Matthews, and James K. Sears for allowing their incredible stories to be told through this volume.

As with every work I've been able to write, I owe a huge debt of gratitude to Dr. Mavis Anne Bryant and Donna Hord Hunt. Much of the information in this book either came from research the two had conducted in the past, or historical articles that they worked so hard to save for future generations. With Donna's eye for historic research and Mavis' uncanny ability to organize information, this duo has saved more history than many of us will ever truly recognize. Denison will always know its unique history due to the tireless efforts of these outstanding women.

Elsie Russell, you are truly amazing. Thank you for editing this work, helping me through numerous typos, and for checking over every photo, all while managing your business! We are blessed to have 2 Chicks Home and Market on Main Street and I look forward to you having the longest running Main Street business in Denison's history someday!

I would also like to thank Elaine Bay for the tremendous job she has done and untold hours she has contributed to the Grayson County Texas GenWeb website. This online repository offers a wealth of knowledge, photographs, and guidance for researchers, thanks to contributors such as those listed above who work so hard to make our history available to the public.

Last, but certainly not least, to my wife, Erin, thank you for putting up with my endless amounts of notes and three ring binders spread all over the kitchen table for months on end. You keep me grounded and never fail to encourage me, no matter what project I decide to tackle. Our son, Nash, is lucky to have you as his mom as I am to have you as my partner on this amazing journey.

With nearly a century and a half of history to document, there are bound to be errors in some shape or form. For these I apologize and hope they do not detract too greatly from the history of this amazing city. Please forgive me and feel free to reach out so that I can make corrections for future editions of this work.

A section at the back of this book features an extensive chronology of Denison history. Every effort was made to record as many events that shaped Denison and the surrounding region as space would allow, and the hope is that this will have value for future generations as they seek to know more about Denison and her history.

Also included are lists of Mayors, Fire Chiefs, Police Chiefs, City Managers, and Chamber of Commerce officials who have served the City of Denison. These individuals formed part of a valuable team as our city has grown throughout the years, serving in leadership roles through many different events that would shape their city in ways they could never imagine.

This has been an incredible work to compile and has imparted a sense of community pride in me that will remain with me for the rest of my life. Despite our differences, our life paths, and our struggles, the people of Denison have always banded together to advance their community and serve one another. This unselfish devotion to each other is reflected in nearly every story told within these pages. May it represent those who came before us and inspire us to continue the work they started so long ago.

Brian C. Hander, City Councilmember Place 6
City of Denison

Figure 5 The home of Brian & Erin Hander at 321 West Gandy Street. Constructed in 1873-1874 and shown here around 1900.

Introduction

"It's true that you can't rewrite history. However, sometimes history simply was never written in the first place, and fortunate are those who have the opportunity to tell about the event at a later date."

This was the opening line from Keith Hubbard Sr. when he began documenting Denison's Golden Spike ceremony from 1873. The event had been lost to history until local historians found evidence that Denison had been the linking of the North-South rail lines in the United States. Hubbard worked diligently to make the story known and a large celebration was held in 1993 to commemorate the 120th anniversary of the event that shaped the nation.

Much like the Golden Spike, there are many other stories from Denison's past that we felt it was appropriate to shed some light on. There are stories of individuals, businesses, industries, and historic firsts that have long been unwritten but are a huge part of what makes our community unique. With the celebration of our 150th anniversary in 2022, there has never been a more appropriate time to celebrate our rich history as we look to the future and all that it holds for our community.

When Denison celebrated its Centennial in 1972, many articles were published in local newspapers and other publications that described various historical individuals, buildings, parks, and events. An additional volume, *Katy's Baby: The Story of Denison, Texas*, was written by Jack Maguire in 1991 and elaborated on our community's rich history.

However, space was limited in what could be published in a newspaper or a book, and it was certainly difficult to tell the city's founding history in great detail while also getting to include a long list of other accomplishments that have taken place. What was needed was a volume that could bridge the gap between our known history and those stories that had not been told or had only been briefly mentioned. The hope is that this work will fill that void and will become a reference to use in conjunction with earlier published stories to help tell the full Denison saga.

Denison's History

In order to fully appreciate any piece of Denison history, it is first necessary to at least have a brief understanding of the basic history of our wonderful community. Denison was founded in 1872 as the terminus for the Missouri, Kansas, & Texas Railroad. The Denison Town Company was quickly organized and was tasked with the layout of streets, blocks, and individual lots of the fledgling town.

Many of the city's early streets still bear the names given to them by this company, headed by W.B. Munson Sr. and R.S. Stevens. As designed, Main Street runs east and west, along with all other streets, and avenues run north and south.

Both Main Street and Woodard Street were designed to hold a large amount of traffic with thoroughfares that stretched eighty-feet across. This would prove invaluable in later years as sidewalks and parking spaces were added to the downtown core. Standard lots along Main were 25-feet wide and 120-feet deep, allowing for a wide variety of different structures to be built as space was needed.

Lots in the residential districts averaged fifty-feet wide and 150-feet deep, with narrower streets and city-ordained setbacks to allow for uniformity amongst the many dwellings that began appearing throughout the community. Additional structures such as churches, club-houses for social organizations, and small grocery markets were also included in these burgeoning residential areas.

Nearly 3,000 souls called Denison home by 1873 when the town was officially incorporated by the State of Texas. A bustling commercial district was quickly established along Main and Woodard Streets while less desirable businesses such as saloons and brothels were required to remain on a side street known as Skiddy Street (later changed to Chestnut Street).

A number of firsts happened during Denison's infancy that are important to note. The first free public graded school in Texas was established in Denison on February 6, 1873. The XXI Club began in 1876 with the distinction of being the first women's club in Texas to own their own building. Denison has the distinction of awarding the first high school academic letterman's honors in the United States and has the honor of being associated with hometown heroes such as T.V. Munson, President Dwight D. Eisenhower, Captain Chesley Sullenberger, and Major Jewel Butler Sr.

Although the MKT was the town's first railroad, it was followed closely by lines such as the St. Louis, San Francisco and Texas along with the Kansas, Oklahoma and Gulf railroad. Between the late 1870's to 1900, five additional rail lines connected Denison to surrounding communities. One of the rail lines included the first interurban electric line in Texas that was added in 1896 and ran between Denison and Sherman.

What began as a small town on the edge of the frontier quickly grew to become the social and economic center of the entire region. The buildings became more elaborate, including the addition of the first skyscraper in Texas when it was constructed at Main and Burnett. By 1908 Main Street was being paved with brick, one of the first thoroughfares to be paved in this manner in the entire state.

Additional schools were built, municipal facilities improved, and state football championships were even won by the Terrell High Dragons and Fighting Denison Yellow Jackets. The local economy witnessed its ups and downs, world wars were fought, and eventually the Katy Railroad, the very driving force behind Denison's founding, was sold and gone. Left to forge a new identity, Denison rallied once again to become a tourism destination defined by Lake Texoma, the longest Main Street District in Texas, and premiere public parks.

Denison, now 150 years old, stands on the precipice of explosive growth that our community has never seen before. Now more than ever is the time to celebrate our rich and vibrant past as we move forward into a brighter future than our forefathers could have ever imagined. May our next 150 years make future generations proud.

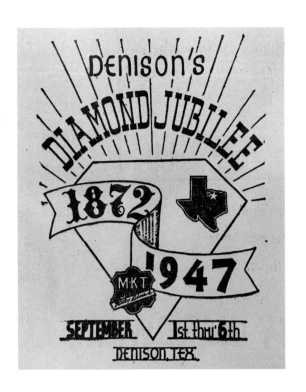

Figure 7 The official seals from the Diamond Jubilee (1947), Centennial (1972), and Sesquicentennial (2022).

This Indenture, Made this 9th day of January in the year of our Lord one thousand eight hundred and seventy four, by and between W.B. Munson of Grayson County, and State of Texas, of the first part, and The City of Denison of Grayson County, and State of Texas of the second part. Witnesseth, That the said party of the first part for and in consideration of the sum of One thousand DOLLARS, to him in hand paid, the receipt of which is hereby acknowledged has sold and by these presents does grant, bargain, sell and convey to said party of the second part his heirs, executors, administrators or assigns, all those tracts, pieces or parcels of land situate, lying and being in D.K. Millers First Addition to the City of Denison, in said County of Grayson, and known and distinguished in a map of said addition, by W. B. Munson, Civil Engineer, dated November 1st, 1872, and duly recorded in Book Y page 539 Grayson County Records, said premises being described on said map as lot number Two (2) Seven (7) Eight (8) Nine (9) Ten (10) Thirteen (13) Fourteen (14) Fifteen (15) & Sixteen (16) of Block number Nineteen (19) in said Millers First Addition

To have and to hold to the said party of the second part, heirs, executors, administrators and assigns, the above mentioned and described lots, together with the appurtenances and all the estate, right, title and interest of said party of the first part therein forever, and said W.B Munson hereby covenant and agree that at the delivery hereof he is the lawful owner of the lots above granted and conveyed and that he will Warrant and Defend the same in the quiet and peaceable possession of said party of the second part, heirs, executors, administrators or assigns forever, against all persons lawfully claiming or to claim the same.

IN WITNESS WHEREOF Said party of the first part have hereunto set his hand and seal the day and year first above written.

IN PRESENCE OF

W.B. Munson (SEAL)

(SEAL)

(SEAL)

(SEAL)

STATE OF TEXAS, ss.
COUNTY OF GRAYSON,

Before me a Notary Public in and for the County of Grayson State of Texas. on this day personally appeared W.B Munson to me well known, and known by me to be the party who signed the foregoing Deed, and who acknowledged to me that he executed the same for the uses and purposes therein mentioned, and the said having been privately examined by me seperate and apart from her said husband, and having said deed fully explained to her by me acknowledged to me that she executed the same freely and of her own accord, and without any fear or compulsion of her said husband and that she wished not to retract it.

IN TESTIMONY WHEREOF, I have hereunto set my hand and official seal this 9th day of January, 1874.

Joseph Perry (SEAL)
Notary Public

Journal Power Press Print, Denison, T.

The 1874 deed to Lots two, seven, eight, nine, ten, thirteen, fourteen, fifteen, and sixteen of Block 19 transferring ownership from W.B. Munson to The City of Denison. This is part of the land in the 700 block of West Main that would become the site of the first free public graded school in the State of Texas.

CHAPTER 1

Service to the Community: Denison's Untold Organizations

"Only a life lived for others is a life worthwhile."
-Albert Einstein

Like many communities, Denison relies on its service organizations to help benefit the public and give back to the community in ways that the city government may not be able to do. Many of these organizations serve a two-fold purpose, first to perform charitable works either by hands-on efforts or by raising funds for defined causes, and second to serve members through social functions, networking, and personal growth opportunities.

Throughout its 150-year history Denison has witnessed the creation, preservation, and dissolution of many different types of service organizations. This chapter seeks to focus on key organizations throughout Denison's past and present that have not been widely discussed in historic documents and prior written works, yet have either made significant contributions to the community or continue to have an impact on Denisonians.

The Denison Chamber of Commerce
By Brian C. Hander

The Denison Chamber of Commerce began a little over a year after Denison's founding and was first known as the Board of Trade. This group met on December 5, 1873 with twenty-five businessmen joining the organization in the hopes of promoting early-day commerce in the fledgling community.

Early officers included President J.W. Jennings, Vice President Sam Hanna, Secretary W.J. Scott, and Treasurer A.C. Terhune. The Executive Committee consisted of J.A. George, Max Grundstein, M.C. Clark, Ed Perry, and J.H. Guy. The very first project of the group was the removal of stumps and tree remains

Figure 8 The first known photo of Denison showcasing the primitive nature of streets and other public utilities.

from Main Street and other surrounding business and residential thoroughfares. The hope was that an ease of travel would make Denison the destination of choice for regional retail needs.

Figure 9 An early token of The Commercial Club (at top) alongside a photo of the Gate City Hosiery Mill (at bottom).

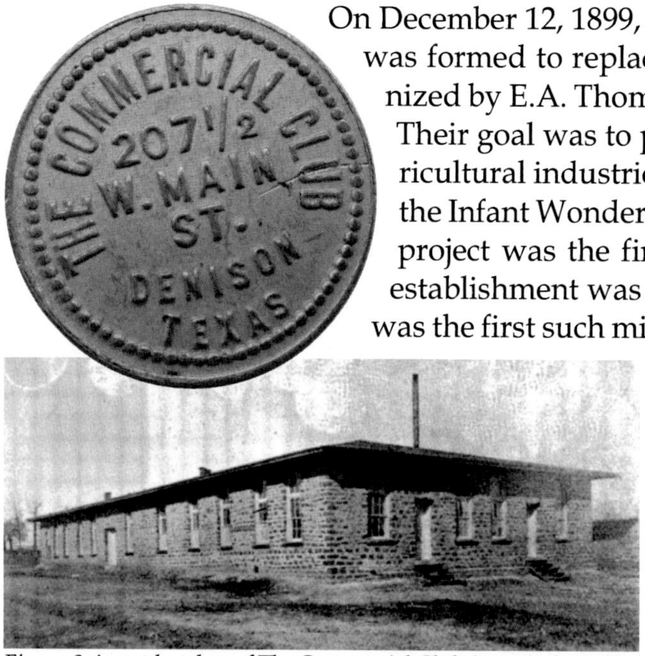

On December 12, 1899, a new club, known as the Commercial Club, was formed to replace the Board of Trade. This group was organized by E.A. Thompson and the first Secretary was F. Kohfeldt. Their goal was to promote businesses, especially Denison's agricultural industries, as viable and to help spread the word that the Infant Wonder of Texas was open for business. Their largest project was the financing of the Gate City Hosiery Mill. This establishment was lured to Denison from Atlanta, Georgia and was the first such mill in the State of Texas. Many of the Commercial Club members were stockholders in the endeavor. Another effort was navigation of the Red River via the steamboat Annie P. which is discussed in a later chapter.

Denison's Chamber of Commerce officially began on February 8, 1912, and was a product of the Commercial Club. Original officers included President P.J. Brennan, Vice President E.H. Lingo, Vice President John S. Knaur, Treasurer G.R. Love, and Secretary E.A. Clymer. An impressive 415 memberships were sold on the night of their first meeting and there was originally a board of 75 directors further narrowed down to an executive board of eleven members.

INCORPORATED UNDER THE LAWS OF THE
STATE OF TEXAS

NUMBER 165 SHARES 1

THIS IS TO CERTIFY THAT
Franz H.Kohfeldt,
IS THE OWNER OF One CERTIFICATES OF MEMBERSHIP OF THE
Denison Chamber of Commerce
OF DENISON, TEXAS
NON-TRANSFERABLE AND NON-ASSESSABLE
THIS CERTIFICATE OF MEMBERSHIP IS ISSUED IN CONSIDERATION OF A PROMISE TO PAY BY THE HOLDER HEREOF, TO THE DENISON CHAMBER OF COMMERCE, AS DUES THE SUM OF ---------One--------- DOLLARS PER MONTH FOR A TERM OF ONE YEAR FROM DATE. SAID SUM PAYABLE MONTHLY.
In Witness Whereof THE PRESIDENT AND SECRETARY HAVE HEREUNTO SUBSCRIBED THEIR NAMES AND CAUSED ITS CORPORATE SEAL TO BE HEREUNTO AFFIXED AT DENISON, TEXAS, THIS 1st DAY OF March 1912

A.E. Clymer
SECRETARY

PRESIDENT

SHARES $5.00 EACH

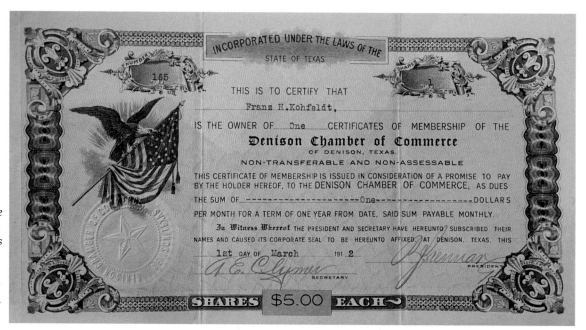

Figure 10 Certificate No. 165 of the Denison Chamber of Commerce. This membership was purchased by Franz H. Kohfeldt on March 1, 1912.

One major program undertaken in 1919 was the acquisition of land for the Katy Hospital. Denison had been vying for the hospital to serve the needs of Katy Railroad employees and their families, and in order to gain the much-needed institution a monetary incentive was needed. The Chamber created a hospital committee and successfully raised $10,000 to purchase land north of Denison that was deeded to the Katy Railroad free of charge. This gift was the driving force that led the Katy to choose Denison as the site of a state-of-the-art hospital facility.

Figure 11 Christmas decorations along Denison's serpentine, ca. 1968.

The first community Christmas decorations in Denison were purchased by the Chamber on November 30, 1925. Originally hailed as a community idea to decorate the downtown district for the holidays, it was quickly discovered that the $600 needed would not be easily found. The Chamber members stepped in and raised over $500 towards the decorations and began a yearly project that the organization provided to Denison for decades.

On December 8, 1934 Denison's most beloved holiday tradition was born, the Denison Christmas Parade. The idea came from the Chamber of Commerce as a way to welcome the Kraft-Phenix Cheese Corporation that had recently selected Denison as the headquarters of their Southwest Division. Despite wars, recessions, and even pandemics, the parade has carried on in some form or fashion and remains an unwavering community tradition.

The Chamber had its own dreams realized in December of 1945 when the organization was able to purchase a lot at 313 West Woodard from Dr. J.A. Mayes for $3,000. The only consideration that had to be made was that Dr. Mayes requested a single-story structure be erected so that it would not block the western view from his loft windows in his neighboring building.

Figure 12 The earliest known photo of the Chamber of Commerce building, ca. 1949.

Ground was officially broken on the structure on January 9, 1948, after an extensive fundraising campaign. Part of this campaign included the purchase of the lot at 315 West Woodard as well so that the building could front fifty feet on Woodard. Donald Mayes, renowned architect, was selected for the design which featured Austin stone, a brick planter bed, and modern façade, all at a cost of $26,000.

Miss Elayne Meador made history on February 28, 1950, when she became the first female to serve on the Chamber's Board of Directors. She announced to the paper that she was excited for the opportunity not just as the first female, but also at the opportunity to get to serve her community as part of such a prestigious organization.

By the end of the 1950's, the Chamber had really begun to dive in deep for future Denison civic projects. In 1958 the Chamber agreed to fund a Junior College feasibility study as well as a study for a new hospital facility.

Both of these endeavors would come to fruition in huge ways when the

Figure 13 Grayson County Junior College, now known as Grayson College, shortly after completion.

new Memorial Hospital opened in 1965 and Grayson County Junior College opened shortly after. Interestingly, the site selected for the new hospital was deeded to Denison by the Katy Hospital and was part of the original land the Chamber had purchased back in 1919. That $10,000 gift decades before was starting to pay dividends for the entire community in new ways.

By the end of the 1960's the Chamber's beautification committee began studying a unique downtown plan that had been implemented in Grand Junction, Colorado. That city had transformed their downtown district into a modern shopping mall with wide sidewalks, a curvilinear street design, and amenities such as lush planter beds and shade structures.

Figure 14 A 1968 view of the Serpentine looking west from Rusk Avenue.

Chamber members embraced this idea and a new organization, Denison Downtown Inc., was formed. Together the Chamber and DDI were able to raise funds needed for Denison to implement their own downtown project. Dubbed "Operation Vision" the project transformed downtown Denison into a picturesque scene that when opened in 1968 was lovingly called "The Serpentine".

A new branch of the Chamber, known as the Gold Coats, was founded on May 13, 1975, to serve as a welcoming force for the organization. Their goal was to serve as ambassadors to the community and attend such events as ribbon cuttings, ground breakings, parades, and other special events. The first leader of this esteemed group was Britt Swain.

In 1979 the name of the organization was changed to the Denison Area Chamber of Commerce as a way of having a more inclusive approach to businesses throughout the Texoma region. With Lake Texoma attracting more and more businesses, hotels, and industries, the Chamber wanted to signify that they were here to serve the entire area and welcomed all who wanted to be a part of moving the region forward.

In 1983, sensing a growing need for trained and engaged individuals to serve as our community's leaders, the Chamber initiated a program known as the Denison Leadership Institute. Participants in the program learn about critical issues facing Denison, Grayson County and the State of Texas while also getting to engage with organizations that work to resolve these issues. The program has graduated more than 450 alumni who have ensured the continued vitality of the Denison community by providing a solid source of motivated leaders.

Figure 15 Above, Gold Coats help open the Butler family's Best Friend's Animal Hospital, ca. 1984. Below, the Gold Coats were so popular that even young children dressed as them in local parades, ca. 1994.

Since its inception, the Chamber had served as the economic development arm for the City of Denison, raising private funds to lure business and industry to the community. However, all of this changed in 1995 when a new sales tax measure was passed that awarded a portion of the tax collected to a new entity formed solely to promote economic development. This would later become known as the Denison Development Alliance and remains next door to the Chamber as the two work closely together to create an attractive environment to prospects looking to locate their business, industry, or employees to the Denison area.

From 2020-2022 the Chamber of Commerce undertook the largest improvement program since the construction of the Mayes-era building. The exterior was restored to its original appearance which included cleaning years of grime and paint from the Austin stone and brick façade. New letters were fabricated to replicate those that originally graced the structure and now the building looks as it did when it was originally completed.

Figure 16 The newly completed Chamber of Commerce exterior restoration, fall 2019.

The interior was redesigned and updated to meet modern standards while preserving key pieces of history, such as an historic brick sign, that were found along the way. For over 110 years the Denison Chamber of Commerce has remained steadfast in their pursuit of a brighter tomorrow for Denison and their commitment to remaining in the heart of our community showcases the organizations steadfast approach to supporting local in any way possible.

The Denison Service League
By Brian C. Hander

In the fall of 1954, a series of meetings was held throughout Denison to begin an appraisal of the existing clubs and organizations available for women. This appraisal provoked serious questions as to whether a Service League could fill a need not yet met by other existing organizations. Sherman had established their Service League a year earlier and the program was providing a great service to the community. The big question that abounded was could Denison do the same?

After the pros and cons of forming a league of their own had been discussed at length, a decision was made, and a letter was written up inviting the women of Denison to a meeting on February 23, 1955. Over 100 letters were mailed, and an open invitation was published in *The Denison Herald* newspaper to reach the widest audience possible.

Seventy interested women attended the first meeting where the program consisted of a presentation by a representative of the Sherman Service League, additional orations by three members of the Dallas

Junior League, and a roundtable discussion of possible needs for the service of volunteers in the Denison community.

Of this initial group, fifty-five women signed up to attend an orientation course to be held March 21-25 to provide additional information on existing agencies such as city and county government, schools, etc. that the originators had not originally thought of before that could be in need of volunteer support.

In total, there were forty-six women who signed up as charter members. Their names can be found at the back of this book.

Mrs. W.B. (Betsy) Munson Jr., who spearheaded the movement for the League, was elected its first President on April 2, 1955, by a unanimous vote. Within one year the membership of forty-six had contributed nearly 6,400 hours of service to and for the community alongside hefty monetary donations.

Early projects of the organization including serving organizations such as the Denison Day Nursery, the Exceptional Childrens' School, and the Hive, a local teen hangout. The League members were also early promotors of the Salk Vaccine Program which provided polio preventative vaccinations to school children throughout Denison. In the first year of the organization, members also assisted with the task of administering free hearing tests to all of the school children in Denison.

To initially raise funds needed to operate and finance their projects, the League first held neighborhood game parties and a benefit silver tea. While successful, League members decided a more consistent and reliable source of funds were needed. Members wanted something that relied less on near-perfect weather conditions so that funds could be raised throughout the year.

On July 15, 1955, the organization opened what would become their largest money-making project, The Bargain Box store, where secondhand clothing, furniture, dishes and other objects could be sold. The Bargain Box was originally located above the insurance office of Mrs. B.J. Lindsay at 406 ½ West Main. Mrs. Lindsay lent the space the to the League free of charge, and Mrs. William G. Wright was the first chairman of the shop. The Bargain Box would move to a new location on North Barrett in 1962 and in July of 1963 moved to an air conditioned and central heated facility (the first for the shop) at 307 West Woodard.

By 1957, the leadership roles for the organization consisted of Mrs. K.J. Mills, President, Mrs. Donald Mayes, Vice President, Mrs. Norman

Bratcher, Recording Secretary, Mrs. Lynwood Massey, Corresponding Secretary, Mrs. Sam Harwell, Treasurer, and Mrs. Hugh Chesnutt, Assistant Treasurer.

Figure 17 Denison Service League logo ca. 2020

The League would go on to operate the Bookmobile under the leadership of Mrs. Bob Cherry, a project aimed at supplying books and magazines to patients of the Katy Employee Hospital. The League also garnered support for the Grayson Family Clinic, a counseling service clinic offered to any couple having marital difficulties. During this time, the League assisted in blood drives with the Wadley Blood Center and co-sponsored a free film on cancer with the Grayson County Medical Society and Cancer Board. The film was shown to over 1600 women, a huge feat for such a new program.

Figure 18 An early postcard view of Denison's Memorial Hospital. The Service League was incredibly supportive with both their time and funds throughout the capital campaign.

During the 1959-1960 term of Mrs. W.E. Wilcox as president of the League, a total of $1800 was donated to purchase seventeen pieces of playground equipment for five city parks. This included four climbers, five water fountains, four jungle gyms, and five basketball goals to Hopkins, Jones, East Sears Lions, Washington Street and Forest parks.

The years 1961-1962 were some of the best of the League. Under the presidency of Mrs. Sam Harwell, the League was able to donate $7,500 to the Denison Memorial Hospital Fund. The following year, the organization would pledge an additional $8,000 to the Denison Memorial Hospital fund for a snack bar and gift shop in the new facility. Ever supportive of health endeavors, the group raised enough funds to donate another $1,000 to furnish a room in the newly completed wing of the Madonna Hospital.

Within the first ten years of the organization, The League had been able to donate $20,000 to community efforts. Mrs. Ben McKinney assumed the role of President during 1964 alongside Mrs. C.B. Middleton, Vice President, Mrs. Lawrence Poole, Recording Secretary, Mrs. Charles Hoffman, Corresponding Secretary, Mrs. Kenneth Mills, Treasurer, and Mrs. David Bayless, Bargain Box Chairman.

Figure 19 The Bargain Box in 2019. The upper level houses the League's meeting space.

In June of 1999 the League released a popular cookbook called *The Dining Car: Collections & Recollections of Denison's First 125 Years*. Part storybook and part cookbook, it featured over 500 recipes paired with pictures and vignettes depicting Denison's history, the railroad town saga, amazing Munson grape milestones, and unique anecdotes. The book gained local fame when it won a 1999 Regional Tabasco Community Cookbook Award and helped the club provide numerous funds for several years to come.

The Bargain Box was eventually moved to 418 West Main Street and continues at this site today. The Service League owns the building and in 2004 renovated approximately one-third of the second-floor loft into a permanent meeting space for members with grants from several foundations and members. Dark wood trim and furnishings along with a kitchen and bathroom helped create an inviting space in the historic loft area.

The League continues to support the community in a variety of ways and is a vital part of many of our non-profits through-out Grayson County. Their mission is to better our community through volunteer work, acts of kindness and financial assistance. To date, the League has given back more than one-million dollars to the community and volunteers have put in more than 360,000 service hours. They currently have approximately 80 members and remain 100% volunteer based.

The Denison Garden Club
By Brian C. Hander

On March 13, 1929, Mrs. Gross R. Scruggs met with a group of civic minded women with a desire to beautify their community, and the Denison Garden Club was born. The purpose of the club was to encourage civic beauty and roadside beautification; to study all aspects of the fine art of gardening; to aid in the protection and conservation of natural resources and to cooperate with other agencies furthering the interests of horticulture and conservation.

Mrs. George O. Morgan was elected first president and within the first seven years the club had grown to 75 members. The initial undertaking of the organization was the landscaping of the United State Post Office on Woodard Street, and the planting of trees on Denison's half

Figure 20 Homes such as the Leeper house on Sears Street were examples of the Garden Club's work to foster civic pride through the planting of rose bushes and flowering vines.

of Highway 75 between Denison and Sherman. Roses and attractive shrubs were planted in the medians along Woodard and Main and miles of highways were planted with flowers and shrubs as well. More than 6,500 patented roses were planted in the organizations first few years with a goal of 10,000 roses planted by its 10th anniversary.

The largest campaign launched the Garden Club was to make Denison the "Crape Myrtle City" when thousands of crape myrtles were planted in yards, on highways, and other spots over the city, including areas surrounding Forest Park. The club went a few steps further and supervised the planting of all shrubbery, red bud trees, and roses in Forest Park. The club worked in cooperation with the Red Bud Association which had the goal of planting a trail of redbuds from Lake Texoma on Highway 75 down to Dallas.

One unique campaign that was begun was the free trash wagon that would come around and help Denison citizens get rid of accumulated rubbish. An annual clean-up campaign was inaugurated and proved so successful that it continues in Denison to this day, although in a slightly altered form than originally done. With the aid of the Boy Scouts, the club established a bird sanctuary at Munson Park and a city-wide campaign was launched to plant crape myrtles and other desirable shrubs throughout Denison.

Through this organization, the "best kept yard" and "most beautiful garden" contests came about that would remain a Denison staple for decades. The Victory Garden Contest was also a successful project of the club and through a partnership with the Chamber of Commerce free seeds were distributed to those who needed them. This resulted in over 3,000 gardens planted by 1944 for the community to assume the full share and responsibility of producing food during the war. J.W. Madden, a local Denison businessman, aided the club by offering cash prizes for the best vegetable gardens grown in the city. Another war time service was the sending of locally grown flowers weekly to the hospital at Perrin Field.

The group celebrated their anniversary with a silver tea in the spring of 1954, and an annual flower show was added as a popular event that was open to the public. In respect to deceased members the club would plant specific trees in their memory.

A garden therapy program was started by the club to aid the physically handicapped from the VA Hospital in Bonham. The group maintained the Post Office flowerbeds and plantings and added the grounds of the Denison National Guard Armory to their territory as well. Plans even included design of the landscaping for the grounds of Denison's Memorial Hospital.

A separate Garden Club to serve the residents of Denison's east end was organized on May 2, 1956. A group of sixteen interested women gathered together with the far-reaching vision of what a program of cleanliness and beautification could do for the rapidly expanding east side of town.

The inaugural meeting was held at the East Baptist Church with Mrs. J.W. Douglass of 601 East Gandy being elected as its first president. Others elected to office included Mrs. Gordon Davis, owner of Davis-Hyland Florist, 400 East Hull, vice-president, in charge of membership and publicity; Mrs. C.A. Robertson, Sr., 504 West Woodard, secretary; Mrs. Felix Grundy, 431 East Sears, treasurer, and Mrs. A.J. Brown, 715 East Sears, councilor. Mrs. Aubrey Hughes, 616 East Woodard, who assisted Mrs. Wilkinson in the organization of the group, was named chairman of a telephone committee.

A contest to decide on a name for the new club was begun and all agreed on a minimum of $1.00 a year for membership dues. Two former presidents of the Denison Garden Club, Mrs. Paul Wilson and Mrs. H.B. Anderson, were guests at the organizational meeting. The name selected for the new group was the Flora O'Maley Garden Club.

The O'Maley Garden Club met at the Eastwood Recreation Center and created a junior club on September 26, 1961. The junior club grew to 87 members at its peak and its goal was to make youth conscious of a clean and beautiful city. The young children of the junior club would make litterbug posters for clean-up campaigns and maintained projects at Raynal Elementary School which included the planting of day lilies, bluebonnets, and a mimosa tree on the site.

The Chelsea Park Garden Club was organized in November of 1958 as a branch of the Denison Garden Club. Mrs. Ann Kubala was the first president with Mrs. June Sager and Mrs. Joyce Page serving as officers. The club originally limited its membership to twenty so that it could meet in the homes of members. In 1962, the organization adopted a vacant lot in the neighborhood of members and began a beautification project of the site.

A Town and Country Garden Club was organized in December of 1964. Elected officers in the new group were: Mrs. M.B. Hodge, president; Mrs. Scott Potts, first vice president; Mrs. T.C. Hooper, second vice president; Mrs. Don Jones, corresponding secretary; Mrs. H.W. Aderholt, reporter; and Mrs. J.K. Shieler and Mrs. Talley Dutton, telephone committee.

The final gardening club to be formed in Denison was the Evening Gardeners. Mrs. Lester Pedigo was elected first president at the inaugural meeting on March 16, 1965, in the home of Mrs. Hardy, president of the Denison Garden Club and sponsor of the fledgling organization. Officers elected were Mrs. Marie Jimerson, first vice president; Mrs. Dan Burns, second vice president; Mrs. Jerry Harvey, treasurer; Mrs. Margaret Patti, secretary; Mrs. Ada Brigham, historian; and Miss Nova Cunningham, reporter.

Throughout the years, these various clubs were combined or disbanded. A city and chamber-initiated effort, an organization known as Keep Denison Beautiful, became the civic-oriented "gardening club" that served as a replacement for the community's historic clubs. The vison of KDB is to make Denison the cleanest, most beautiful city in which to live, work and visit. Their mission is to engage individuals to take greater responsibility for improving their community and environment.

Figure 21 The Keep Denison Beautiful Logo, unveiled 2021

Just like the garden clubs of old, this organization has planted hundreds of Crape Myrtle trees along highways throughout Denison as well as the planting of shrubs and flowers in parks and civic centers. One program, known as "Operation Daffodil", saw the planting of over 25,000 daffodil bulbs that continue to bloom faithfully throughout Denison each spring. This all-volunteer organization placed fourth in the Governor's Community Achievement Award in 1990, third in 1991, and finally first place in 1992. Keep Denison Beautiful was named a Keep Texas Proud Community in 1993.

Denison VFW Gate City Post 2773
By Brian C. Hander

Denison's Veterans of Foreign Wars Post 2773 was created on January 18, 1933, with twenty-five charter members. The first commander of the VFW was Clayton Evans, and the first meeting place was the IOOF Hall at 609 ½ West Main. A full list of the original charter members is included at the back of this book.

A Ladies Auxiliary was chartered on December 4, 1933, with twenty-two members. The first president was Mrs. David Fennell. A list of these charter members may also be found at the back of this book.

One of the largest projects of the Auxiliary included the erection of a large signboard at Forest Park during World War II containing the names of all area men in the service. Gold stars were placed by the names of those who died in service. The three main points stressed by the Auxiliary were community service, youth activities, and hospital work.

In 1935 the VFW group moved to the Woodmen of the World Hall at 201 ½ West Woodard, and then moved again in 1936 to the Labor Temple. The or-

Figure 22 The VFW Ladies Drill Team.

ganization flourished and was able to build their own building at the corner of Mirick and Crawford in 1947. A modern brick edifice was erected with the main entrance on Crawford Street highlighted by cast stone masonry features that still remain today.

Two remodeling programs followed in the late 1940's and again in the 1960's. 1947 was a banner year for VFW leadership as Roger Q. Evans, of Denison, was elected to serve as the State Commander of the Veterans of Foreign Wars. This was the highest office ever held by a representative from Denison.

Figure 23 A 1960's aerial view of the VFW post building (at left) prior to large additions that would consume the two homes to the East.

The organization reached its peak in 1968 with a membership of 1,214 members, making it the largest VFW post in Texas at that time. This number would begin to decline following the closure of Perrin Air Force Base.

In 1975 a $60,000 addition was unveiled that added a new kitchen and doubled the size of the auditorium. Two homes to the east of the original structure were demolished to allow for the new building's footprint. By 1976 the post still boasted 1,070 members, bumping it from its number one slot but still ranked among the largest in Texas.

Early projects for the organization included uniting the Sherman and Denison VFW's for parades, annual decoration of the graves of veterans at Memorial Day, and the celebration of Buddy Poppy Day. Membership in the post was further impacted when the MKT Railroad was sold and ceased all operations in Denison. The post closed in 2015 following several more years of declining membership.

Denison Kiwanis Club
By Brian C. Hander

Denison's Kiwanis Club began in 1946 with a banquet meeting at the Tropical Gardens, a local nightclub in Denison's early history. The club set a record for the Kiwanis district with approximately 600 persons in attendance. The early mission of the group was to provide business networking while focusing on community service-specifically driven towards service to children.

The charter was officially signed on April 9, 1946, and the group was formally designated Club Number 23 of Division Two by Lieutenant Governor Otis Milstead of Mt. Pleasant, Texas. Elected officials for the new group included L.J. Womack, president; Fred Hahnel, first vice president; Richard Hankins, second vice president; and James Woodruff, treasurer. The sponsoring club, Sherman's Kiwanis Club, presented the newly chartered group with a flag, gavel, and bell.

Figure 24 The Tropical Gardens played host to the first meeting of the Kiwanis group and their official charter signing banquet in 1946.

The Kiwanians secured a meeting place in the basement of the old Security Building, the first skyscraper in Texas, but quickly outgrew this site. In 1948 the organization purchased a lot at 728 West Sears Street and moved a two-story building onto it at a cost of about $8,000 and remodeled the structure into their new meeting place. This site was later donated to the Camp Fire Girls organization for construction of a new building.

The club was most known for its annual Chili Day, the Easter Egg Hunt for local youngsters, and Pancake Day which was held for the first time in 1971. The organization also installed gumball machines all throughout Denison and donated all proceeds to help the city's youth and underprivileged.

The Kiwanis Club served Denison with fundraisers that supported such organizations as the American Cancer Society, Grayson County Shelter, and the Helping Hands food bank. Each year the group sponsored a circus that typically performed at either Denison's Main Street or at the Mayor Arena at Loy Lake Park. The group, now down to seven members according to the Kiwanis website, remains active and provides scholarships for Denison High School seniors.

American Legion Fred W. Wilson-Sam Patillo Post 62
By Brian C. Hander

On September 12, 1919, a call was made in *The Denison Herald* for all interested to meet at the Denison Chamber of Commerce to organize an American Legion Post. Abner Lewis was in charge of the organization and anticipated a great turnout. Congress was expected to incorporate the American Legion on September 16, 1919, and Denison organizers wanted to be prepared. The intent of the organization was to focus on service to veterans, service-members, and their communities.

Denison's group was created soon after Congress officially endorsed the Legion, and immediately members voted to name their post in memory of Denison-born Fred W. Wilson who served and died in the U.S. Navy in World War I. Fred attended Denison public schools and graduated from Harshaw's College, finding employment at Denison's First State Bank soon after graduation.

Wilson was aboard the USS President Lincoln when she was hit by three torpedoes in the Atlantic Ocean at 9:53 am on May 31, 1918. Wilson was the first Denison boy to give his life in the service of his country during WWI.

Many posts across the country were named after the first person from that town killed in service, however some small towns such as Denison, selected the first native from their community to die in service.

A temporary slate of officers was chosen and included Post Commander Roy Henderson, U.S. Army; Vice Commander O.J. Sanders, U.S. Navy; Post Adjutant Ralph Geisenhoner, U.S. Army; Post Finance Officer James White, U.S. Navy; and Post Chaplain Reverend Fred Cochran.

On September 22, a preamble to the Legion's constitution was drawn up and read:

The objects of this organization shall be: To uphold and defend the constitution of the United States of America; to maintain law and order; to foster and perpetuate a hundred percent Amercianism; to preserve the memories and incidents of our association in the great war; to inculcate a sense of individual obligation to the community, State, and Nation; to combat the autocracy of both the classes and the masses; to make right the master of might; to promote peace and good will on earth; to safeguard and transmit to posterity the principles of justice, freedom and democracy; to consecrate and sanctify our comradeship by our devotion to mutual helpfulness.

Figure 25 A photo of Fred W. Wilson, ca. 1917

With a preamble adopted and a hearty group of men ready to become a part of the organization, the post was formally chartered on September 30, 1919, with 54 members. Roy Henderson served as the first official Post Commander.

Feeling like they had everything in order, in November of 1919 the Legion was ready to institute a membership campaign. A committee consisting of Roy D. Henderson, Floyd Ford, Oliver Hayes, Abner Lewis, Farley Reasonover, C.E. Eggleston, Sidney Goldman, Lingo Platter, A.A. McCarty, Clarence Scott, Bill Jackson, James White, Ralph Geisenhoner, W. T. Brown, and Britton Smith was formed with the task of finding members to join the fledgling group.

The campaign stated that the Legion's ranks were open to any person who served in the American Army, Navy, Marine Corps, or Nursing Corps as well as Americans who served in any Allied Armies. The membership fee was $1 per year with 25 cents going to the national association, 25 cents to the state organization, and 50 cents to the local post. Meetings were originally held in the auditorium of the Denison Chamber of Commerce. The extensive list of charter members is located at the back of this book.

A Women's Auxiliary Unit was organized on May 6, 1921, with nearly 100 charter members. Mrs. C.R. Eggleston was charter president. The five main objectives of the auxiliary included rehabilitation, child welfare, hospital service, community service, and Americanism.

Following a period of immense growth, a building was erected at 419 West Crawford Street in 1934 with 16-inch-thick brick walls in Alamo fashion.

The deed to the five lots that the Legion came to own stipulated that the property would revert to the City of Denison if ever it became a public nuisance. Further, the property could not be mortgaged without the direct consent of the City Council. The title also could not be transferred to any other party, and if and when the post ceases to function the property would become the city's.

Figure 26 Denison's Little Symphony Orchestra performs in the new American Legion building, 1934.

In 1933 the post had $52 in its operating fund and yet in 1938 had raised enough funds to pay off the mortgage on the original building. By 1947 the roster had grown to 1,300 as veterans of World War II returned home. During this time, in accordance with the constitution and by-laws, both the Post and the Auxiliary added the name of Sam Patillo, a hero of World War II.

Patillo served as a 2ⁿᵈ Lieutenant in the U.S. Army Air Corps. He was a navigator on a B-17 E bomber that was shot down over the Java Sea by Japanese fighter planes on February 8, 1942. Lt. Patillo received the Silver Star and the Distinguished Service Cross for gallantry in the South Pacific prior to his death.

Figure 27 A photo of Sam Patillo, ca. 1941

Patillo was actually not the first man from Denison to perish during WWII. Denison's first casualty was actually Jesse Lee Roy Adams, a 21-year-old who was killed in action in the Pacific theatre following the Japanese attack on Pearl Harbor, However, Adams was not a native of Denison so his name was not selected for the post.

The Legion maintained a membership of 1,000 or more for the greater part of a decade before it dropped to around 741 members in 1971. Much of the decrease in membership was due to the closing of the Perrin Air Force Base on Denison's western edge. As seen previously with the VFW, the closing of the base had devastating consequences for the fraternal clubs that catered to veterans and active service members.

Around this time, the club undertook a $35,000 capital improvement campaign that included paneling the auditorium and construction of a completely new kitchen with the old kitchen area changed into an entrance and trophy room. The basement, long a victim of seepage and rotting timbers, was filled in and new central heat and air conditioning was added. The project was rounded out with the addition of new restrooms and the lowering of the building's cathedral ceilings.

Figure 28 An early view of Denison's American Legion building.

To date, the post remains active in Denison and Grayson County. They serve their members through bingo, costume parties, Veterans Day steak nights, and special events focused on Memorial Day. The group annually participates in Denison's Fall Fest and is a member of the Denison Area Chamber of Commerce.

Denison Lion's Club
By Brian C. Hander

The first meeting of the Denison Lion's Club was held on April 20, 1921, at the Union Station dining room in the MKT Depot. The club had been the talk of the town with twenty-five members on its rolls by the first meeting. The impetus of the organization came when a Lions International field man, Mr. Kinney, came to Denison, and with the help of B.F. Shepherd was able to recruit the nucleus membership.

While they had met before, the Lions Club was officially organized on June 1, 1921, and Dr. W.A. Lee, a local physician, was elected as the President. H.H. Cummins, an attorney, was first Vice President; C.D. Kingston, druggist, second Vice President and E.M. Beazley, garage owner, third Vice President.

H.A. Newsom, a co-owner of Newsom's Women's Wear in downtown Denison, was the first Secretary. Elected Lion Tamer was J.J. Loy, then an employee at Madden's Department Store who later served as State Senator and Grayson County Judge. Reverend T.L. Huffstuttler, pastor of Waples Methodist Church, was Yell Leader. Directors included J.T. Scott, B.F. Shepherd, Dr. H.T. Walker, and A.P. Linn.

Figure 29 The first meeting of the Denison Lion's Club was held in the dining room of the MKT Depot, seen here ca. 1920.

The original number of members was thirty-four at the time of the charter, and meetings were to be held every Wednesday at noon at the Union Station dining room. Their names appear at the back of this book.

One of the earliest projects of the group was to raise money to buy blankets for the 1922 Denison Yellow Jacket football team. That was the year the Jackets endeared themselves to all of Denison by defeating the Sherman Bearcats for the first time in years.

The Lions played a key role in organizing outside support of the early Yellow Jackets. Few adults attended the games in the early years, but with the help of the Lions Club, supporters of the Jackets began to flock to the stadium for games.

In the beginning the club met in various churches and headquartered at the dining room of the Union Station for several years until the Hotel Simpson was completed in 1924. Ever in support of Denison enterprises the group chose to hold their meetings at the new hotel and would remain at the site for decades.

Figure 30 The Hotel Simpson as it appeared in 1924. This site would remain as the meeting place of the Denison Lion's Club for decades.

The club found its niche in a broad social program that included glasses for needy school children, sponsorship of Little League baseball, Christmas toys for underprivileged children, and other activities oriented towards the youth of the community.

In fact, the Denison Lions Club was said to be only the second or third club in the world to adopt eyesight conservation as a local club project in 1930. Glasses were provided for children as a year-around project and the club sponsored annual events that benefitted the fund. By 1972 the Lions had donated more than 845 pairs of glasses to local children in need at a cost of more than $8,078.38.

The Lions Club began sponsorship of the Denison Little League baseball program in 1952. Shortly after beginning, it was discovered that Denison offered no adequate parks for baseball games, so the Lions Club acquired two parks for play. One was on Woodard Street and the other was at Waterloo Park. The club furnished the field, chain-link fencing, lights, concession stands and press boxes without any cost to taxpayers. A girls' softball league was also begun by the Denison Lions Club and a new field was built at Waterloo Park for their benefit as well.

The Lions later built a small building at 1030 West Crawford Street to serve as their Toy Shop and storage facility. Toys that were damaged or in need of repair were restored to working order by members of the club and gifted to needy children for Christmas.

Figure 31 The Lions Club Toy Shop on West Crawford, ca. 2010

For more than 60 years, the main fundraiser for the club was the annual Lions Club Carnival that was held in Forest Park each May or June. The carnival began in 1947 and ran for decades before it was discontinued in the early 2000's. It was estimated that the carnival raised between $15,000 to $20,000 each year for club projects.

In September of 2020 the Lions Club Toy Shop building on West Crawford Street was sold to Denison's Homeless Empowerment Actions Team, H.E.A.T., for use as a resource center. Work on the building is currently underway, leaving a lasting legacy of the Lions and the work they did to serve our community.

Denison Rotary Club
By Brian C. Hander

One of Denison's oldest clubs, the Rotary Club was established on June 1, 1916, as Club Number 227 after five Denison business leaders gathered to launch the endeavor. The driving force behind the group was Dr. J.E. Aubrey, the minister of Denison's First Presbyterian Church and prominent member of the Chamber of Commerce. Joining him at lunch was George O. Morgan, manager of the Denison Peanut Company, Harry E. Ellis, editor of the Denison Herald; Guy Alexander, an insurance man; and Jack Tinsman, druggist.

Each meeting the group would invite others and tell them of the plan and by the summer of that year they had enough interested to begin the organization. Dr. Aubrey served as the first president of the group, and the first official meeting of the club was held in the boardroom of the State National Bank.

Rotary International had been founded eleven years earlier and the Denison club was the 227th to join. A list of the club's charter members may be found at the back of this book.

In its infancy, the club held their meetings in the auditorium of the Chamber of Commerce, then located on the second floor at 330 West Main Street. Once the Hotel Simpson (now Hotel Denison) was completed in 1924, the club moved into the elegant banquet room.

Over 3,000 Rotary luncheons were held in the hotel until they voted to move to the new Holiday Inn on Highway 69/75. Somewhere in the move from the Hotel Denison to the Holiday Inn, the original copy of the charter was misplaced.

Early services the club worked to aid included the Salvation Army and the formation of the Denison Public Library. The club is also said to have sponsored the first boy scout troop in Denison.

Figure 32 Thelma Braun, the first female Rotarian in the United States, accepts her award as a Paul Harris Fellow in 1976.

Miss Thelma Braun, the pianist for Rotary Club meetings for nearly fifty years was awarded a membership as the first female Rotarian in the country. She was invited to play for the club in 1931 and would remain their dedicated pianist for decades, attending over 2,500 meetings without one absence. She was honored with the club's Paul Harris Award on March 25, 1976 and was only the third person to receive the honor in the club's history.

The Rotary Club celebrated its 100th anniversary in 2016 with a kick-off for a new playground at Denison's Forest Park. The project was valued at $300,000 with $100,000 coming from the Rotarians. The club sold corporate sponsorships, hosted a golf tournament, and sold bricks harvested from Denison's Chestnut Street to pay for the project. The new playground included a splashpad and train-themed equipment for children of all ages to enjoy.

Figure 33 A rendering for the new playground at Forest Park, sponsored by the Rotary Club as part of their Centennial Celebration.

The Rotary Club remains active in the community to this day, and continues to serve Denison through volunteer opportunities, charitable funding, and scholarships.

Boy Scouts of America
By Brian C. Hander

On January 29, 1913, an article appeared in *The Denison Herald* stating that the organization of a Boy Scout group in Denison was wanted and was hoped that an effort would be launched within the next few days to start a troop.

While no available content could be found that mentioned the movement, an article did appear on March 22, 1913, alerting Denison that a clean-up army had been mobilized consisting of forty Boy Scouts under the direction of Scoutmaster George Redwood Shane, a staff member at the Denison YMCA.

The first Scout troop known to have been organized in Denison was sponsored through the YMCA and was created sometime before 1915, so it is very possible that the 1913 group was Denison's first. Although formed, Denison would not register the troop with a national council until 1919. There were two troops registered in 1919, and both were sponsored by the Denison Rotary Club. Lute Loy was Scoutmaster of Troop 104 and Ben Burget was Scoutmaster of Troop 101.

In 1920 Denison's Scout troops joined the Grayson County Council, which was later expanded to included parts of Fannin and Bryan Counties, at which time it was renamed the Texas-Oklahoma Council. Around 1938, following Sherman's removal to form its own council,

Denison entered the Chickasaw Council with headquarters at Ardmore, Oklahoma.

Another merger occurred in 1940 when the Denison, Bryan County, and Cooke County Scout districts merged to form the Red River Valley Council. The year 1944 marked a milestone for Denison scouting troops with 241 boys in all levels of scouting throughout the city. This growth would continue well into 1947 when the scout troops played a key role in the celebration of Denison's 75th Anniversary.

The final merger for the troops occurred in 1949 following the bankruptcy of the Red River Valley Council, when they joined the Circle Ten Council with headquarters in Dallas. Denison was originally represented in this Council by vice-president Ben Munson III and Council members at large J.V. Conatser and Joe Dusek. Clark C. Harp served as the district scout executive serving Denison.

Later, J.V. Conatser would serve as President, E.J. Lilley and Frank Dyer would serve a Vice Presidents, Evans Wood would serve as Commissioner, and H.P. Watkins would serve as Treasurer. These men would greatly shape the early days of Denison's involvement in the Circle Ten Council, paving the way for future troops to expand and flourish.

At one time Denison had nearly 740 youth in the scouting program with a large number of troops. They and their sponsors are as follows: Pack 601, Layne School PTA; Troop 602, St. Patrick's Catholic Church; Pack and Troop 603, Parkside Baptist Church; Troop and Pack 604, Trinity Methodist Church; Pack and Troop 605, Waples Methodist Church; Troop and Pack 606, St. Luke's Episcopal Church; Pack and Troop 607, First Presbyterian Church; Troop 608, Denison Lions Club; Pack 609, First Christian Church; Pack and Troop 610, First Baptist Church; Troop 611, Hyde Park Baptist Church; Troop and Pack 612, Raynal PTA and Dad's Club; Pack 613, Golden Rule PTA; Pack 635, Hyde Park PTA; Troop 642, Imperial Heights Methodist Church; Troop 643, Grace Evangelical Lutheran Church; Post 644, VFW; and Pack, Troop and Post 403 from Terrell School.

In 1971, it was announced that through the combined efforts of the various scout troops, over 800 young men had joined the program and had become affiliated with troops. With the closing of Camp Texoma in 1978, the Red River District (Denison, TX and Bryan County, OK) seceded from Circle Ten Council and joined the rest of Grayson County in the Texoma Valley Council, BSA. With the pending bankruptcy of the Texoma Valley Council in 1993 the Denison troops once again became affiliated with the Circle Ten Council and remain so to this day.

Throughout the years, some of these organizations have merged, disbanded, or reformed under different charter numbers. However, the scouting tradition continues in Denison with countless projects undertaken by local Packs, Troops, and Venture organizations to move Denison forward each day.

Denison Alumni Association
By Brian C. Hander

Denison's Student Alumni Association held its first meeting in May of 1901 on the lawn of the T.V. Munson home, known as Vinita, on South Mirick Avenue. Miss Carrie Johnson, an 1888 graduate, served as the organization's first president.

Any graduate of the High School could become a member of the Association by a payment of a yearly fee of fifty cents. The original intent of the association was "to bring together yearly the graduates of Denison High School in order to renew old associations and to cultivate and maintain an interest in Denison High School."

The 1908 meeting was held in the XXI Club Building on Gandy Street with 150 members in attendance.

Figure 34 Vinita, the home of the T.V. Munson family, as it appeared ca. 1900.

The following resolution was adopted: *"Resolved that the Alumni Association heartily endorse the plan of building a modern and efficient high school building by means of a special tax; and that this association collectively, and individually, use its good officers in calling the attention of the people of Denison to the need of the new High School building."*

Future meetings included discussions regarding sponsorships of fountains to be added to the new Denison High School and the Raynal Monument Fund. By the 10th annual meeting there were 125 graduates in attendance and the 11th annual meeting saw a committee formed to write a constitution and by-laws for the organization. This constitution was unanimously adopted at the 12th meeting in 1912.

Annual meetings were held the second Wednesday in June with a reception for the most recent graduating class. These soirees were held at various locations including public parks, church facilities, and private homes. An alumni newspaper was published from 1908 to 1914 but no known copies exist to this day.

In its early days, the association used its considerable influence to get the "new" High School built in 1913. These early students, benefiting from an education in Texas' first free public graded school, saw the need for a new building and were happy to help advance the project in any way.

One unique program that was undertaken by the former students was a Student Loan Fund that was incorporated in 1916. These loans were awarded to students to help them pay for tuition in their last year of college. The hope was that these same students would return and add to the fund for future generations.

Figure 35 The "new" 1913 Denison High School that the alumni association advocated for, seen here around 1918.

In the beginning, annual alumni gatherings were considered the top social events of the year. However, as classes became larger and more students had access to college educations, interest dropped to an occasional class reunion.

The parent organization of the Alumni Association is the Denison Education Foundation, a nonprofit, 501C-3 tax-exempt corporation founded in 1997 that operates under its own board of directors. The foundation was created to support the educational programs of the Denison ISD and to enhance the quality of education for all students. To date the foundation has awarded $853,373 in grant funds and $537,293 in scholarship funds.

After many months of planning, a mobile museum was unveiled by the Association on October 6, 2001. The museum was housed in a school bus no longer used by the school district. Seats were removed to make way for memorabilia that had been donated throughout the years, and the bus made appearances at many of Denison's festivals and events.

By 2003 the organization had 275 members and plans were in the infancy stages to being gathering historic memorabilia to preserve for a possible brick and mortar museum. Dorothy Rushing, an archivist and alumnus, was in charge of preserving and storing the items. This work would become incredibly important just a decade later when the group received the ultimate gift from the Denison Independent School District.

Figure 36 The Denison Alumni logo featuring the artwork of Penny Case, a student at Denison High who designed the Yellow Jacket in 1973.

With the opening of Denison's new high school campus on Highway 91, the school district set about selling or donating surplus buildings and materials that had made up the former high school complex. A building 1710 S, Mirick Avenue was formally donated to the museum for use by the Denison ISD School Board on February 18, 2014. The group maintains this site as an Alumni Museum and it is open upon request for reunions, class field trips, and other special occasions.

The purpose of the Association has changed throughout the years and now includes three basic principles:
- To provide activities, communications, and other services for alumni of the Denison ISD and other members of the association.
- To foster and support educational and related activities of the Denison High School and/or other DISD schools.
- To support the purpose of the DISD Education Foundation.

Denison's Black Chamber of Commerce
By Brian C. Hander

Denison's Black Chamber of Commerce was founded in 1942 as a way to serve black-owned businesses and interests throughout the city. In the early days of the Chamber, members advocated for equal addition of playground equipment to all parks in the city, not just those whose patrons were predominately white, and also worked to create and grow black-owned businesses.

In March of 1949, the Black Chamber of Commerce announced the beginning of construction of a community center at the corner of Washington Street (now MLK Street) and Armstrong Avenue. The building was to be used for all civic and social organizations that served the community of color and would also serve as a youth center on two nights of each week. President. S.M. McCollum was President of the organization during this time.

At a membership drive in 1955 the objectives of the Chamber were to include closer cooperation with the health program of the city, be a part of the Civil Defense program, assist in welfare work and improve the youth programs of their people, encourage the establishment of homesites on Lake Texoma, help promote better labor conditions, help to promote cultural arts, aid in the promotion of black-owned businesses, encourage payment of poll taxes, increase interest in African American schools, work toward better race relations, and to liquidate the indebtedness of the Chamber of Commerce building.

Officers of the Black Chamber of Commerce (Date Unknown)

President-Wesley Dennis
President-Elect-Michael Braxton
1st Vice President-Melton Kemp
2nd Vice President-Marvin Smith
3rd Vice President-Tommy Pruitt
4th Vice President-Thressa Malvern
Recording Secretary-Imell McCollum
Executive Secretary-Van Withrow
Treasurer-Viola Walker
Assistant Secretary-Dolly McDonald
Parliament-June Garrett

Figure 37 The seal of the Denison Black Chamber of Commerce, 1981.

In 1960, the Chamber successfully advocated for a portion of the storm sewer fund that had been approved in a city-wide bond program to cover the cost of a storm sewer from the 500 block of West Morton to Austin and up to a portion of Johnson Street.

In 1985-1986 the fifty-member Black Chamber worked towards two main projects. The first was the creation of a community youth center and the second was the restoration of the Mercy Hospital building at 1030 W. Munson. Chamber President Frank Harper said while the youth center was open during the summer the Chamber hoped to have it open all-year-round for students to have a place to go after school.

One publication released by the Black Chamber of Commerce is reprinted below and gives great insight into some Denison's black-owned businesses.

Black Businesses of Denison

This is a list of the black-owned and operated businesses in the Denison area.

There is a total number of 27 businesses within the black community in Denison, Texas.

There are (2) Service Centers, (2) Mortuaries, (4) Beauty Salons, (1) Beauty Supply Store, (2) Package Stores, (3) Barber Shops, (1) Grocery Store, (1) Washateria, (1) Auto Garage, (2) Auto Repair Shops, and (2) Night Clubs. (1) Car Cleaning Center, (4) Snack Bars, and (1) Nursery.

The following is a compiled list of names and addresses:

Auto Garage
1. *Jeff's Garage*
    408 West Johnson St.
    Jeff Cyrus-Owner

Auto Body Shops
2. *Polk's Body Shop*
    815 West Elm
    Eluster/Cleo Polk-Owners

3. *Springfield Auto Body Shop*
    215 East Nelson St.
    Cornell Springfield #3rd-Owner

4. *Texoma Auto Cleaning*
    Aaron Hunt-Owner

Beauty Salons
5. *Adorable Beauty Shop*
    302 West Johnson St.
    Dollie McDonald-Owner

6. *Baker Beauty Salon*
    527 West Elm
    Elzona Baker-Owner

7. *Community Beauty Salon*
    908 West Elm St.
    Evelyn Braggs-Owner

8. *Pruitt's Beauty Salon*
    511 North Fannin Ave.
    Willie M. Pruitt-Owner

9. *Parker's Beauty Supply*
    701 South Mirick Ave.
    Clyde/Edward Parker-Owners

Barber Shops
10. *Braxton Barber Shop*
    718 North Mirick Ave.
    Michael Braxton-Owner

11. *Douglas Barber Shop*
    Eldorado A. Douglas-Owner
    402 West Walker St.

12. *Kelly's Barber Shop*
    117 South Burnett Ave.
    Charles E. Kelly-Owner

Grocery Store
13. *Groce's Food Market*
    720 North Mirick Ave.
    Wm. Groce-Owner

Mortuaries

14. McDonald Funeral Home
    729 West Walker St.
    Paul/Vasteline McDonald-
    Owners

15. Smith's Memorial Chapel
    515 North Burnett Ave.
    James E. Smith-Owner

Nursery

16. Jack/Jill Nursery
    800 West Washington St.

Package Stores

17. Cut-Rate Liquor
    1126 West Washington St.
    T.H. Wrenn-Owner

18. Frazier Place
    817 N. Fannin Ave.
    Lorenzo Frazier-Owner

Restaurants

19. Hollywood Garden Drive Inn
    600 West Morton St.
    Mrs. Lonnie Bunkley-Owner

20. Green's Take Out
    213 West Bond St.
    Mary Green-Owner

Snack Bars

21. B. Snack Bar
    917 North Fannin Ave.
    Albert/Knola Bryant-Owners

22. Lamar St. Grill
    606 North Lamar Ave.
    Jewell Pough-Owner

Service Centers

23. Jimmy's Amoco
    800 West Main St.
    Jim Fleming-Owner

24. Norman's Texaco
    1431 West Morton St.
    Norman-McGee-Owner

Night Clubs

25. Poor Boy's
    319 West Walker St.
    Tommie Pough-Owner

26. Elmo's Pough #845
    American Legion Post Club

Washateria

27. Groce's Coin Operated
    720 North Mirick Ave.
    Wm. Groce-Owner

This makes a total of 27 businesses in the Black Community, below is a list of the various organizations in the Black Community.

1-The BPW
President-Mrs. Cora L. Bell

2-The Mandingo's Social Club
President-Mr. Marvin Thomas

3-The Denison Black Chamber of Commerce
President-Willie V. Harris

4-The Entire Masonic Family

CHAPTER 2

The Playground of the Southwest: Denison's Untold Parks

"There are no words that can tell the hidden spirit of the wilderness, that can reveal its mystery, its melancholy, and its charm."
-Theodore Roosevelt

Since its inception, Denison's citizens have always had access to outstanding public park facilities. Our very first park, Forest Park, was one of the first public parks in the State of Texas and was a gift from our community's founders who recognized the benefit public spaces can have for a growing city. After all, parks are a reflection of the quality of life in a community and our forefathers wanted Denison to be the community of choice for this region.

As the city grew, so did our parks system. What was one park in 1872 that encompassed roughly thirteen acres now includes eighteen parks with a combined 667 acres of space. With this amount of greenspace for residents, Denison leads North Texas in parkland per capita and is currently utilizing the renowned firm of HALFF and Associates to develop a long-range parks and trails master plan to protect and enhance these spaces for future generations.

This section begins with our oldest park and also includes several parks that are no longer found in Denison. These early-day parks were either lost to development, the elements, or reverted back to their original owners when the city could no longer utilize them as intended. However, many of Denison's early parks still exist as memorials to those who came before us and serve as symbols for how our community has benefited from these gifts of green spaces.

Forest Park
By Brian C. Hander

Forest Park was the brainchild of Robert S. Stevens and the Denison Town Company and was conceived with the hopes of attracting a more cultured and refined group of citizens to the fledgling town of Denison. Stevens donated thirteen acres of land to Denison in 1872 with the stipulation that the city keep the park in good condition and that the land never be used for anything other than a park. If the city failed on either end of the

Figure 38 Robert S. Stevens, head of the Denison Town Company.

bargain at any point in time the land would revert to Stevens or his heirs.

The park was mentioned in local area newspapers just a few months after the first town lots were sold and was commonly referred to as City Park before given its official name. In 1873 the fledgling city hosted a barbecue in the park to celebrate the First Anniversary of Denison with hundreds of people in attendance, cementing the park as the city's official public gathering place for events and festivals.

In 1875, the park was improved upon with help from the Texas Gift Concert Association and featured a stone walking path of a quarter mile in length encircling the park. The Gift Concert Association was unique in that there was a concert, but there was also a lottery-style drawing at the event that allowed those who purchased tickets to be entered for a chance to receive a "gift" of winning cash money. This proved to be a successful fundraiser for the park although Texas law was soon changed to make this type of lottery endeavor more difficult to conduct.

Figure 39 An early view of the entrance to Denison's Forest Park. Note the density of the trees in the park.

The official name of the park, Forest Park, was announced sometime prior to 1875, and the name is thought to have originated from the dense amounts of forested woods that covered the park grounds at that time.

By the 1880's, many of the trees were diseased and had been removed; it was thought that they were victims of chemicals coming from the smoke at the Katy machine shops located one block south of the park. Although many improvements had been made to the park over the years, it wasn't until 1882 that the land was officially deeded to the city from the Denison Town Company; the reason for the delay is unknown and is thought to have been a simple error of omission.

By 1895 an attractive park entrance was constructed and the whole park was enclosed in new fencing to prevent stray livestock from wandering around the grounds. During this time an impressive cast iron fountain was erected in the center of the park for the enjoyment of Denison's citizens. The fountain would stand for decades and housed a number of goldfish in its waters before it was removed in the 1970's.

In 1910-1911, a zoo was started in the park with the addition of two whitetail deer in a large new enclosure. The zoo was projected to have a total of eighteen enclosures that would hold the most complete animal collection in Texas at that time. Denison resident, Roy Finley is credited with attempting to bring this metropolitan attraction to the people of Denison, even going so far as to write to Colonel Theodore Roosevelt requesting he send a lion from his recent trip to Africa.

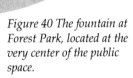

Figure 40 The fountain at Forest Park, located at the very center of the public space.

Animals at the zoo eventually included a badger, a baby lynx, a coyote, six deer, several civet cats, an armadillo, a wolf, three monkey-faced owls, a bald eagle, South American monkeys, and prairie dogs. Although a great attempt was made to make the zoo a reality, it ultimately was discontinued only a few years after its founding.

The following years brought a time of great prosperity for Denison's recreational jewel. By 1914, an impressive masonry gazebo with a unique hipped roof replaced the wooden Victorian-styled bandstand from the 1800's. In 1915, the Denison Civic Association erected a grand brick entrance to Forest Park that is still in existence to this day. The entrance was originally equipped with lights atop its large columns, but these were removed sometime in the 1960-70's.

Following the City Beautiful movement, massive quantities of crape myrtles, irises, flowering trees, and lush landscaping was added to the park. Wading pools were constructed for children to play in and a day at the park was strongly encouraged by local newspapers.

In 1922, a nationwide strike of shop-union employees against the Katy Railroad made its way to Denison. When the strike began, physical violence was seen throughout the country. Texas Governor Pat Neff declared martial law and sent the National Guard to Denison, a major railroad center, to help keep order of nearly 1,400 Katy Railroad workers.

The National Guard erected a large tent city in Forest Park, known as Camp Leeper, due to its close proximity to the Katy car shops. The Third Battalion, 142nd Infantry camped at the park from August 10, 1922-October 21, 1922 and made almost 300 civilian arrests during that time.

Figure 41 National Guard tents erected in Forest Park. Note downtown Denison in the background.

Construction of Munson Stadium, a large football stadium, was undertaken by the Works Progress Administration in 1938. The design featured large stone bleachers for the home team and corresponding stone dressing rooms for both the home and visiting teams. The stadium complex eventually grew to occupy the entire eastern half of the park, and was named for Benjamin Munson Jr., longtime school board president and early advocate for Denison's school district and athletics.

During this time, tennis courts were added on the south side of the park along with a clubhouse and restrooms that were constructed in

Figure 42 General Eisenhower addresses a crowd at Forest Park on April 20, 1946.

the Mission Revival style. On April 20, 1946, Denison native Dwight David Eisenhower, then a five-star general, addressed a record crowd of 10,000 at Forest Park. He would later become the President of the United States.

In 1979, the City of Denison was approved for a UP ARR grant totaling $447,777. This fund was used throughout the park to upgrade walkways and playground equipment. Additional parking for autos was also added along the northern edge of the park's boundary.

In 1980, various renovations and updates to the park were undertaken at a cost of $122,700, this time funded by the City of Denison. In 1982, picnic tables and grills were added, and other renovations were undertaken including reroofing the 1914 gazebo, new sidewalks, renovations to the tennis courts and restrooms, and new landscaping.

In 1983, the eastern half of Forest Park (416' x 620' tract), which contained Munson Stadium and its axillary buildings, was exchanged to the Denison Independent School District for the Raynal School Annex on Maple Row. In 1988 a therapeutic playground was added and in 1989 six electrical risers were added to the park for activities.

In 2003 a skate park, estimated at a cost of $50,000, was constructed by the city with Park Bond Funds. The skate park was located on the southern perimeter of Forest Park and utilized one of the old tennis court structures that was no longer in use.

In 2013, $5 million in community donations was raised to demolish the aging Munson Stadium to make way for a new press box and stands on the home side of the field. The new Munson Stadium and

Figure 43 The new entrance to Forest Park as designed by la terra Studio in 2013-2014.

Dr. Rene and Eva Gerard Field were completed in 2014 and stands as a testament to the generosity of Denison's citizens.

During the time of the stadium renovation, the City of Denison completely revamped the western half of Forest Park. The tennis courts and clubhouse/restroom, skate park, and outdated playground equipment were all removed in an effort to restore the park to its turn-of-the-century appearance.

The bandstand was completely restored and repainted, new brick and concrete walkways were added and were accompanied by historic-themed lighting. The historic brick entryway at the northern end of the park was restored and repainted, and a new cast iron fountain was installed to replicate the one that was originally located at the center of the park.

Recent additions include copious amounts of landscaping featuring dozens of new trees and shrubbery, and a train themed children's playground and splash pad valued at $300,000. This unique addition was made possible with a matching gift from the Denison Rotary Club as part of the celebration of their centennial in 2016.

With thoughtful renovations and care, the City of Denison and her citizens have ensured that Forest Park will continue to serve future generations for many years to come.

Munson Park
By Brian C. Hander

The spring of 1908 was a banner year for Denison when it gained a public park, free of charge, that was hailed as second to none in the state. Mr. Joseph Theodore Munson, one of city founder W.B. Munson's brothers, began working on the idea several months prior as a way to give back to his community and to create one of the largest public parks in a city at that time.

The deed for the property states:

State of Texas, County of Grayson.

Know all men by these presents, that I, J.T. Munson, a bachelor of the County of Grayson, State of Texas, for in consideration of the use, improvement and maintenance perpetually by the City of Denison and its citizens, the premises hereinafter described as a public park, have this day sold and do by these presents grant, bargain, sell and convey unto the City of Denison, a municipal corporation located in the County of Grayson, and State of Texas, all that certain tract of land described as follows: Situated in the County of Grayson, and State of Texas, on the water of Duck Creek, being part of a survey originally granted Ramon Rubio and described as follows to-wit:

Beginning in the center of Lamar Avenue extended north 770 feet from the north line of Washington Street; thence north along the center of Colberts' Ferry road, 1791 feet to the Southwest corner of the Catholic Cemetery; thence north 4 degrees 15 minutes east along center of said road at 2450 feet center of the east fork of Duck Creek, at 2930 feet, a large bois d'arc stake; thence south 83 degrees 10 minutes west 1700 feet, a stake in the west line of the R. Rubio survey; thence south 7 degrees 50 minutes east with said Rubio line 4561 feet to a stake 60 feet north of the south line of Anne Street extended east from the Cuff addition; thence east parallel to and 770 feet distance from the north line of Washington Street, 815 feet to the place of beginning, containing about one hundred and thirty acres of land, subject to a road reservation of 15 feet wide alone as line of said street and a road reservation 15 feet in width along the west line of the before described tract;

Figure 44 J.T. Munson, date of photograph unknown. From the T.V. Munson Collection on The Portal to Texas History.

it being hereby stipulated as a condition of this conveyance that in the event that the City of Denison shall at any time fail to maintain said premises as a public park, and its driveways, as planned and platted by man and A.N. Rhamy, city engineer, with such additions as the city may add thereto, then all right and title thereto shall revert to me or my legal representatives, together will all and singular the rights and appurtenances to the same belonging, or in any wise incident of appertaining, to have and to hold, all and singular the premises above mentioned, unto the said City of Denison, forever.

And I, the said J.T. Munson, do herby bind myself, my heirs, executors and administrators, to warrant and forever defend all and singular the said premises unto the said City of Denison against the lawful claims of all persons.

Witness my hand this 7th day of February, A.D. 1908
J.T. Munson

Acknowledged before J.R. Handy, a notary public in and for Grayson County, Texas, Feb. 7, 1908.

In presenting the deed to the Council Mr. Munson stated that in his opinion a most important adjunct to every city of any size was a park or playground for its people. Mr. Munson stated that he had made some observations of parks in and near various cities and this it was his belief that Denison would have a better park than any city in the Southwest.

The new public area was so large that it was estimated that two miles of driveways could be added in the park alongside miles and miles of walking trails. Initial plans also called for the impounding of water in two different places to create a sizeable lake, known as Munson Lake.

Within a matter of days of accepting the park, city leaders voted to annex the area into the city limits and to fence the park as soon as possible. In 1913 Mayor C. T. McElvaney and Aldermen Davis and Cole went to Munson Park to make arrangements to clean out the underbrush from the park and to build a dam for an artificial lake.

By 1915, the lake had not yet materialized, and the local newspaper ran an article stating that under the stipulation of the deed instructions, the park's lake had to be completed by the end of the year in order for the City of Denison to be able to remain owners of the property. However, the Munson family was more than willing to work with community leaders to set a realistic timeline rather than let the park revert to the family.

In 1919 a contract was let to George Kessler, a well-known St. Louis landscape architect to design a masterplan for the park. The undertaking called for by a joint task force of W.B. Munson Sr., the City of Denison, and the Denison Chamber of Commerce. The task force was to meet and discuss wants, needs, and visions for the park space so that appropriate plans could be drafted.

Later in the year, Kessler had completed three sets of plans that were intended to make Munson Park into a "park beautiful" following the excitement surrounding the City Beautiful movement. W.B. Munson provided a considerable cash gift in memory of his brother, and that paired alongside a fund left from what was known as the MO&G Donation Fund created a total balance of $17,000 to use towards the park improvements.

Figure 45 The entrance to Munson Park, ca. 1921.

The plans called for four sperate tennis courts, three separate picnic grounds, a baseball diamond, an athletic field with a quarter-mile long track, and small club houses. Other anticipated improvements involved massive amounts of landscaping with grading throughout the park to create a gentle slope.

The plans further called for restroom and other accommodations for ladies and gentlemen at the main entrance to the park with a drive that would rival the capital corridors in Austin. A lake was expected to cover an area of sixteen acres and would be arranged to as to allow both swimming and boating. Bath houses erected in the mission style and boat houses of the same were expected along the lake shore.

Munson Lake was finally completed in January of 1921 under the supervision of engineer Julian Feild. Although it did not make it to the sixteen acres that had been hoped, at twelve acres the lake was still one of the largest man-made lakes in Texas at that time. The dam was 300 feet long and twenty-six feet deep allowing for boating and swimming in the water body.

Figure 46 A fishing scene at Munson Lake from The Denison Guide, 1938.

A gun club was soon formed and in 1921 improvements were made for the convenience of club members. A club house, gun racks, seats, and stands for the shooters were constructed in order to conform with the club's policy to make the Munson Park grounds the best in the state regarding convenience and efficiency. The club boasted more weekly members than any other similar club in Texas with a membership of forty-three.

That same year also saw 45,000 men, women, and children who hailed from points as far north as Canada and west to the Pacific, east to the Atlantic, and south to Mexico visiting Munson Park to camp. The travelers came on motorcycles, in automobiles, in covered wagons, and all other manner of device to visit the Gate City.

The Chamber of Commerce had erected a tourist home with equipment at a cost of $1200 that was known far and wide as a hospitable place to stay. The tourist home consisted of a summer kitchen and dining room, shower and toilet facilities for men and women, electric lights, water, and fuel.

In 1922 bathhouses for men and women were added to the park. The cost was estimated at $2,400 with the National Bank of Denison donating half of the needed amount. The plans called for the houses to be fourteen feet wide and ninety-two feet long with lockers, verandas, and other accommodations. Jack Becker, of Denison, was awarded the contract for construction.

Tragedy struck in July of 1923 when Melvin Marion Gaines, aged 13, drowned in the Munson Park Lake. Gaines was swimming with his younger brother in the shallow water of the lake when he suddenly stepped into deep water. His brother, Elvin, went to his rescue but was unsuccessful in his attempt, nearly drowning himself. W.J. Murley swam to the boys but could only return one to the bank at a time. He swam the younger brother to shore and by the time he went back the lad had expired. He was buried in Fairview Cemetery.

Figure 47 The entrance to Munson Park from the 1929 DHS Yearbook

The Munson Lake dam had to be rebuilt in the spring of 1925 following torrential rains that posed a danger to the structure. Pat Tobin was in charge of the construction that would involve several feet being added to the dam. It was also hoped that this would allow the lake to hold more water, which was becoming a problem as lake levels decreased in previous years making it difficult for swimming and boating.

The concrete entrance into Munson Park was destroyed on January 11, 1946, when a driver by the name of Bob Palmer, from Dallas, crashed his truck into the structure. The truck cab was demolished when the 20-ton concrete archway was pushed over onto it after the trailer failed to clear it. Palmer had apparently been looking for a place to sleep and the archway was not visible when he struck it at 3:00 a.m.

In 1956, thirty acres of Munson Park on the north end near the lake were deeded to the heirs of W.B. Munson with the stipulation that the

Highway 75 right-of-way along the west edge be deeded to the highway department by the Munson's. The highway department had requested the land, but Denison was unable to provide the property with clear title due to stipulations in the original deed that required the property be maintained as a park. By deeding the thirty-acre portion back to the Munson family, the highway department would be able to complete their project through the area.

Joe C. Clark, Senior Resident Engineer for the Texas State Highway Department, wrote the City Council of Denison to request that the department have the privilege of filling in the lake to facilitate the construction. Mayor Glidden presented the question to the council saying, "We never have been able to develop this park, and probably never will be, and I recommend we let the highway department build their road through it." The recommendation was approved by Councilmen Weideman and Lebrecht.

However, all was not lost as the year 1967 saw some improvements to the park including the rebuilding of some of the old stone picnic tables that dated to the early days of the property, along with road grading and clearing of areas of heavy undergrowth. A concession stand was added to the baseball diamonds to provide refreshments for patrons at games. It was around this time that a swimming pool was added as well, one of two municipal swimming pools meant to serve Denison. The Munson Pool was meant for one end of the city while the Waterloo Pool serviced the other end.

By 1970 the historic lake was removed to make way for the incoming Highway 84 alignment. The dam was broken, the water was drained, and today little marks the site of what was once one of Denison's premiere city lakes.

A baseball field, lighting, fencing, and backstop were added in 1982 at a cost of $32,196. Other improvements at this time included new picnic tables, grills, and general clearing of brush and debris on the north end of the park.

The Munson Pool was closed in 1985 due to significant structural deterioration caused by a ground fault line that ran underneath the structure. The solution was to fill in the area and an asphalt overlay was completed on the site. A playground was built, and the original covered picnic area retained so parents could watch their children play from a comfortable position.

To make up for the loss of the pool, a Bicycle Motorcross (BMX) track was constructed in 1987 with a $9,721 grant from the UPARR. This was a relatively short-lived amenity as no further mention is made of the facility.

The Munson Foundation continued to aid the park through the early 2000's by awarding nearly $265,000 to help with general improvements to the park and baseball fields. The Aubrey W. and Clara Blackford Smith Foundation also aided the park effort by awarding $5,800 in 2003 to help with the baseball facilities.

Figure 48 A map of the 18-hole disc golf course at Munson Park.

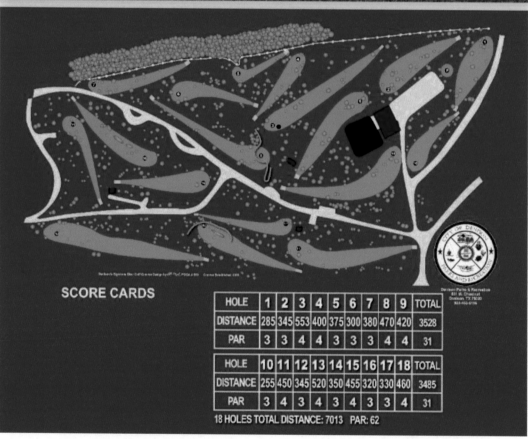

HOLE	1	2	3	4	5	6	7	8	9	TOTAL
DISTANCE	285	345	553	400	375	300	380	470	420	3528
PAR	3	3	4	4	3	3	3	4	4	31

HOLE	10	11	12	13	14	15	16	17	18	TOTAL
DISTANCE	255	450	345	520	350	455	320	330	460	3485
PAR	3	4	3	4	3	4	3	3	4	31

18 HOLES TOTAL DISTANCE: 7013 PAR: 62

An 18-hole disc golf course, designed by noted golfer H.B. Clark, was added to the park in July of 2011. The par 62 course totals over 7,000 feet in length and challenges even the most skilled disc golfer with rolling hills and numerous trees. The area continues to serve as a valuable community asset along one of the main entry points into Denison.

George G. Hopkins Park
By Brian C. Hander

George G. Hopkins was born in Sussex County, Delaware on March 8, 1864, the son of Mr. and Mrs. Selby Hopkins. He was married in Sedalia, Missouri on September 22, 1898, to Miss Dorothy Allcorn. George became an engineer for the Katy Railroad at Sedalia, and eventually made his way to Denison where he became an active member of the First Christian Church.

Hopkins would remain a locomotive engineer for forty-five years before he retired in 1937. He passed away at the MKT Employees Hospital in Denison on December 21, 1956, leaving behind one child, Mrs. Walter Bryant, one grandchild, Mrs. Harvey Walter in England with her husband, Captain Harvey P. Walter, and one great grandchild, Kathy Walter.

On March 20, 1959, the Denison City Council accepted a gift of eight city lots in the 200 block of East Murray from Mrs. Walter Bryant for a recreational park. Mrs. Bryant gave the property with no restrictions except that it be called the George Hopkins Park when developed, in memory of her father.

The city's Park Playground Committee was quickly engaged to study the terrain and make recommendations for development. Picnic facilities were the first to be installed, designed to match those at Forest and Munson Parks, followed soon thereafter by various pieces of playground equipment.

The one-acre wooded site became a beloved neighborhood park and today consists of night lights, a shade structure, playground equipment, three picnic tables, and a basketball court.

Figure 49 Descendants of the Hopkins Family at the entrance to Hopkins Park, 2022. From left to right are Dane Walter, Kathy Coulter, Dorothy Wyskup, and Stanley Walter. Photo courtesy of Kathy Coulter.

Jones Park
By Brian C. Hander

Jones Park, bounded by Shepherd Street, Day Street, Eddy Avenue, and Perry Avenue, was gifted to the city by Minnie M. Jones in 1947 in memory of her daughter, Janis Jones. With this gift, the park became the first in Denison to be named after a female.

Janis, the only child of Minnie and Charles Jones, died tragically from a heart attack in 1932 at the age of 28. Minnie donated the land to be used as a public park and left a large portion of her estate to be used for playground equipment and maintenance of the park property.

A monument was dedicated on July 30, 1947 and reads: *This Playground is Dedicated to the Children of Denison in Memory of Janis Jones by Her Mother.*

Figure 50 The monument to Janis Jones in Jones Park, 2021.

In 1948, a motion was made before the city government to purchase Jones Park for the purpose of expanding Houston Elementary. However, this was found to be in violation of the intent of Mrs. Jones, and the proposition effectively died.

The Boy Scout troop at neighboring Parkside Baptist Church requested the erection of a Scout Hut on the grounds of Jones Park in 1951, but once again this was seen as a violation of the use of the park for the public. With a clear intent that it was meant to serve all no further requests were brought before the city.

Jones Park was given the gift of light in 1952 when the lights that formerly lit Denison's Commercial District along Main Street were relocated to the park. The lights added greatly to the uses of the park and helped light up an area of the city that had no streetlamps of any kind.

In 1953, the Denison Garden Club received permission to plant dozens of redbud trees in a designated spot within the park's boundaries in honor of one of their longtime members, Leona Morgan. The club hoped to beautify areas throughout the city by planting flowering trees and shrubs in parks, along highways, and at public facilities. Sadly, none of these trees survive in Jones Park today.

For much of its early life, the block remained a grassy playground until a park improvement project was launched as part of the 1957 City of Denison Plan of Work. A ball diamond was added, and playground equipment was erected throughout the park, making it a true park for the neighborhoods surrounding the parcel of land.

Figure 51 Newly installed lights at Jones Park, 1952.

In 1985 a grant helped pay for an obstacle course to be installed around the perimeter of the park, and the Jones Trust donated $3,500 in 1991 to help construct a basketball court and goals.

By 2001 the obstacle course had deteriorated and had to be removed from the park. To help make up for this loss the Denison Leadership Class of 2002 helped provide funds for a pavilion and picnic table. Today, the three-acre space boasts playground equipment, a basketball court, a pavilion, and a softball practice field. The marker erected to the memory of Janis still stands among towering post oak trees in the park.

Figure 52 A 1972 view of Jones Park.

Layne Park
By Brian C. Hander

Layne Park was purchased by the City of Denison in 1963 in an attempt by the city to distribute park facilities so that each section of Denison would have at least one available open park area where children could play.

The original area was developed by David H. Coffman Sr. and Joseph Layne who donated land for a school, cemetery, and church in the area northwest of Denison in 1879. The Layne area operated as its own community with its own school until 1956 when it was annexed into the City of Denison. At this time, Layne School became part of the Denison School District and would serve as an elementary school for decades.

The park was filled with playground equipment and a ball diamond was laid out. While the park is not mentioned any further in newspaper articles, it is assumed that the land was donated to the Denison ISD for future school purposes. Once Layne Elementary was closed, and subsequently demolished in 2012, the land was sold, and the park space was no more. Future developments for the area have indicated greenspace could return to this portion of the city, bringing a safe place for children to play once again.

Figure 53 A scene at Layne Park, 1965.

Terrell-Griggs-Marshall Legacy Park

By Dr. Mavis Anne Bryant

Located at the corner of North Mirick Avenue and West Bond Street, the recently established Terrell-Griggs-Marshall Legacy Park occupies the site of the historic Hopewell Baptist Church. The church, a Recorded Texas Historic Landmark, was demolished in 2008.

The State of Texas historical marker remains at the site in a monument erected from remnants of the historic church structure. The park sits just across the avenue from the current Hopewell Baptist Church. Also at this intersection, at 530 West Bond Street, stood Anderson School, one of Denison's first African American schools.

Legacy Park is named after three men much revered in Denison's African American community:

AUGUSTUS H. TERRELL (1861-1929) was an educational, community, and church leader in Denison's African American community. After teaching for several years, he resigned in 1893 to operate a grocery store until his death. Terrell Elementary School is named in his honor.

SUTTON ELBERT GRIGGS (1872-1933), son of Allen R. Griggs, was a noted novelist and minister who lived in Denison when his father was a minister here.

THURGOOD MARSHALL (1908-1993) was the first African American to serve on the Supreme Court of the United States. He addressed an NAACP convention at Hopewell Church in 1952.

Figure 54 The monument sign for Legacy Park incorporates pieces of the historic Hopewell Baptist Church.

W.B. Munson Memorial Recreational Playground

By Brian C. Hander
Miller Park information contributed by James W. Burden

One unique playground in Denison that has been in nearly constant use since its inception is the W.B. Munson Memorial Playground. The land was donated by Munson's daughter, Eloise Munson, in memory of her father. However, in earlier years the park was known by another name, Miller Park.

Originally bounded by the Texas Electric Railway track on the east (Mirick Ave.), fields to the west, and abandoned nursery to the north (the former T.V. Munson vineyard and nursery) and Coffin Street to the south, the area was essentially an unclaimed piece of land that the Cotton Mill community saw as community property. A major shift for the area occurred when Clyde Smith, Walter Boatright, Limly Coffin and a host of volunteers joined together to build a fence, grandstands, dugouts, and a diamond.

Much of the supplies were donated or bought as surplus and when completed the structures boasted many bent nails mismatched boards, and crooked sections. However, it was a thing of beauty to those who had worked so hard to create their own little piece of recreational paradise. All work was completed in 1936 and Miller Park was born. A team was soon formed, known as the Miller's, and soon rallied the small community around them in support.

Figure 55 An early view of Denison's Miller baseball team.

On days when the team was at work, young boys would use the park, playing with bare feet, tennis shoes, ragged clothes, worn gloves, and cracked bats. Much of the time the children used worn baseballs that were made from waste thread from the Cotton Mill. Several of these youngsters would go on to join the Miller team once they were old enough, continuing a tradition that spanned several decades.

The park, as donated by Miss Eloise, opened in 1951 and was the early-day home for the Denison City League, a baseball league for local youth. The playground, which included new and improved baseball grounds, was intended to be open for public use at all times.

With this information, and at the urging of the W.B. Munson Park Committee, the city approved to run water to the site as well as furnishing the park with lights. In 1952, early day Boy Scouts, representing the Denison District Boy Scout Camporee, held their event at the park. Approximately twenty-five patrols, representing every troop in Denison, were expected to participate in the event.

In 1957, commencement exercises for Denison High School were held at the ballpark. This was to be the first instance graduation was held in the open instead of the high school auditorium where graduates from more than half a century had received their diplomas.

The class of 1957 voted to unanimously to go through with the new idea and their selected graduation theme was "Our American Heritage". However, the weather did not turn out well and the graduation was moved to the auditorium of the Junior High at the eleventh hour on account of wet grounds and more rain in the forecast. Undaunted, future classes voted to hold their commencement exercises outdoors and a tradition was born that still continues today.

Figure 56 The flagpole and original base at the Munson Playground, 2021.

Beginning at the end of the 1950's the playground became the home of the annual Denison Cotton Mill employee reunion and would continue as such for several decades.

Over time Denison High School was expanded to include portions of the playground and the ball diamond became the home of the Fighting Yellow Jacket baseball team. The memorial flagpole and base still remain at the site as a lasting tribute of the gift that the Munson family gave to the south side of Denison.

Oldham Park
By Brian C. Hander

The first mention of Denison's Oldham Park occurred on June 17, 1888. The park was the brainchild of Colonel W. M. Oldham who hoped to garner a street railway extension to his property where he planned to develop a large subdivision.

The public was invited to the park each Sunday where watermelons on ice and cold lemonade and sodas were available. Swings and hammocks were set up beneath large shade trees for families to enjoy and many friendly games were played during an idle Sunday afternoon. While the park itself was free, omnibuses run by Harnest and Co. did charge 25 cents for the round trip to the site.

The area was meant to coincide with the posh suburb known as The Boulevards which had seen large mansions built on well-spaced lots. Oldham Park was near the end of Shepherd Street, and Colonel Oldham was so committed to the cause that he was willing to put himself into debt to help finance the rail line.

While intentions were good, the privately owned park and surrounding land never became the area that Colonel Oldham had envisioned. Following the Panic of 1893 and Denison's Night of Terror that saw unspeakable tragedy at The Boulevards, the entire area was essentially abandoned. Once beautiful homes were either moved to other parts of the city or left to deteriorate, and the dream of Oldham Park with its surrounding development became lost to time.

Local architect Donald Mayes would re-envision the wild and untamed space at the end of Shepherd Street as the Edgehill addition in the middle of the 20th century, creating one of Denison's most unique and sought-after suburban developments that would have made Colonel Oldham proud.

Lelardoux Park
By Brian C. Hander

Denison's Lelardoux Park appears to be the shortest lived of all of Denison's parks. The name first appeared in 1891 and the site was described as being located at the corner of Mirick Avenue and Elm

Street. The Sons of Hermann, a local German fraternal organization, used the park to observe their first anniversary on July 26, 1891.

The park encompassed several acres that made it the perfect venue for a picnic and reception area and was generally accepted to run from Washington (now MLK) Street to Johnson Street and Mirick Avenue to Fannin Avenue.

The land that comprised the park area was owned by Pierre Lelardoux, a French born architect well-known in Denison's elite circles. He was credited with the design of the Leeper/Security Building, the State National Bank, the Waples-Platter Building, the Acheson home, and the J.B. McDougall home, among several other extraordinary structures.

Lelardoux eventually retired from design-work and went on to try to develop his land in north Denison. By 1898 he was offering lots for sale on the former park, now known as the Lelardoux Addition, at half price. As the lots were sold and developed Denison lost one of its gathering places. With only seven short years of existence the park faded from public knowledge.

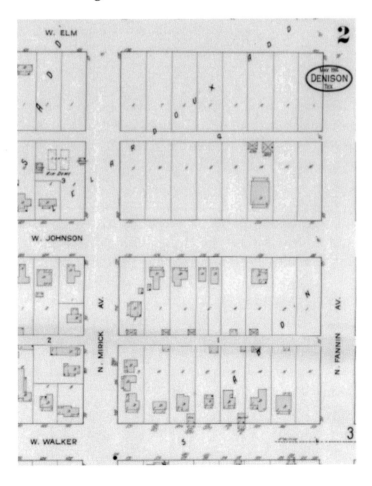

Figure 57 The 1914 Sanborn map showing the location of the Lelardoux Addition.

Lions Club Park
By Brian C. Hander

In 1953, Miss Eloise Munson, on behalf of the W.B. Munson Foundation, donated an entire city plot between Woodard and Main Streets in the 1600 block to the Denison Lions Club for the site of a playground. Sponsorships of playgrounds by the Lions Clubs had become a nation-wide project alongside the club's eyesight conservation work.

Figure 58 Two neighborhood girls play with their dog in the new Lions Club Park shortly after it was donated by the Munson Foundation.

The piece of land had historically been occupied by a large Katy Railroad water reservoir that served the old Ray Yards area. After being abandoned for a number of years, the reservoir was filled in and the site graded into what was assumed would make an ideal playground area.

Shortly after the donation of the block, Lions Club member Ed Winter made the following statement before the Denison City Council, "it may be rather unusual, but I have come before the city council to give the city something rather than ask for something."

Winter wanted the city to assume title of the plot of ground to help aid the organization in upkeep and management of the playground. The gift was received by the city and could be kept so long as the property remained in use strictly for park purposes.

Mr. Winter made the request that the name of the park be "Denison Lions Club Playground Park." This was requested since the local Lions Club had agreed to maintain the property for use as a Little League ball field alongside city efforts to improve the block.

It was anticipated that the ball diamond was only to be the first of the improvements that would include tennis courts, wading pools, and other facilities. The steering committee to make the improvements included Jack Barker, Hub Brown, and Fred Sneed.

A Boy Scout hut was moved from South Fannin to the park in 1955. While the hut was moved, no mention was ever made of when it was removed from the park as it does not exist at the site today. The City of Denison still retains ownership of the park and ballfield that occupies the site.

There is a monument sign at the northeast corner of the park that reads: *"Lions Club Park. May 11, 1965. The Lions Club of Denison, Texas, recognizes the devoted service of its members to the Little League and the youth of this community. W. E. (Bill) Byrd, Lonnie D. Legg Sr., Clayton B. Smith, Curley O'Donnell, W. L. Hightower, A. L. Strickland, Wesley Moss."*

Katy Golf Course
By Brian C. Hander

Denison's Katy Golf Club came into existence in the late 1920's following an explosion of public interest in golf throughout the country. Prior to this, golf was seen as an exclusive sport for the well-to-do, however, it quickly became popular as a recreation sport for the masses.

Figure 59 The monument sign at Lions Club Park, 2022.

The site near the intersection of the Katy tracks and Crawford Street was owned by the Katy Railroad and had previously been used as the old Ray Yards. The railroad outgrew the space and relocated the yards to a larger plot of land on Mirick Avenue, leaving a large area of undeveloped property in the heart of the city. Citizens of Denison had been on the hunt for a municipal course of their own and this site would fit the bill wonderfully. The golf club was allowed to use the property under a lease agreement with the railroad that involved a token payment only.

The idea for the course was the brainchild of W. H. Hall, superintendent of the Katy Telegraph Department for many years, and the original intent was that the club would serve employees of the Katy Railroad. Hall was joined by the Chief Clerk of the Telegraph Department, Herman Krattiger, who played a pivotal role in developing the idea into a reality.

Beginning in 1933, the club organized a traveling team that played against neighboring towns in 18 rounds of golf at various venues. The first friendly game occurred against Durant with 26 members of the Katy Club making their way to play the links of the Durant Country Club.

The Katy course was remodeled and improved through the years and was able to meet the needs of a very large number of regular players and transient guests. By 1947 the club had grown to an astonishing 165 members and boasted a very active women's group. This group was headed by Mrs. Helen Brooks as President; Mrs. Maxine Crowson,

Vice President; Mrs. Willard Overbeck, Secretary-Treasurer; Mrs. Leonora Bunch, Tournament Chairman; and Mrs. Frances Tignor, Food Chairman.

The Katy Golf Club held an annual club tournament and alternated with the Rod and Gun Club in hosting the yearly city tournament. By 1948 the club was at a low ebb and the Denison Kiwanis Club came to the rescue. The organization held their annual fundraiser and donated 25 percent of the proceeds to the Katy Golf Club to help build back the golf course and fairways.

One of the final recorded events held at the golf course was in 1982 when the Denison Jaycees sponsored a 3-mile run at the site. The once prosperous club was abandoned following the sale of the Katy Railroad to the Union Pacific Railroad Company and, except for the development of soccer fields on a portion of the property, has remained largely undeveloped since that time.

Current plans call for a large investment in the soccer field area to create a multi-use sporting venue for the community. This investment will include upgraded fields and lighting, basketball and pickleball courts, a walking trail, and playground area.

Figure 60 An aerial view of the Katy Soccer Complex plan as presented before the City Council in 2022.

Denison Rod & Gun Club
By Brian C. Hander

The Denison Rod & Gun Club was created on May 14, 1890, with J.J. Fairbanks as chairman and A.F. Platter as secretary. The first meeting was held in a building identified as the "Philosophical Hall" with quite a number of gentlemen arriving at the appointed hour. At the initial meeting, fifty men gathered and agreed to pay $100 each to form the club. There were no dues charged to members with funds expected to be raised from members as the needs of the club evolved.

The membership selected a site on Clear Creek, 18 miles west of Creede, Colorado in an area known as Antelope Park, San Juan, Colorado. This location was deemed highly favorable due to its plentiful fish and wild game. The first clubhouse was a two-story stone and frame log building that had been occupied as a family residence by a man named C. Mason.

Following the adoption of by-laws, the group commissioned R.S. Williams of Del Norte, Colorado to haul six loads of lumber to the cabin site to begin the building program which included a large expansion of the former Mason residence.

The first President of the group was Major L.L. Maughs, with "Uncle" Ben Merrell the Vice President; A.F. Platter, Secretary; J.T. Munson, Treasurer; W.A. Hollenbeck, Steward; and Levi Lingo, Dr. W.H. Mills, T.B. Waldron, J.J. Fairbanks, and Platter as directors. Members were assessed when needs for financing arose. During the first decade the assessments were around $25 each, and when some of the original group failed to pay up, they were promptly ousted from the membership rolls and forfeited their $100 investment.

The lure of big game and fish in Colorado waned throughout the years and in 1905, under the urging of W. B. Munson, Sr. the Colorado site was sold, and 205 acres Northwest of Denison were purchased for a new club. Munson proposed raising the capital

Figure 61 A view of the first Denison Rod & Gun Clubhouse in Antelope Park, Colorado, 1894.

structure to $12,500 to finance the construction of a dam for a club lake and a clubhouse.

Amenities for the new club location included a gun range for trap and skeet shooting, duck blinds for hunting, a fishing pier, and a place for swimming. By 1908, more financing was required, and the stock was raised to $25,000.

Even before the clubhouse was completed, J.W. Madden built a cottage on the grounds, and E.J. Smith (father of Aubrey W. Smith) and Jim Haven formed a partnership to build a second. These two cottages were widely used to house hunting parties and social gatherings before the clubhouse and basement was built. An African American couple identified only as George and Nora were the first formal stewards of the club, and their tasks included cooking for members and keeping the clubhouse in good working order.

A golf course was added to the club grounds in 1922 and included a nine-hole layout. This was accomplished thanks to the shortening of the work week from 72 hours to 60, allowing more leisure time. The original layout was nine holes with Munson taking the lead on the project. The layout of the first nine holes remains the same to this day.

Following the addition of the course, the name was formally changed to The Denison Rod & Gun Country Club. The organization quickly became the social center of Denison and North Texas.

Figure 62 A view of the original clubhouse in Denison, ca. 1918.

In the spring of 1923, a building committee was formed with the purpose of approving remodeling plans of the clubhouse and property of the Club. The plans called for nearly $5,000 worth of improvements, including quite a few changes to the facilities. The ceilings on the ground floors of the clubhouse were lowered to allow for a more inexpensive heating system. A kitchen was to be added with the old kitchen and dining room torn out to make way for 76 lockers and showers for men, and 30 lockers and showers for women.

A winter and summer dining room were planned, and a new porte-cochere was anticipated at the entrance to the clubhouse building. Charlie Bengle was the architect on the job with local contractor W. B. Pyburn overseeing the work. A new manager, Mr. D.S. Cuthbert, took over the club as well. He was to be a golf instructor, repair broken golf clubs, make clubs, and oversee all clubhouse and dining room concessions.

A fire in 1924 completely leveled the historic clubhouse, however, the members would not be deterred. They rallied together to raise the capital stock for the fourth time, raising $37,500 to finance the new building. The Club was well attended for decades, retaining an important place in the social lives of its membership.

Figure 63 A view of the newly rebuilt clubhouse, ca. 1929.

The capital stock was hiked once more in 1956 to $62,500 following a 95-4 vote of the membership to approve an $85,000 expansion program that included a complete remodeling of the interior of the club, installation of central heating and air, and the construction of a swimming pool.

A 5-year oil lease was signed with C.H. Nicholson, an independent oil operator in 1963.The five-year lease totaled $6,965.65 and a $1 per acre per year renewal was included for the following four years. This income proved invaluable as shifting social past-times began to cut into the club's normal membership base.

Fire seemed to be an ever-present threat for the club for on May 14, 1972, the clubhouse once again was destroyed in a fateful blaze. A new clubhouse with a restaurant and banquet facilities was added just over a year later, and within five years four tennis courts were constructed for member use. The course was expanded to a full eighteen holes in 1978.

Over time, the name of the organization was changed to the Denison Country Club, although many locals continue to call the site the "old Rod and Gun Club."

The club was purchased in 2013 and a reported $7 million was spent on restoring the fairways and club buildings. However, club memberships continued to wane, and the Denison County Club closed for good in the spring of 2020.

Figure 64 & 33 Above, the Denison Rod and Gun Club's lakeside clubhouse, ca. 1968. Below, an ariel view of the club's lake and clubhouse structures.

In August of 2021 local entrepreneurs with Carrus Health purchased the club and grounds with plans to open a venue in the renovated clubhouse by October. While the amenities such as the tennis courts and pool were planned to reopen there were no plans announced for the golf course. Now the future of Denison's great recreational paradise hinges upon the promising new vision for the historic property.

Figure 65 A 1950's aerial view of the Denison Rod and Gun Club lake and golf course.

Riverside Park
By Brian C. Hander

One of Denison's most unique parks was located along the Red River. No photos of the site have ever been located and no infrastructure exists along the banks of the river to allow viewers to see Denison's lost paradise. All we have are stories that have been passed down and early newspaper accounts of a park that truly faded from existence.

The following appeared in the *Sherman Daily Democrat* on January 30, 1919, "Denison people are to have a park and playground of about forty acres fronting on Red River. W.B. Munson, capitalist and philanthropist of that city who has already made several substantial donations of park property to the City of Denison, has offered to deed a forty-acre tract of land near the old Annie P. landing to be used as a riverside park, conditionals upon the tract being improved and a road opened to it from the J.T. Munson Park. Mr. Munson's offer has been accepted and it is expected that Denison will soon have a delightful picnic ground and park on Red River. The proposition of employing George F. Kessler to plan the improvement of the tract and also the cemeteries recently acquired by the city is receiving consideration, it is said."

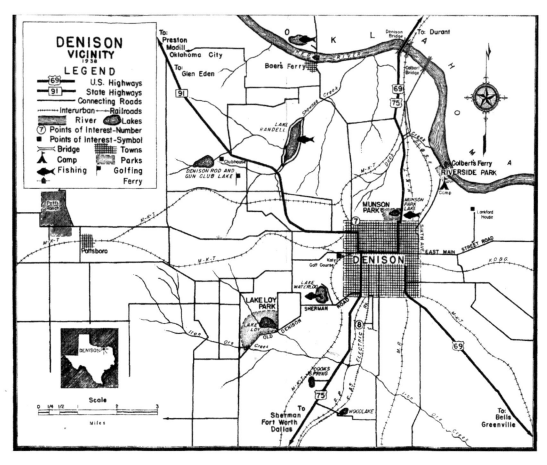

Figure 66 A 1938 Denison map showing the location of Riverside Park near Colbert's Ferry.

A large Fourth of July program was expected to be held at the new park shortly after the January 1919 announcement. There were to be power boat races, water sports, and other "doin's" to make for a great old-fashioned celebration. A new roadway was to be constructed and Dr. A.W. Acheson stated that W.B. Munson, Sr. would put men to work erecting a fence to enclose both the roadway and the new park.

Following the celebration, the east end of the park was decided to be devoted to commercial purposes. The idea was that it could be an area of service to the planters along the river. At this time, the Riverside Park Committee consisted of Alex W. Acheson, Chairman; B.J. Lindsay, Treasurer; W.J. Scott, Secretary; and Franz Kohfeldt.

While the park had been in use for some time, it wasn't formally dedicated until June 9, 1924. The ceremony began near a flagpole known locally as Flagpole Hill. Those in attendance included Mayor Walter S. Hibbard, Captain J.P. Leeper and the 36th Division Signal Corps, the American Legion men, local Boy Scout Troops, and the DeMolay band under the direction of Tommy Herron. Special tribute to the park was paid to Dr. Alex W. Acheson with the naming of Fort Acheson at the site. It was noted that this was a unique fort as it had no cannon, no bayonets, no ammunition, or soldiers. Only the ammunition of patriotism, justice, and fight.

Figure 67 The 1939 WPA Denison Guide that featured directions to Riverside Park.

The park continued for decades as a hidden gem in Denison. By 1934, the Denison Relief Bureau was able to provide twenty men for 12,000 hours to repair roads and bridges within Riverside Park. Several months later an additional 2, 560 hours for twenty men to each receive $768 was approved for the grading and widening of the road from Denison to Riverside Park.

The only known directions to the park were published in a WPA guide in 1939. The directions stated that the driver should start at Main Street and Houston Avenue in Denison, head east on Main Street to North 5th Avenue, the left and west four blocks to a gravel road where another left is to be taken. The last turn was to take the traveler to Riverside Park and Colbert's Ferry Landing.

It appears that the park was eventually abandoned with a portion of the property reverting back to the Munson family. The other portion became the home of Denison's wastewater treatment plant and operates as such to this day.

Templemeyer Lake
By Brian C. Hander

One of Denison's lost pieces of paradise was created by Fred and Emma Templemeyer on a 20-acre tract in the 2300 block of West Walker Street in what was then far west Denison. In 1915, the enterprising couple began construction of their own lake. This required the manual labor of friends, family, hired hands, and teams of horses to dig out the 100-foot by 200-foot lakebed and accompanying earthen-rolled dam. The lake was fed by both an underground spring as well as copious amounts of run off, quickly filling the area to its 20-foot-deep capacity.

With the completion of the lake came the need for amenities to attract crowds. Several species of fish were stocked in the lake and diving boards were added along the dam. Bath houses were put up and by the summer of 1916 the area was ready for visitors. Crowds flocked to the new outdoor venue for swimming, fishing, and even baptismal services.

While the lake proved popular in the beginning, other swimming holes such as Bush Pool began to draw vital business away from the lake. The dam was weakened by heavy run-off from seasonal rains and eventually split, sending most of the water and fish to a pond northeast of the site. The dam was rebuilt only to break once again. The third time proved to be the charm and the rebuilt dam still exists to this day.

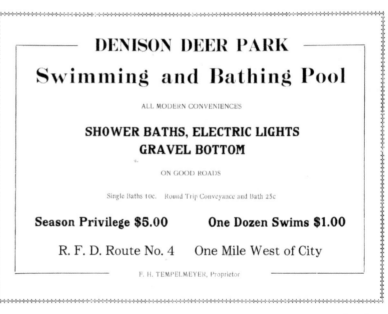

Figure 68 An early advertisement for Lake Templemeyer, sometimes referred to as the Denison Deer Park.

Fred Templemeyer died in February of 1934 and the lake was closed to the public following his passing. Several smaller ponds were dug around the lake and the entire area became one of the largest fish hatcheries this side of the Mississippi. The property was eventually sold in 1966 and was expected to be redeveloped in the 1970's into Manning Plaza, a multi-unit retirement village.

The lake, now only twenty-five percent of its original size, still exists to this day. Plans were approved in 2021 for a large housing addition that would take up much of the 40-acre site. Several of the smaller ponds will be leveled to make way for homes, although green space and park-like amenities will be built throughout the new neighborhood. The area, Denison's first pleasure resort, will continue to serve as a type of paradise, just in a different manner than originally conceived.

Grayson County's Castle-Loy Lake Park
By Donna Hord Hunt

"What is that big castle-like thing out at Loy Lake?" is a familiar question for anyone who has ever ventured to the park in west Denison. The mysterious tower that stands on the highest point in Loy Lake Park frequently catches the eyes of travelers.

The answer is that it once was a water tower constructed by the Civilian Conservation Corps in 1933.

The water tank and pump equipment were removed years ago, but the distinctive, castle-like structure still attracts the interest of anyone who sees it. I have no doubt that hundreds of photographs of the tower are floating around. I think I have a few of those photos myself.

The old rock water tower once held equipment and stored the water for use by the park superintendent at his nearby house and at the concession stand not far away. It was used when swimming at the lake was in its heyday in the late 1930s, '40s and early '50s.

Figure 69 Judge Loy, the namesake of Loy Lake Park.

In my file is information from a brief article that was sent to me in case I wanted to use it in a story. Today is a good time to share it. The article came from *The Dallas Morning News* in 1937 and is headlined "Denison Loy State Park Improvement to Begin."

I may be getting a little ahead of myself here, talking about improvements since the park was only a few years old at that time. Grayson County actually purchased 350 acres of land for the park in nine tracts in 1931, mostly from the McCarthy Estate.

Work on building the lake was done by the CCC, an agency of President Franklin D. Roosevelt's New Deal that provided employment during the Great Depression. The park first was known as Grayson County Park, then was changed to Loy Park in honor of County Judge Jake Loy, who had spearheaded the establishment of the lake. A bronze bust of Judge Loy sits at the entrance to the Texoma Livestock and Exposition Grounds.

Camp first was set up by the CCC and the workers began digging rocks out of the lakebed. The rocks were used to build the superintendent's house, concession area and dressing rooms, sidewalks and a stairway that led up the hill from the swimming area to the concession stand, as well as a wall at the water's edge and along the beach.

The rocks also were used to build the water tower.

Figure 70 The Loy Lake Park water tower, February 2014. Photo by Larry D. Moore.

The government spent $150,000 improving the land for a county park with the understanding that the improvements would become the property of the county when the work was completed.

But success was not immediate because the lake remained dry for months until a 5-inch rainstorm drenched the area on a summer day and in about two hours the dry basin held water. Times were pretty tough then, and money was in short supply. On Oct. 15, 1934, Judge Loy called a special session of Commissioners Court and the park was dedicated to the State of Texas.

Commissioners, in their dedication, said it seemed that the public was interested in completing, improving, and decorating the park. Several thousand dollars in improvements had been made by the Federal Government, but the county still didn't have the money to complete the project. By dedicating the park to the state, the county had access to all the advantages and conveniences while the state bore the expense of upkeep to the park in keeping with other state parks. Past records show, however, that the state didn't accept the park.

So, on May 14, 1937, commissioners rescinded its dedication because more than two and a half years had passed and the state parks board had ignored the agreement, allowing the spillway to become badly damaged as well as roads, bridges, fences, land and buildings to show neglect.

Then, as if to make up for lost time, the court got busy and set up rules for the park. In August of that year electric power was installed to light the beach, picnic area, and concession stand. That's about the time the 1937 article was published, saying that a CCC project that had employed men in a $21,509 improvement program at Loy State Park would begin with Grayson County appropriating $12,826 toward the project, covering much equipment and material that already had been purchased.

The CCC "boys" became known as "The boys who made Roosevelt Famous" for their work that had begun in 1933. I was told by a Denison woman several years ago that her brother was a CCC worker and was paid $30 a month of which $25 was sent home to his family. He lived on the remaining $5 a month, but his food and lodging were provided, mostly in Army tents.

Usually, the CCC workers weren't hired to work on projects in the area where they lived, but in the case of Loy Park projects, officials brought in 48 young Grayson County men and assigned them to the project. It was this group that built the castle-like tower to house the water well and an elevated storage tank. All the buildings and the superintendent's house were built with native rock dug out of the lakebed.

At that time the tower, which still stands on a high point of the park, was built, it was the most outstanding feature of the CCC construction. About 4 million people saw service in the CCC, many from right here in Grayson County. Among the accomplishments of the CCC were the 40,000 people who learned to read and write, soil erosion was arrested on 20 million acres of land, trees and brush were cleared for more than 39,000 acres of reservoir sites and many more achievements all over the state by the different CCC camps.

Today, the concession stand and dressing rooms are gone, as is the fishing pier and the sandy beach by the swimming area, and the dance floor and its jukebox. There are no more Fourth of July political rallies that brought thousands to the lake to hear what was called "speakings" by those seeking office. There are no more Girl Scout camps, where scary stories about the water tower were imagined in the middle of the night by a bunch of scared young girls.

The best thing that has gone away is the unorganized Fourth of July fireworks display that turned into a virtual "World War III" every year with the fireworks going in all directions. That was pretty scary if you were in the area.

These activities have been replaced by a Christmas Lights display every year that is free to the public. Grayson County Frontier Village that is the county's official museum, the annual livestock show and various other events that take place in that area. The picnic tables still draw families on outings in nice weather, and frequently you can find a fisherman somewhere around the lake. I'm sure I'm leaving something out, and if I do, I apologize. Loy Lake was the "stomping ground" for many teenagers growing up before there was Lake Texoma.

BATHING BEACH, LOY LAKE

Figure 71 A 1938 view of the Loy Lake Bathing Beach from The Denison Guide.

Loy Park still is a special place in Grayson County and that old castle-like, rock building continues just as mysterious looking today as it has been for years.

Iron Ore Creek Cemetery
Researched by Tina DiToma

This cemetery, sometimes referred to as the Iron Ore Baptist Church Cemetery or the Pool Cemetery, dates to the founding of the Iron Ore Baptist Church in 1871. The congregation formed their church in an area known as Honey Run (sometimes referred to as the Ellsworth Community), located between present day Denison, Texas and Sherman, Texas.

During the early days of the church, the congregation numbered 500 in membership, and it is thought that their first place of worship was a brush arbor in this area.

In 1922, Iron Ore Baptist Church moved from the Honey Run/Ellsworth Community to the 1500 block of West Dubois in Denison. Once again church services were held under a brush arbor until a more permanent structure could be acquired.

A small frame school building was purchased from the Golden Rule School on April 6, 1922, for $100.00. The first choir was organized in 1926 and a remodeling effort took place in 1943. The church was rebuilt in 1968 and a fellowship hall added in 1979. Over the years, this small Baptist Church has continued to serve its community and congregation.

The earliest burials in the cemetery are unknown due to aging of the sandstone or iron ore markers, none of which bear any discernible identification. The earliest known burial dates to 1882 with the last recorded in 1940. Many of the burials were recorded by the George Shields Funeral Home. There are approximately forty-five known grave markers in the cemetery including cast stone and marble headstones, funeral home markers, and markers made of iron ore or sandstone.

The cemetery lay forgotten for many years until development of surrounding parcels of property unveiled the sacred place. Realizing the importance of our cemeteries as part of our community's story, local historians researched the history of the area and graves, applied for, and earned recognition of the Iron Ore Creek Cemetery as an official Historic Texas Cemetery in 2010. The site received the honor of having the first City of Denison Historical Marker bestowed upon it in 2019.

Figure 72 The entrance to Iron Ore Creek Cemetery, 2021.

Denison's Lost Fountain
By Brian C. Hander

Denison's Women's Christian Temperance Union was organized in 1881 to promote total abstinence from alcoholic beverages which was viewed as a leading cause of the plight of abused and neglected women and children at the turn of the century. A water fountain was erected in Denison in 1890 by the W.C.T.U. to discourage men from frequenting saloons with an alternative to alcohol.

The fountain was installed at the intersection of Main Street and Rusk Avenue just outside of the Madden Department Store. As originally designed, the fountain had a place where people, dogs, and horses could drink. Two large granite troughs were placed at the base of the fountain for horses while different heights of basins on the main structure were meant for dogs, children, and people.

The large statue of a woman that had stood guard atop the fountain for many years was torn off in the early 1920's when a farmer allowed his team to ram the monument with the wagon tongue while the horses were drinking. Subsequently, the fountain was cut off from the water supply and did not operate for several years. In July of 1925 friends of Sarah Acheson, a long-time leader of Denison's W.C.T.U., thought the fountain should be moved to a public location to better serve as a token to her memory.

Figure 73 Members of Denison's W.C.T.U. during the dedication of the water fountain at Main and Rusk.

The fountain was moved to Forest Park within a matter of days where it was hoped to remain in memory of Mrs. Acheson. The granite basins were also moved to locations that were deemed appropriate to serve the community. One granite basin bearing the name Acheson resides at the former home of T.V. Munson in south Denison. Based on knowledge of the fountain it is believed that this trough was once part of the original configuration of the W.C.T.U. fountain on Main and remains the last known piece of Denison's lost fountain.

Figure 74 The Acheson memorial trough, once thought lost, now resides at Vinita, the historic home of T.V. Munson in south Denison.

Figure 75 The rebuilt remains of the W.C.T.U. water fountain once it was relocated to Denison's Forest Park, ca. 1930.

CHAPTER 3

From Boomtowns to Ghost Towns: Denison's Untold Communities

"Great cities are not static; they constantly change and take the world along with them."

-Edward Glaeser

Denison was always destined for greatness from its very inception. A rough and tumble patch of growth located along a rail line quickly grew into the Gate City of Texas. At one point in the beginning of the 20th Century, Denison was even anticipated to outgrow Dallas and Fort Worth. While growth-stunting events such as the Railroad Strike of 1922 and the Great Depression greatly inhibited the once grand vision of what Denison could be, her citizens never stopped working to move their community forward.

However, with the growth of any community can come the absorption, reorientation, or even loss of nearby communities. This was seen in Denison when both the Layne and Cotton Mill communities were annexed into the city limits and became part of Denison and its school system. The same also happened for the Hyde Park community. Growth was inevitable, it was how community leaders worked to ensure that all involved could grow together that made the difference.

For one community though, Denison's very existence negated any development that had occurred and relegated the once-bustling little enterprise into nothing more than deep ruts along the Red River's bank. This similar fate also occurred to Denison's first suburban shopping center, Sugar Bottom. As the community grew, the suburbs reached further away, and Denison's little space of mom-and-pop shops became just another row of vacant buildings along a once-thriving highway. This chapter hopes to tell the stories of these two lost communities that they not be forgotten.

Red River City
By Brian C. Hander

Red River City began as a store that was built by Benjamin, Jim and Frank Colbert and Charles Gooding on the Texas side of the Red River across from the popular Colbert's Ferry stop. The store was called the "First Chance, Last Chance" and marked the beginning of what would become Red River City. The merchandise consisted of grocery items, dry goods, and whiskey.

By 1867, the community had grown and was an important stop for the Butterfield Overland Mail and Stage service. The bustling, rowdy settlement consisted of transients, cowboys, and wagon masters looking to cross at Colbert's Ferry into Indian Territory. The little town traded in buffalo hides and acted as an important supply point that afforded gaudy entertainment to travelers across the river.

A claim was made that a man was killed on every 25 feet of the business blocks, and a group of ex-Confederate soldiers were organized into a makeshift police organization to preserve some semblance of peace.

Plans originally called for the M, K & T Railroad, and the Houston & Texas Central Railroad to construct a terminal at Red River City, thus cementing the small settlement as an important trading center in North Texas. The townspeople were so excited and sure of future success that they built a post office, the only permanent structure in the community at that time. The post office was built before filing with the U.S. Postal Service was even approved.

However, the settlement ultimately missed out as the M, K & T opted to choose a site further south of Red River City and 217 feet above the level of Red River, creating an environment free of the diseases that plagued the river bottoms. This new town would be named Denison. To add insult to injury, the U.S. Postal Service denied the request for a post office in Red River City, citing that another community already had that name in Texas.

While the M, K & T Railroad pushed south to Denison, the Houston & Texas Central Railroad ran tracks parallel to the Katy and into Red River City. The animosity between the two railroads was evident from the start over which would be superior in developing a town.

The Houston and Texas Central was chartered in the State of Texas and felt it was their right to build a line into Indian Territory. The company sought an injunction against the Katy Railroad demanding that they cease construction of their line into Texas from the north since they weren't chartered in the state. The founders hoped this would force the Katy to use the H&TC lines and thus end the establishment of Denison.

An agreement was eventually reached between the two railway companies which allowed the Katy to have its station in Denison and the H&TC to remain in Red River City. The Texas Central finally arrived at Denison on March 10, 1873. Cars coming from the south to be transferred to the Katy were taken on to Red River City where the Katy picked them up. Likewise, cars coming from the north for transfer to the Texas Central were brought into Denison, then back down the hill to Red River City.

This revitalized the community somewhat and the railroad even began construction of a two-story hotel. However, after the foundation for the new structure was laid, the Texas Central began looking for a private developer and found no one willing to invest in the project, ultimately leading to the abandonment of the enterprise.

After just three months of transferring the cars, the Texas Central relented and began to stop in Denison. However, the rivalry remained, and it is said that when Katy trains would drive through Red River City that residents would come out of their homes and throw rocks at the trains. This lasted until 1874 when an agreement was reached that any citizen of Red River City that moved to Denison would be given a lot by the Denison Town Company free of charge.

For many residents moving was easy, all they had to do was pack their tents and move to their new location. Others just rolled up blankets and it was reported that some only had to rise from the ground and shake themselves in the morning before starting their trek southward.

The first mayor of Red River City was a Captain Faulkner, General Passenger Agent for the Houston and Texas Railroad Company. One prominent citizen and short-term postmaster for Red River City, John Ourand, began a mercantile in Red River City but left for Denison in 1874, becoming wildly successful in all manner of business pursuits and building a stately home that remains today.

It was announced in the local newspapers that Ourand was moving his buildings from Red River City to Denison and would set up shop in the 100 block of West Main with a fine stock of

Figure 76 The Ourand home in the 100 block of West Sears Street, ca. 2009.

liquors. George Cutler, a prominent newspaper publisher, moved his printing equipment into the settlement and started publication of the Red River City Journal, publishing the first edition in red ink.

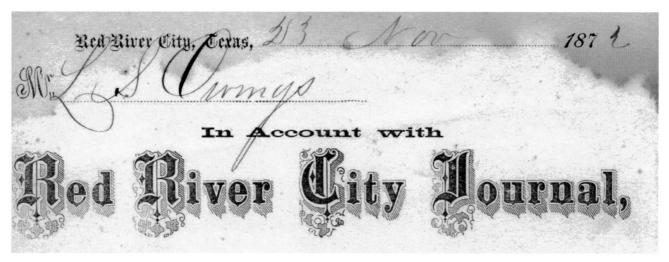

Figure 77 A receipt from November 23, 1872 with the Red River City Journal masthead. The receipt is made to L.S. Owings who became the first mayor of Denison.

Once the new town of Denison was announced, Cutler loaded his press on a wagon and headed south to the Infant Wonder, switching his masthead to the Denison Journal.

The small town's final demise came in 1876 when torrential downpours caused the Red River to swell and leave its banks. The floodwaters overtook Red River City, and the H & TC abandoned their lines and from then on ran on Katy rails. Only one log cabin remained after the flood and on March 14, 1876, and the Texas Central began pulling up their tracks for use in other projects in Houston.

The final portion of Red River City made its way through Denison on August 8, 1877. What was left of the depot had been dismantled, loaded onto three railcars, and was being taken to Houston. The present site of Red River City is estimated to be on the East side of Highway 75 where the Munson family has their Red River Sand Company. Nothing remains of the tiny community that tried, but ultimately missed out once Denison began to shine.

Getting to the Bottom of "Sugar Bottom"
By James K. Sears

Figure 78 A view of Sugar Bottom by Jenkins Studio. Source: Maguire, Jack. Katy's Baby: The Story of Denison, Texas. Austin, TX: Nortex Press, 1991, p. 41.

The area of Denison, Texas, that lies in or near the 600 block of South Armstrong Avenue has been known as Sugar Bottom for longer than anyone can remember. How did it get its name?

The two most widely repeated versions of the origin of the name can be found, like the above photo, in *Katy's Baby: The Story of Denison, Texas*, a book written by Denison native Jack Maguire and published thirty years ago.

A Sweet Place Called "Sugar Bottom"

In truth, Denison from early times had been one of the very few small towns that had a "suburban" business district. It was a stretch of a few blocks along south Armstrong Avenue and adjoining streets which the townspeople called "Sugar Bottom." Exactly why this small commercial area developed some distance from downtown and how it got its name are facts lost to history. There are two versions, both probably apocryphal, as to how its unusual designation originated.

One story is that a gang of rowdy boys who called themselves the "Huckleberry Gang" became angry with Gideon Stephens, the cantankerous owner of the neighborhood grocery. One night they broke into his store, took a barrel of sugar and dumped it along South Armstrong. From then on, the name "Sugar Bottom" stuck.

The other — and more likely — story is that a Katy crew was switching freight cars where the tracks still cross Armstrong Avenue. The main line had not been cleared when a passenger train rounded the curve and splintered a freight car loaded with sugar. The sweet cargo spilled into the street. At any rate, Sugar Bottom got its distinctive monicker and some little fame. Shanty Morrell, who grew up there and went on to become a well-known orchestra leader in Texas, wrote a ballad called the "Sugar Bottom Blues." It was a mild hit in the state.

Maguire, Jack. *Katy's Baby: The Story of Denison, Texas.* Austin, TX: Nortex Press, 1991, p. 104.

Figure 79 The original Sugar Bottom story from Jack Maguire's Katy's Baby.

The first step in gauging the authenticity of either of Maguire's stories is to ask whether it could have happened prior to January 13, 1876, when the name "Sugar Bottom" first appeared in print.

By that measure the second version, which Maguire considered the more likely of the two, is actually less likely. Sugar spilled from a freight car requires a train, which in turn requires a track. The 1876 bird's-eye map of Denison shows no railroad track in the area that we now know as Sugar Bottom. On the 1886 map a track is clearly visible crossing Armstrong Avenue just above Nelson Street, but at the start of 1876 the neighborhood had already acquired its name, and the track had yet to be laid.

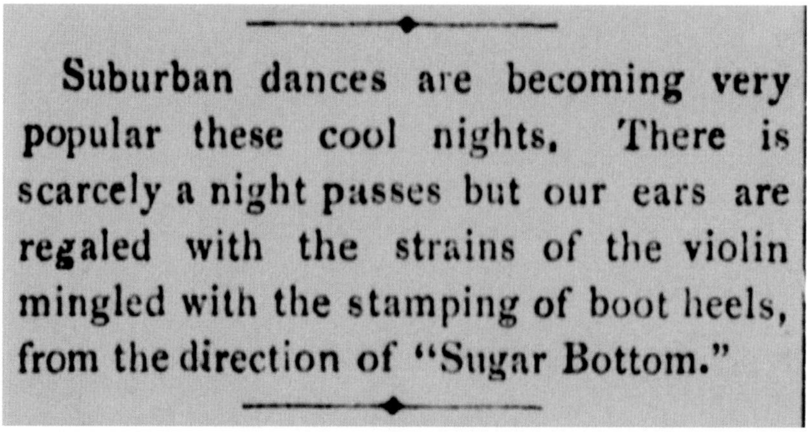

> Suburban dances are becoming very popular these cool nights. There is scarcely a night passes but our ears are regaled with the strains of the violin mingled with the stamping of boot heels, from the direction of "Sugar Bottom."

Figure 80 An excerpt from the Denison Daily News. Vol. 3, No. 275, Ed. 1 Thursday, January 13, 1876, Page 3

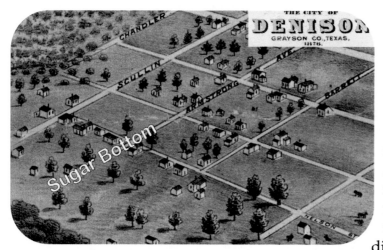

Figure 81 A view of the 1876 Bird's Eye View Map of Denison, TX. Morse, D.D. The city of Denison, Grayson Co., Texas. [Denison, TX: D.D. Morse, 1876] Map (detail with overlays). https://www.loc.gov/item/2013592212/.

The first version is only slightly more likely than the second. Gideon Stephens came to Denison from Butler County, Kansas, in late 1875 or early 1876. His first appearance in a Denison City Directory is in the 1876 edition, compiled in the fall of that year. He and his son Sidney are both listed as farmers residing at the southeast corner of Barrett Avenue and Nelson Street. The directory does not list a Stephens-owned store. Gideon appears to have started out in Denison as a farmer instead of a merchant.

In any case, he would have needed to arrive and open his store prior to early January in order to be considered for a role in the origin story of Sugar Bottom. The earliest known mention of him in print in Denison is on March 11, 1876, in a *Daily News* report of his being fined for disturbing the peace. That is two months too late to have been early enough. What, then, is the earliest date that he could have been in Denison? Before he left Kansas he sold his farm there to a man from Tennessee.

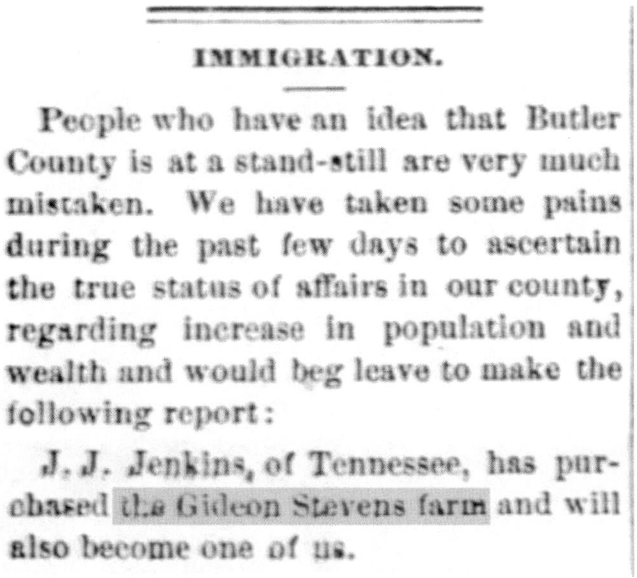

The date of the newspaper is December 24, 1875, only twenty days earlier than the first mention of Sugar Bottom in the *Denison Daily News*. What is the likelihood that Stephens could have moved his family to Denison, opened a store, got on the wrong side of the Huckleberry Gang, and had his store burgled, all in less than a month's time? Perhaps the break-in happened at a later date. If the Huckleberry Gang took its name from Mark Twain's character, Huckleberry Finn, the gang would have been formed after December of 1876, when *The Adventures of Tom Sawyer* was first published in the United States. Assuming that the story is accurate in most of its other particulars, we can safely conclude that it is more likely that a barrel of sugar was selected by the gang to be dumped precisely because Stephens' store was in Sugar Bottom than that the neighborhood derived its name from the contents of the barrel.

IMMIGRATION.

People who have an idea that Butler County is at a stand-still are very much mistaken. We have taken some pains during the past few days to ascertain the true status of affairs in our county, regarding increase in population and wealth and would beg leave to make the following report:

J. J. Jenkins, of Tennessee, has purchased the Gideon Stevens farm and will also become one of us.

Figure 82 An excerpt from the Walnut Valley Times (El, Dorado, Kansas) Friday, December 24, 1875. Page 2.

Maguire admits that both stories are "probably apocryphal." Keep in mind that, when he published the book, he had been reading and writing about Denison and Texas history for more than fifty years. In all that time he was unable to gather any tangible evidence to corroborate either story, both of which he probably heard as a boy growing up in Denison in the 1920s and '30s.

There is persuasive evidence, apparently unknown to Maguire, pointing to an altogether different origin story. Denison pioneer B. C. Murray, editor and publisher of the *Denison Daily News,* and later of the *Sunday Gazetteer,* left us a valuable clue when he identified the man who gave Sugar Bottom its name. He was John W. Pecor, alias Patsey McJackson.

Denison (TX) Daily News
Vol. 4, No. 16, Ed. 1 Friday, March 10, 1876, Page 3

Patsy McJackson has the honor of naming Sugar-Bottom. When he gave that locality its name he little thought it would become so notorious.

The Sunday Gazetteer (Denison, TX)
Vol. 22, No. 49, Ed. 1 Sunday, March 20, 1904, Page 4

Early Days in Denison.

Items of Local and General Interest Taken From the Columns of the Denison News

WEEK ENDING MARCH 11, 1876.

........Patsy McJackson (Pecor) gave South Denison the euphonious name of Sugar Bottom, which it retains to this day.

Figure 83 Two excerpts, published 28 years apart, that state the Sugar Bottom origin lies with Patsy McJackson.

These two items appeared in Murray's newspapers twenty-eight years apart. In the second one the "Pecor" in parentheses confirms that Patsy (often spelled "Patsey") McJackson's real name was John W. Pecor. Why he chose to call himself Patsey McJackson is unknown, but it suggests that he had an affinity for nicknames. A native of Richmond, Virginia, he was in Denison by June of 1875. At that time he was about twenty-three years old. Not long after he arrived, he was hired by Murray to deliver copies of and to solicit subscriptions for the *Denison Daily News*. Their business relationship developed into a friendship that lasted until Pecor's death twelve years later.

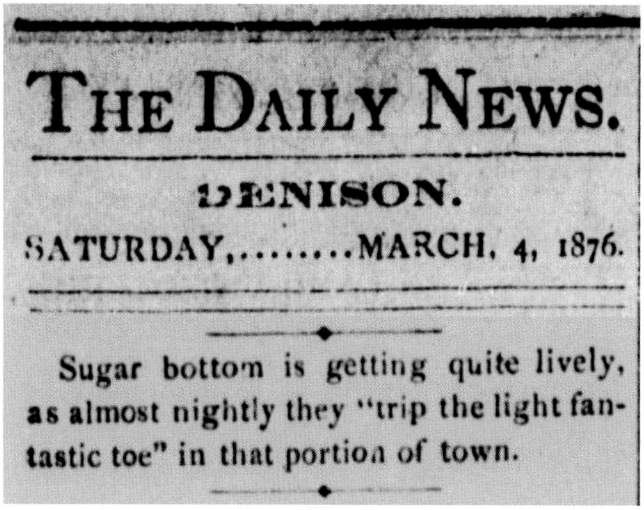

THE DAILY NEWS.

DENISON.

SATURDAY,........MARCH. 4, 1876.

Sugar bottom is getting quite lively, as almost nightly they "trip the light fantastic toe" in that portion of town.

Figure 84 An excerpt from the Denison Daily News. Saturday, March 4, 1876.

The map of Sugar Bottom shows that South Armstrong Avenue was near the southern and western city limits in 1876. Around the time that Patsey McJackson arrived in Denison, the neighborhood had acquired or was rapidly acquiring a reputation for rowdy revelry.

Sugar Bottom retained its unsavory reputation through at least the end of the decade.

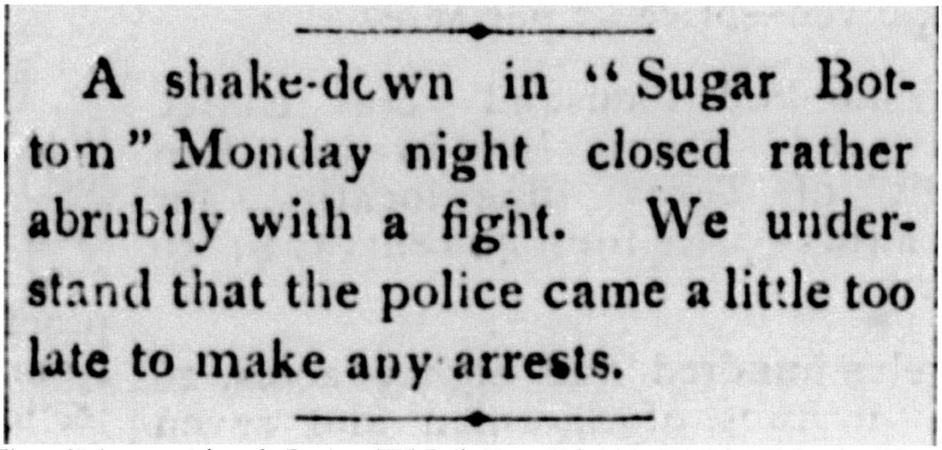

A shake-down in "Sugar Bottom" Monday night closed rather abrubtly with a fight. We understand that the police came a little too late to make any arrests.

Figure 85 An excerpt from the Denison (TX) Daily News. Vol. 6, No. 294, Ed. 1 Wednesday, February 5, 1879, Page 4.

Although the word "shakedown" connotes a type of extortion today, in early Denison newspapers it referred to an evening of boisterous dancing.

The name "Sugar Bottom" almost certainly came, like J. W. Pecor himself, from the city of Richmond, Virginia. Around the time of the Civil War the Confederate capital included several seedy neighborhoods.

They persisted throughout the war and for at least a decade beyond. Pecor, who was eighteen years old in the 1870 Census, would have been familiar with their colorful names, even if not with the neighborhoods themselves.

Byrd Island has a wide but unsavory reputation. The neighborhood, as popularly known, lies between the river and the canal, bounded on its eastern side by the Haxall Mills and its western by the Tredegar Works. It includes within its limits such disreputable places as Sugar Bottom, Rummersville, Horse Alley, and Glory Hole. There are a few respectable people living within its limits, and there are many honest workmen who are employed over there in the day-time, but the great majority of its denizens belong to the lowest dregs of our population. Here vice raises its hideous front and is not abashed. Here lewd women and worthless men congregate to spend the night in drunken orgies. Here squalid poverty and hopeless misery confront the passer-by. Many of the houses are dilapidated. Those backing on the canal between Tenth and Twelfth streets are notorious in the annals of crime. At this row Mary Holmes was murdered, and soon afterwards her friend Mary Melton, weary of the world, without a friend to point her to a new and better path, rashly resigned her life and went forth to meet her Maker with all her sins upon her head. Her companions survive and follow in the old, old way. Byrd Island has few redeeming features. Its streets are begrimed with coal-dust; its pavements are ragged; and altogether it is little favored by the City Fathers. A more unpromising yet a richer field for Christian labor is nowhere to be found in Richmond.

Figure 86 An excerpt from the Richmond Dispatch of Richmond, VA. May 29, 1875. Page 1.

Newspapers in both Denison and Richmond used the phrase "lewd women" in stories about their respective Sugar Bottoms. Pecor, noting that and other similarities, probably began using the borrowed nickname as a joke. Murray apparently liked it well enough to use it in print, and the name stuck. After his competitor paper, the *Cresset*, picked it up, he was quick to give credit for the sobriquet to his own employee.

Although Sugar Bottom in Denison could claim a consensus on respectability by the end of the nineteenth century, its sister suburb in Richmond struggled with its reputation until relatively recently. Within the last five or six years increased demand for new housing has finally led real estate developers there to begin improving that long-benighted neighborhood.

And what became of "Patsey" Pecor? He had the misfortune to contract pulmonary tuberculosis in his early thirties, and he died in Denison at the age of thirty-five. He lies in an unmarked grave somewhere in Fairview Cemetery.

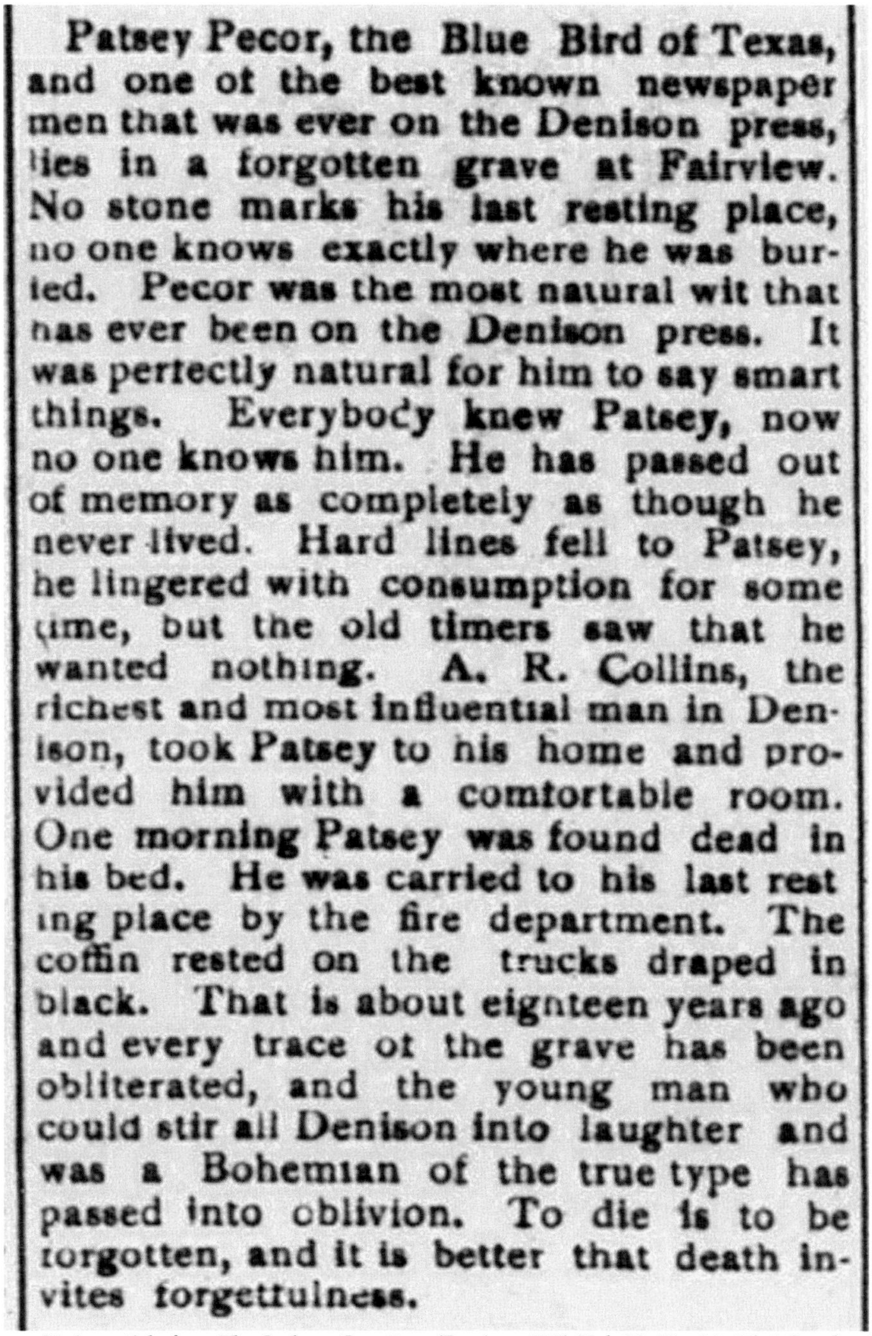

Patsey Pecor, the Blue Bird of Texas, and one of the best known newspaper men that was ever on the Denison press, lies in a forgotten grave at Fairview. No stone marks his last resting place, no one knows exactly where he was buried. Pecor was the most natural wit that has ever been on the Denison press. It was perfectly natural for him to say smart things. Everybody knew Patsey, now no one knows him. He has passed out of memory as completely as though he never lived. Hard lines fell to Patsey, he lingered with consumption for some time, but the old timers saw that he wanted nothing. A. R. Collins, the richest and most influential man in Denison, took Patsey to his home and provided him with a comfortable room. One morning Patsey was found dead in his bed. He was carried to his last resting place by the fire department. The coffin rested on the trucks draped in black. That is about eighteen years ago and every trace of the grave has been obliterated, and the young man who could stir all Denison into laughter and was a Bohemian of the true type has passed into oblivion. To die is to be forgotten, and it is better that death invites forgetfulness.

Figure 87 An article from The Sudnay Gazetteer (Denison, TX) Vol. 23, No. 34, Ed. 1 Sunday, December 4, 1904, Page 4.

Having now read this explanation, the next time you hear that spilled or dumped sugar was responsible for naming the neighborhood around the 600 block of South Armstrong Avenue in Denison, it will be your civic duty to speak up and give proper credit to the "worthless" male and "lewd" female inhabitants of the place a century and a half ago. Try to remember to mention Patsey McJackson, too.

CHAPTER 4

Into the Wild Blue Yonder: Untold Transportation

"A mile of highway will take you just one mile...but a mile of runway will take you anywhere!"

-Author Unknown

While the railroad may have given birth to Denison, it by no means defined it as the only mode of transportation that the city would offer. By the beginning of the 20th Century, Denison was joining the Good Roads Movement and undertook major public projects to ensure that roads throughout the community would be ready for the automobile. Travel proponents also diligently worked to see the Red River made navigable, even going so far as to charter a steamboat, The Annie P., to make its way up the river to Denison.

But through these all, the thought of flight held the biggest promise of hope. Planes could take people further and faster than any train track or road, and the surrounding topography proved to be a great resource for the creation of runways. This would later be proved when Grayson County was selected as the site for the Perrin Air Force Base, and Denison was one of only a handful of contenders that was considered when a site was being selected for the United States Airforce Academy. However, before all of this was ever even a dream, there was a tiny airfield in the middle of a pasture. This chapter pays tribute to the tiny airport and its underdog fight to become known far and wide.

Gray Field
By Brian C. Hander

While Denison has a long been a railroad town with industries and infrastructure meant to further this mode of transportation, it also has a history of innovation through air travel. The first airfield in Denison was Gray Field, named for Dick Gray, a reporter for *The Denison Herald* and Denison's Fire Marshal. The future in air travel was clear, and Gray wanted to see that growth brought to Denison.

In 1926, he began seeking financial support for the endeavor and with private donations, alongside fundraising efforts of the Denison Junior Chamber of Commerce, funds were raised, and 100 acres of land were leased two miles east of the city. The property, owned by Clarence Richardson and formerly a part of the Richardson Dairy enterprise, was easily accessible with its location between East Main and East Texas Road.

Very little clearing of the property was needed, and a hangar was quickly constructed. By the fall of 1928 the airfield was opened with the arrival of a squadron of Army/Air Corps fighter planes from Randolph Field. By the end of the day, hundreds had come to the airfield to view the latest flying technology close up.

The airfield did well for over a decade with groups going out on the weekends for flights and Braniff Airlines stopping during the week to refuel on trips from Tulsa to Dallas.

The Chamber of Commerce had the airfield resurveyed in June of 1939 in the hopes of further expanding the location's offerings. Charles Hayden was contracted for the survey and was expected to submit the blueprints to the government, after which the field could be placed as a landing spot on government air maps.

Figure 88 A postmark advertisement from 1929 boasting the formal opening of Denison's Gray Field.

Within two months' time, runways had been marked off and graded and a huge 100-foot circle to help fliers locate and land had been constructed. The airfield was expected to be included in the Aeronautical Authority's "Weekly Notices to Airmen," that was sent to all recognized airports throughout the nation. A great deal of expectations was placed on the airport becoming busy during the construction of such projects as the Denison Dam.

Further improvements made to the airfield included the addition of a three-plane hangar and the widening of runways. The new hangar was meant to house passenger planes and private planes that may need to stop at Denison. Roads to the airport were also regraded in the hopes of spurring further travel to the site.

However, no amount of growth and construction could prepare the airfield for what lay ahead. The outbreak of war in 1942 caused the shutdown of all operations at the site. Fuel was in short supply and pilots were needed for the war effort, and the airstrip returned to pastureland for cows once more. The main hangar, once used to hold the pride of Denison's small fleet now held only hay.

All was not lost though! The airfield reopened in July of 1944 under manager and flight instructor Tom McBee. The unerring Mr. McBee would bring in planes and helped gain enough support to have more hangars built for the growing enterprise.

Sixteen German Prisoners of War were brought in to build the hangars each day then would be returned to their camp at the future site of Lake Texoma each night. Ingenuity such as the use of this readily available labor would be a hallmark of McBee's tenure.

Figure 89 Planes at Gray Field from the collection of Grayson County Frontier Village.

In January of 1946 the Civil Aviation Authority and Veterans Administration approved Gray Field as a civilian and veteran flight school location. Within one year of the certification, there was a total of fifty-eight flight students enrolled in courses. By 1947 over twenty private planes were maintained at the airfield and Denison celebrated its Diamond Jubilee with a giant, old-time air circus. Over 1,000 spectators came out to view planes from all over the United States.

Post-War Aviation became incredibly popular among men and women, and Gray Field was no exception. Four Denison women became students and soon flew planes all along Denison's airspace. The women included Miss Lorene Doane, 1220 West Main, a cashier at the Rialto Theatre; Miss Zoe Rutherford, 200 East Hull, a trumpetist hoping to have a professional music career in New York; Miss Anita Doyle, a Physical Education teacher at Denison High School, and Mrs. Ouida Self, an employee of the Denison District of the U.S. Corps of Engineers.

Alongside the women learning to fly was Air Scout Squadron Number 204, referred to as the Denison Eaglets. This group was learning to fly as part of the Boy Scouts of America program and included Donald McBee, Leonard Isom, Epifanio Vaillareal Jr., Raymond Myers, Vittie

Corthron, Bradford Mott, Ralph Mullikin, O.M. Pearson, Eugene Barens, Glenn Neidert, and Ed Briggs.

In September of 1949 the airport, which had gone inactive for nearly a year, was sold to Frank and Henry Wilburn of the Wilburn Brothers Grocery and Meat Market. The two brothers, owners of an airplane themselves, planned to maintain two runways and a workshop for the convenience of local flyers.

The Denison City Council hoped to help with the endeavor by promising to help gravel and level Gray Field by supplying both excess gravel and the use of a grader. The airfield had to furnish their own truck to haul the gravel and the grader could only be operated by a regular city driver, as was the rule of the council. It was hoped that the grading effort would enable chartered passenger trips to take off and land at the field, thus bringing a greater number of planes and funding to Denison.

Hangar fires in the 1950's strained the airport's finances and maintenance of the property began to decline. The field, running north and south with no professional grading of any kind, was no longer desirable or well adapted for modern and sophisticated aircraft. The airfield slowly drifted out of the public eye and nature began to take over.

The remaining hangar was used to store hay for livestock until it too succumbed to fire in the 1960's, leaving nothing but a partially visible slab that still exists today.

The land eventually became the home of a family vineyard, known as Hidden Hangar Vineyards, in the 1990's. In 2017, the vineyard and grape supplier became a producer of its own Texas wines and in 2020 opened a tasting room onsite as well. Hidden Hangar pays homage to the lost airfield while carrying on a wine-making tradition spanning three generations.

Chaos in the Streets of Denison
By Natalie Bauman

Today, modern drivers believe highway traffic is crazy and chaotic. People in Denison in the late 1800s had to, at times, face even more terrifying scenes of chaos in their once tranquil downtown streets and sidewalks. The Denison Daily Cresset on March 27, 1877 reported that rampaging horses were making incompetent fools out of the local Austin city police and causing major upset in the town. Actually, what really occurred is, a driver was arrested for leaving his team of horses standing unhitched on the street, and it served him right in the words of the Austin Leader newspaper. The Denison newspaper wondered what a place Austin must be. Suppose every man who left a team unhitched on the streets of Denison were arrested? Wouldn't there be fun? Oh no, the newspaper cried, Denison ain't that kind of a place. Our officials don't care if two or three teams a day run away, jeopardizing both life and property. Mayhem and chaos reigns, there were many runaways causing much injury, death and destruction on the streets. Let 'em run, say they – our most sublimely impotent officers.

They really knew how to throw out an insult in grand style back in those days, didn't they? It would almost put you in such a good humor, you would forget to be offended -- almost. But wait, it gets better, or worse, according to your point of view.

Back in those days, animal menageries were a huge fad in Denison, including Boland Saloon and Dyche's Menagerie at Pickwick's Saloon. These wild animals being kept right on the Main Street of town was a ticking time bomb as well.

A huge rattlesnake measuring four feet in length and about six inches in circumference was killed on Rusk Avenue near the State National Bank in downtown Denison on October 15, 1895. A well-known citizen suggested that an investigation be instituted to ascertain, if possible, which of the two contiguous saloons had permitted the dangerous reptile to escape from their animal menageries - Sunday Gazetteer. Was it possibly Dyche's Menagerie at Pickwick's Saloon? Was it Boland's saloon in the Atlantic Gardens on the corner of Main Street and Houston, with its zoological collection? Was it one of the other saloon's collections gone wild? The businessmen and patrons of Denison were uneasy about what might await them around the next corner on the streets of Denison. Had some dangerous wild animal or venomous reptile escaped to wreak havoc on the innocent population? Were proper precautions being taken to contain them?

It seemed the answer was often – No. You know what that meant – more chaos on the streets of Denison.

John Boland had a bull buffalo hanging out right on Main Street in Denison as an attraction at his saloon according to the Denison Daily News on February 6, 1880. It was also reported that he had added a raccoon to his zoological collection, one of the least frightening of the assortment. Boland's Saloon also displayed live venomous snakes, monkeys, bears and cougars. Would you want to meet any of those on your stroll down the city street?

Inevitably, John Boland's bull buffalo took a notion into his massive wooly head one day that he would enjoy the air of freedom for a while.

He broke loose from his fastening and sauntered onto the downtown Main Street. The fact that a buffalo was running loose, created a ripple of excitement, to put it mildly. The buffalo took things as easily as if he was roaming in his native wild. He walked majestically up Gandy Street in Denison, with about one hundred young urchins rapidly following, but at a respectful distance. Several times the buffalo turned, lowered his head and charged, scattering the pursuers. He was captured near the Washington school after a lively chase. (It sounded like all the school children were out chasing the buffalo, what could go wrong there?) After some trouble, he was driven into the back yard of Boland's saloon.

There were people living in Denison then who could recollect when buffalo grazed in the wild almost in sight of Preston Bend. Now and then, an immigrant wagon would pass through Denison's streets with a buffalo cow and calf trailing behind it, instead of the expected domestic cow. This caused a stir in the streets for various reasons when it occurred, depending on how tame the buffaloes in question had become.

The buffalo, once numbering in the millions, were made almost extinct by the efforts of the ubiquitous buffalo hunter in the 1870s and 80s. This was done for profit, and in an effort to force the Native Americans onto reservations by slaughtering their main source of food and supplies, the buffalo. This made Indians and buffalo hunters mortal enemies and set the stage for war between them. A buffalo hunter named "Chet" Finney who went from Denison told of a narrow escape he had from a Comanche war party. He was chased many miles, but when the Indians got too near, he would turn on his horse and stand them off with his big gun. He escaped to a creek bottom where many other buffalo hunters were in camp, and the Indians, consisting of a very small number, abandoned the chase.

It sounds implausible, but one of the most successful buffalo hunters on the range was an English woman. She was a dead shot, a fearless rider and able to protect herself against rough associates and outlaws. The story was, that she was the daughter of an English Lord, who arrived in the country with her husband and was deserted by him. Her life would furnish material for a good novel – that is, if the story is true. She disappeared from the range, and it is said, was finally reconciled to her husband, and returned to England.

The Sunday Gazetteer on November 28, 1909 confirmed that many buffalo hunters had passed through Denison and the surrounding area over the years.

Many of the buffalo hunters were rough, dangerous men, many of whom passed through nearby Red River City and Denison. Killings were a huge problem in Red River City just to the north of Denison. The Denison Gazetteer reported at the time: Mr. Budlong was in Denison and stated that at least 100,000 buffalo pelts had been received here, he being the largest buyer, and as many more went to Fort Worth and other markets, but Denison was the largest buyer. That was the largest buffalo train that ever arrived in Denison. Many other smaller ones followed. On one day on November 20, 1875, Mr. Holland alone, purchased 1,400 dried buffalo hides, which were brought in from the far west. The hunters and wagon drivers were paid off at Denison and turned their money loose with a lavish hand. They went down on old Skiddy Street (now Chestnut Street) and made a lively time in the saloons and houses of ill repute. Chaos, anyone?

Chaos comes in many different forms. Whether it be rampaging horses, venomous serpents, charging buffalo bulls in the street, out of control hunters looking for a good time or speeding cars driven by texting teens; chaos and vulnerability to serious harm seems to be a timeless ordeal we must all face. However, the odds are vastly against any of these chaotic occurrences, so relax and enjoy your day!

Annie Peruna followed Annie P. on Red River
By Donna Hord Hunt

Figure 90 The Annie Peruna, a tribute to the first steamship to reach Denison on the Red River.

A lot has been written through the years about the *Annie P.*, the first steamboat to navigate the Red River. It was early in 1905 that the *Annie P.* plowed up the river from New Orleans to Denison, proving the Red River was navigable.

Now we learn that a Denison-built boat also had its day on Red River a short time later.

What was intended as a whimsical, but not mocking parody on the voyage of the *Annie P.*, the *Annie Peruna* was built in Denison later the same year and used on the river for a while. Bert Ford, one of

- 102 -

Denison's earliest gasoline motor mechanics, and Lon McAleer, owners of a Sugar Bottom coal and wood yard, were builders of the boat. An unbylined and undated yellowed article clipped from *The Denison Herald* said "the two were always ready for anything that broke away from the humdrum."

Bert died in Denison and Lon died a few years later in Red River County, where he had purchased a sizeable tract of land after he left Denison.

The article said that the *Annie P.* probably was the inspiration for the *Annie Peruna*, and the Denison builders undoubtedly took their cue from the former in selecting a name for their 25-foot boat.

The Annie Peruna was powered by a one-cylinder gasoline engine of early design that rotated the stern wheel that moved the boat. It was built in town, then taken on house-moving blocks to the Colbert crossing, where it was launched.

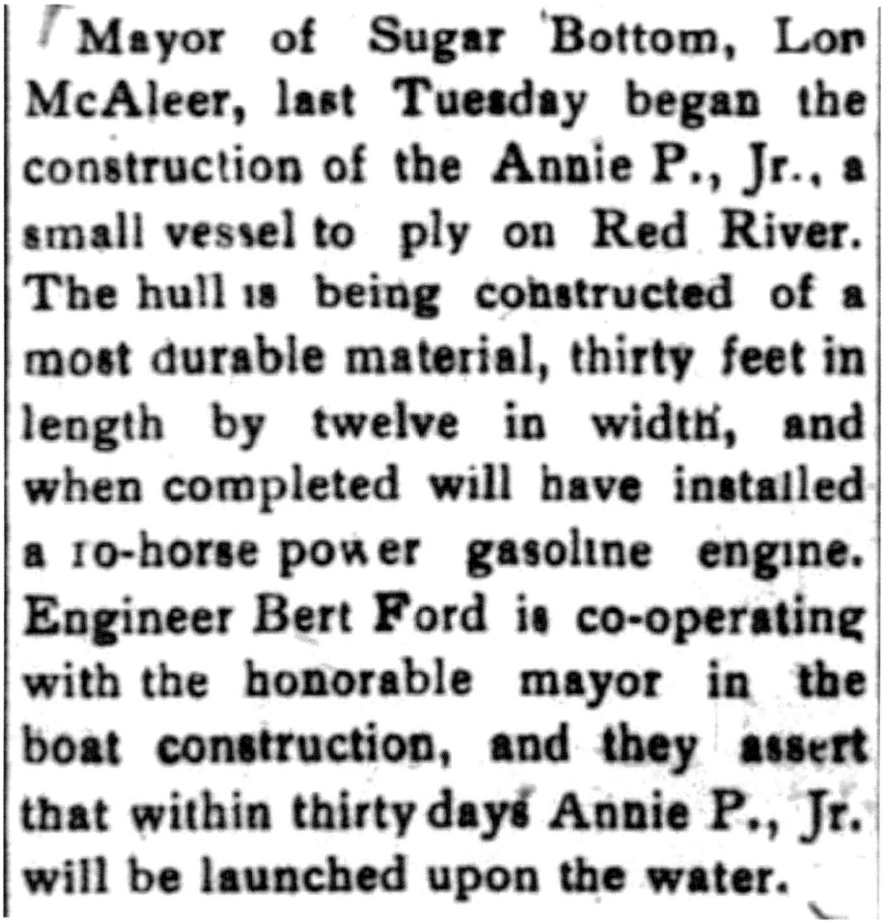

Mayor of Sugar 'Bottom, Lon McAleer, last Tuesday began the construction of the Annie P., Jr., a small vessel to ply on Red River. The hull is being constructed of a most durable material, thirty feet in length by twelve in width, and when completed will have installed a 10-horse power gasoline engine. Engineer Bert Ford is co-operating with the honorable mayor in the boat construction, and they assert that within thirty days Annie P., Jr. will be launched upon the water.

Figure 91 A description of the Annie Peruna from The Sunday Gazetteer, May 28, 1905.

A picture taken by Carl Davault was taken as the boat was being inched toward the river. The flat-bottomed craft drew only a few inches of water and could negotiate the sallow stretches of the river with pretty good safety. The boat was christened by the two builders who broke two bottles of beer on it.

The men had hoped to fight their way upstream as far as possible, but after the Annie Peruna sat on the surface in its first "sink or swim" test, they were joined by T. E. Horan, and headed west up the river at a snail's pace.

Mr. Horan had been in ill health for some time and became violently ill before the Annie Peruna reached Gainesville. The boat headed back downstream to return the ill member of its crew to Denison. He died the next day after his return. [He died on August 6, 1905 and was buried at Fairview Cemetery.]

After that Ford and McAleer made jaunts up and down the river. The *Annie Peruna* had its day at churning the river into foam and finally was dismantled.

I'm no boat expert, but the article said the *Annie Peruna* had "fore and aft compartments, one housing the engine and the other the crew's quarters." Between the two compartments was an open space where meals could be cooked and the crew could "lounge." The wheel at the "prow" controlled two rudders, one on either side of the paddle wheel at the stern.

McAleer dubbed his coal and wood yard in Sugar Bottom "Fort McAleer" and loaned atmosphere to the shop with a towering flag mast, where colors fluttered on every occasion. A couple of improvised cannons always could be relied upon to furnish the percussion for a celebration.

The Annie P. was built by a ship contractor in Shreveport, Louisiana, for W.M. Porter and named for his wife, Annie. A former Denison resident, Walter C. Sanders, a veteran river pilot, joined Porter in going 40 miles below Shreveport and helping cut trees that were sawed and used in construction.

As work on the hull was completed, just like with Noah and his ark, the rains came, the river rose and the boat floated off its stand. It was towed to Shreveport, where the superstructure was added.

In the spring of 1903, the boat, which was said to have cost $1,000, passed federal inspection and was approved for a 71-ton cargo. However, the boat spent most of 1904 as an excursion craft taking passengers from Shreveport to Ruby Park. The fact that liquor could be sold on water, but not on land, may have helped its high passenger interest.

Then through a contract with Porter, the boat was to be delivered to Denison for $2,000 and Porter, the owner, was to receive the proceeds from the sale of freight on

Figure 92 A crowd of people rides the Annie P. as it puffs along the Red River.

o sale on the boat until it docked in Denison.

At Shreveport the boat was loaded with a variety of cargo, including plows, grindstones and whiskey. But Porter got a little scared of trouble over the whiskey and dumped it overboard, according to an early story.

On board the boat for its historic voyage were Porter and his wife; Tom Grimshaw, a reporter for the Denison Herald; ship captain and pilot Tom White; assistant pilot, carpenter, and watchman Sanders; engineer Ed Holden and eight crewmen.

The Annie P. docked north of Denison on April 21, 1905, but news didn't get around until morning. Then people came from far and wide to see the steamboat. Town leaders came for speech making led by Dr. Alex Acheson and E.A. Thompson, publisher of *The Denison Herald*.

Figure 93 The steamship Annie P. the day after it arrived at Denison on the Red River.

Figure 94 Denisonians celebrate in early day autos. Above, a photo from the Moose Parade in 1912. Below a photo of the impromptu parade honoring the Denison Dam after Congress approved funding in 1939.

CHAPTER 5

A History of Healing: Untold Medical Stories from Denison's Past

"Wherever the art of medicine is loved, there is also a love of humanity."
-Hippocrates

Denison's first step into the acquisition of a hospital occurred in 1873 when the community was less than a year old. The structure was located just off of Austin Avenue on Skiddy Street (now Chestnut Street) and featured fifty beds for patient care. However, a cholera outbreak in September of 1873 led to widespread death and a very real image problem for the fledgling community.

The citizens felt the hospital had failed to control the epidemic and no longer supported the institution, causing its closure within less than a year of opening. Denison would have no true hospital services for nearly forty more years.

Once medical services became more readily available, a variety of healthcare establishments opened within the community. Many of them shaped neighborhoods and helped craft Denison into the regional healthcare hub that it is today. While none of these previous facilities exist, their stories are worth telling.

Denison City Hospital
By Brian C. Hander

The ever-increasing need for quality healthcare finally led the citizens of Denison to begin plans to build their own institution in 1910. The citizens voted to purchase property on East Hull Street and construction began in 1913 with an open house for the community held on January 25, 1914.

Figure 96 A postcard view of the Denison City Hospital, ca. 1920.

Originally known as the Denison City Hospital, the life-saving institution was equipped with the latest and most up-to-date medical technology and occupied an impressive three-story edifice.

The hope was that the Katy Railroad would purchase the building and see both employees and residents, however, the Katy officials turned the proposition down. Their statement was that the Railroad was not financially able to take on the added responsibility of serving both their own employees and the public at large.

By the 1930's the hospital structure was in dire need of repairs. The estimated cost of repairing the building and equipment came out to $50,000, a seemingly insurmountable sum of money. The City of Denison sought a bond election, but the measure failed, and with it state and federal funds were also denied. Something had to happen in order for healthcare to continue for Denison residents which is when the Sisters of Divine Providence came to the rescue.

Figure 97 An early view of Denison's City Hospital before operations were taken over by the Sisters of Divine Providence.

The Sisters agreed to take over operations of the hospital if Denison's citizens would deed the property to them. The citizens overwhelmingly voted for the transfer and the hospital was closed on July 16, 1944, for a major remodeling project. The interior was completely gutted and rebuilt, and landscaping of the grounds was completed. While construction was underway the Katy Hospital agreed to accept patients so that Denisonians would not have to go without care. The new hospital, now known as the Madonna Hospital, opened on September 1, 1945.

As originally designed during the renovations, the hospital's floors were divided up and named as halls. The main floor of the hospital, known as the St. Ann Hall, housed the administration offices and a nursing unit for medical and surgical patients. Madonna Hall on the third floor was the site of the maternity ward and surgery suite with accompanying rooms for surgical patients. The ground floor housed St. Joseph's Hall where the lab, x-ray department, drug room, central service room, blood bank, emergency room, laundry, and additional patient rooms were located.

A Convent for the Sisters was connected to the hospital and the main kitchen was also located in this wing. A chapel was also provided in the Convent for use by the Sisters, patients, and visiting public.

Figure 98 Two architect's renderings of the Sisters' proposed changes to Denison's City Hospital. Several of these desired changes and additions would not occur for another decade. Design is attributed to Easterwood & Easterwood Architects based out of Waco, TX.

WELCOME
to
MADONNA HOSPITAL

Sisters of Divine Providence
Denison, Texas

Figure 99 The cover of an early-day welcome brochure at the Madonna Hospital.

In its first year, the hospital had treated 2,929 patients and 501 babies had been delivered. Within just a few years the hospital admitted 16,500 patients in a single year, marking the need for more rooms and space.

The hospital flourished under the direction of the Sisters, and by 1951 was in need of an expansion to keep up with the patient demand. Miss Eloise Munson donated $30,000 towards the effort that covered the gap that grants and loans weren't able to cover. Ground was broken on January 26, 1951 for what would be the largest expansion project the hospital would ever face.

A new two-story addition was built on the north side of the structure shortly after the donation. The new structure was dedicated on October 11, 1951, and increased the hospital's capacity to sixty-five beds. This annex would later become known as the Munson Wing following another gift from Ms. Eloise in the mid-1960's towards the hospital's building fund.

In 1958 the hospital began its own program for the training of Licensed Vocational Nurses. The first class graduated in September of 1959 and the program was deemed a resounding success. The school was formally incorporated in 1965, although it did not remain under the leadership of the Madonna much longer after this point. The program would eventually become part of Grayson County College and remains to this day.

Figure 100 A view of the Madonna Hospital shortly after the 1951 Munson Annex expansion.

Near the end of the 1950's, the hospital began to suffer from declining revenue and rising costs for service. A professional hospital consultant was employed, and his recommendation was that Denison needed a new facility entirely. However, the city had reached its borrowing limit and could not issue any additional bonds necessary for the construction of such a structure.

The decision was made to appoint a hospital authority of eight members including Robert Baker, Vernon Beckham, J.D. Bond, Fred Conn, Charles Gullett, Sam Harwell, Miss Eloise Munson, Ralph Porter and R.R. Rutherford. One member, Mr. Conn, had very personal reasons for being part of the Authority's board of directors. In the early 1950's, his young son was admitted to the Madonna Hospital for emergency surgery. As Conn waited anxiously for his child to go to the operating room, he overheard two nuns discussion whether or not some of the instruments had been sterilized with neither of them seeming to know the answer. The Conn child died shortly after the surgery and Fred vowed to do everything he could to help Denison get a modern hospital.

By 1961, plans had been drawn for a new eighty-bed hospital with enough room to sustain a 150-bed operation. This was the beginning of Denison's growing interest in the healthcare field and would lead to a competing hospital to rival the Madonna and Sherman's Wilson N. Jones Hospital.

In 1962 a single-story wing for thirty-six patients was added to the north of the historic Madonna building. The new wing added private rooms, baths and showers, as well as examining rooms, a medicine room, and a new nurse's lounge. New equipment was provided for each department, including a large expansion of the laboratory that allowed the department to include services found at any of the larger hospitals north of Dallas.

The Madonna Hospital Auxiliary was organized in March of 1965 with a dedicated group of volunteers ready to raise funds for necessary improvements to the facility. Some of its projects were piped oxygen to all the rooms, a furnished surgical waiting room, the purchase of anesthetic equipment and an electrocardiograph, and the complete redecoration of all rooms in the 1945 and 1951 wings.

The Madonna was able to boast nearly 8,236 babies birthed during the time from when the Sisters began ownership of the facility until 1966. The hospital also spent an average of $37.86 on each patient compared to a $20.34 per patient average in 1955.

Figure 101 The decorative imagery of a Madonna Hospital birth certificate.

In 1967 the maternity ward was closed, which made space for a much-needed physical therapy department as well as a classroom set up for the nursing students from Grayson County College in the old maternity ward. A fully equipped emergency room evolved in the process of these changes as well.

Many of the doctors and staff of the Madonna Hospital transferred their practices to Denison's new Memorial Hospital that had been constructed a mile away in the 1960's. In 1974 the nuns left the hospital and turned the management over to a group of Denison physicians; however, this would not be enough to turn the tide for the small healthcare institution. The Madonna could not compete in the new healthcare market; therefore, an administrator, Mr. Frank Silverwise, recommended that the hospital cease operations. The Sisters relented and sold the Madonna site in 1974 to Denison's Memorial Hospital for $400,000.

Texoma Medical Center, the former Memorial Hospital, began demolition of the historic structure in October of 1985. The building could no longer meet fire codes and renovation costs proved too costly. The building had also been empty for a number of years and had become the target of vandalism. The decision was made to demolish the original portion of the Madonna Hospital while saving the Munson Wing for use as TMC East.

Following the razing, the Munson Wing was going to see improvements including landscaping and more parking areas for patients and visitors. The demolition of the Madonna was intenionally kept quiet until the day the wrecker showed up. Officials with the hosptial felt it best to not make a big deal of the demolition in order to avoid public outcry. The razing began at 7 am and was completed within one day.

Figure 102 The 1985 razing of a large portion of the Madonna Hospital.

Once renovated, the remaining 1965 structure served as the headquarters for TMC's drug and alcohol unit. By the 1990's the building served as a psychiatric care facility under the guidance of Texoma Medical Center. The building was later left unused and was essentially vacant for nearly twenty years.

Figure 103 The last remnants of the Madonna Hospital building, ca. 1998

The last piece of the once-revered institution was demolished in 2016 by the City of Denison following safety concerns, marking the final chapter for Denison's historic Madonna Hospital. The hope was that the land could be developed into single family homes once demolition was completed.

Mercy Hospital
By Brian C. Hander

Denison's Mercy Hospital, built to serve the African American community, was originally owned and controlled by a fraternal organization known as the Sons and Daughters of Mercy. The organization operated on a membership basis with their own insurance plans that paid $7.00 per week in case of disability from either sickness or accident, while room, board and nursing were covered expenses if the patient used Mercy. The plan also paid its members a $150 burial benefit. All of this was included for the premium of $1.25 per month. Dr. Roscoe C. Riddle was President and his wife, Mrs. Marie S. Riddle, was the Secretary-Treasurer of the organization.

The hospital formally opened in 1925 at the corner Tone Avenue and Munson Street with great fanfare. Several hundred members of the community, both white and black, were in attendance. The award winning African American Woodmen band played a selection, "The Star-Spangled Banner" was sung, and an invocation was delivered by Pastor C.C. Choice, a Baptist minister.

Figure 104 Dr. Roscoe Riddle, founder of Mercy Hospital

Mayor W.S. Hibbard, *Denison Herald* editor H.E. Ellis, and Dr. Riddle all gave congratulatory addresses. The master of ceremonies was Mr. J.H. Owens, the editor of the esteemed *Gate City Bulletin*, a publication devoted to people of color. As built, the hospital contained four wards capable of accommodating twenty patients. There was a check-in area and nurses' station in the main lobby, an operating room upstairs, and patient rooms scattered throughout as space allowed. While the original architect is unknown, it is assumed that John Tulloch designed the structure as he was called on shortly after it was completed to design a bungalow for Dr. Riddle and family.

Dr. Riddle was initially assisted by a man named Dr. Holloway and a nurse, Susie Foster, who trained alongside eighteen other nursing students in the hospital. Marie Riddle originally served as a dietician for the hospital and would later tackle many of the managerial duties of the organization as well.

At this point in history there were very few hospitals that treated African American patients, especially in the southern half of the United States. To have a facility of this size in Denison was an incredible asset to the African American community. Patients would travel from as far away as Lufkin and Clarksville just to receive care.

Dr. Riddle's station wagon was used to transport patients to and from the hospital, and whenever the building became overcrowded patients would stay at the Riddle home in the same block.

The hospital briefly closed in the mid-1930's when the Riddles moved to another city. By 1937, they were back, and Dr. Riddle announce he would stage a comeback for the organization offering hospitalization and healthcare at the lowest possible cost for the people of his race.

The Riddles stayed in Denison for nearly a decade before they sold the hospital and moved to Benton Harbor Michigan in 1946, where Dr. Riddle went on to serve as chairman of the executive board of the NAACP. Dr. Riddle died on December 23, 1950 and is buried in Magnolia Cemetery in Denison.

Dr. C.U. Franklin Sr. purchased Mercy Hospital following Dr. Riddle's death and practiced there for several years. Dr. Holloway opened his own private practice at 1001 West Munson and would remain there until he also retired. By 1953 Dr.

Figure 105 A 1940's view of Denison's Mercy Hospital.

- 115 -

Franklin would be the only doctor of color to hold an MD degree in the Grayson County area.

Dr. Franklin's health began to decline rapidly in 1954 due to diabetes. Eventually he was unable to practice, and he ultimately passed away from the disease in 1963.

The hospital was later converted to the Haven Home for the Aged, known to many as the Franklin Rest Home, and was operated by Pinkie Franklin until her retirement in 1971. The primary means of supporting the home was in the form of retirement pensions. There was no money given from the state at that time, or if there was, it was unknown to Pinkie.

The building was closed for good shortly after Mrs. Franklin's retirement and the property was willed to Dr. Franklin's son, a doctor in Kansas City. The historic building was eventually purchased by a group of investors, represented by Dallas real estate broker Joy Tarver. Several unsuccessful attempts were made to raise funds to preserve the historic landmark, but after five long years the building was no closer to renovation and was slated for demolition.

Don Mace of Denison purchased the building at a sheriff's sale after an unpaid lien of $8,100 was recorded on the property. Bowing to pressure from neighbors, community members, and City of Denison Code Enforcement, Mr. Mace agreed to have the structure removed. In October of 1988 wreckers began their work on the site and a Denison landmark was no more.

Katy Hospital
By Brian C. Hander

Katy Railroad employees had tried for nearly fifteen years to negotiate for the construction of a Katy-owned hospital facility in Denison. Around 1920, the Katy's directors finally voted to allow the hospital on the condition that land was purchased and provided for said construction, free of charge. As soon as news broke of the directors' decision, the Denison Chamber of Commerce raised funds from its membership, purchased twenty-five acres of land in north Denison, and donated the entire portion to the Hospital Board for that purpose. The Katy Hospital, completed at a cost of $214,000, opened on November 1, 1921.

Dallas architects Robertson and Griesenbeck are thought to be the firm behind Denison's Katy hospital as they built a similar structure in Parsons, Kansas for use as a Katy Hospital shortly afterward.

At its opening, the hospital could accommodate sixty-five patients and could be so arranged to add fifteen more patients into care if needed. The building was constructed of reinforced concrete, steel, and brick and was deemed fireproof. The interior was finished in battleship gray with furnishings that were considered top of the line. Dr. T.J. Long became the Division Surgeon and Dr. A.G. Sneed served as the Resident Physician.

Figure 106 A postcard view of Denison's Katy Hospital, ca. 1925.

The hospital was constructed and maintained by fees from the railroad's employees. Katy Association members paid dues ranging from $.55 to $1.75 per month, much like modern-day insurance premiums. The fees were collected by the MKT Railroad Employees' Hospital Association which was chartered in 1913 "to provide medical and surgical treatment and care for the employees…and erect and maintain suitable buildings for hospital and other purposes at suitable points along the line." In total, the Katy had three hospitals along its line, one in Parsons, Kansas, one in Sedalia, Missouri, and the Denison hospital.

For decades, the hospital served as the main healthcare facility for employees of the Katy. In 1951, the Employees' Association voted to make an astonishing $40,000 worth of improvement to the Denison and Parsons hospital facilities. All Katy hospitals opened to the general public in 1957 following the hospital associations severance with the railroad.

The hospital headquarters and accounting department moved to St. Louis, Missouri around 1960. Following a decline in membership and a reduction in Katy forces, the organization began dwindling down services. The board of the hospital voted to deed a portion of the property to the Denison Hospital Authority with the understanding that Katy Employees could utilize any hospital that was built on the site.

The Hospital Authority purchased the Katy Hospital and utilized it for administrative offices and pharmacy space. The hospital board tried gallantly to reuse the building for psychiatric services, or physician's offices but these were not feasible due to structural limitation of the building, the most pressing being the low ceiling heights which would not allow for new equipment necessary for modern procedures.

The historic building was demolished in November of 1987 shortly after the Katy Railroad Employees' Association was dissolved. The demolition made way for a new south entrance and outpatient surgery center for the Texoma Medical Center.

Figure 107 Denison's Katy Hospital with houses in the foreground, ca. 1928.

Figure 108 The Katy Hospital and Nurse's Quarters (at left) ca. 1940's.

CHAPTER 6

Made in Denison

"There are no secrets to success. It is the result of preparation, hard work, and learning from failure."

-Colin Powell

Denison has always been incredibly proud of those early-day institutions that rose above and created products that had a lasting impact on society as a whole. Some Denison-made products still exist to this day while others faded over time, however, they are all celebrated as part of our community's rich heritage.

Some products that were made in Denison were not retail products as we think of them, but rather products such as laws-specifically one unprecedented legal case over groundwater rights that remains the basis for all cases of its type to date. These are the stories that are also proudly made in Denison.

Industrial Denison
By Donna Hord Hunt

Manufacturing companies have come and gone in Denison, leaving some very interesting products carrying the "Denison, Texas" stamp. Whether it be clothing, salad dressing or maybe even potato chips, the products have been endless. We're still working on the chips.

"The Denison Guide," an American guide series published by the Denison Chamber of Commerce in 1939 discusses in depth activities and industries in Denison at that time.

General information from the guide gives an insight to the city's makeup with the Missouri, Kansas & Texas, the St. Louis & San Francisco and the Kansas, Oklahoma & Gulf railroads, all with stations here. There also was an interurban passenger station for the Texas Electric Railway, a Greyhound Bus Terminal and a station for Dixie Trailways.

Figure 109 The cover of The Denison Guide.

There was a taxi service and a dime would get you to any part of the city. If you wanted to go outside the city limits, the fee was an additional 10 cents a mile.

Denison had an airport three miles southeast of the city that was utilized by local and private planes only. The city had street cars and city buses with nickel fares.

There were three modern commercial hotels with rates running from 75 cents to $3.50 a day. Four tourist courts listed rates from $1 to $2.50 a day.

KRRV (1310 kc) was the only listed radio station, and television and cell phones hadn't made their debut yet.

You could fish at Munson Park free or at Loy Park for 50 cents a day. All you needed to fish at Waterloo or Randell lakes was a permit from the city engineer's office, but you had to be a member to fish at the Denison Rod & Gun Club.

You could swim at Loy Lake, Denison Rod & Gun Club, Bush's swimming pool or the Kraft Athletic Club inside what now is the Barrett Building. Last I heard, the pool still was there, but hadn't had a swimmer in it for years.

The Patterson Manufacturing Co. overall plant employed 275 people at 216 North Houston. Overalls and dungarees for men and boys, farmerette suits for girls and women and children's sportswear were put together at the plant that used principally Texas products and catered to the wholesale trade.

It certainly sounds better than all the "Made in China" or "Made in Bangladesh" tags we see these days, doesn't it?

Figure 110 A postcard view the Kraft-Phenix Plant in Denison.

Much later, and not listed in the guide, came Levi Strauss, where the very popular blue jeans were put together for many years.

The Kraft-Phenix cheese and mayonnaise factory, forerunner of Kraft Cheese, at 1406 West Washington, was the southwestern division headquarters of the Kraft-Phenix Cheese Corp. The operation of 28 plants in eight states in addition to the local plant was directed from Denison.

Total floor space in the local plant was 61,000 square feet and approximately 26.996 million pounds of cheese were produced annually in the Denison plant. Around 50,000 pounds of Roquefort cheese was imported every year from France to Denison, along with 100,000 pounds of Swiss cheese and large quantities of other varieties from Denmark and Holland.

In the Denison plant, 53 different products were manufactured including mayonnaise, spreads, French dressing, salad dressings, varieties of cheese and by-products from whey for poultry and stock feeding.

At that time, the plant employed 156 men and women with an average monthly payroll of $18,000.

The Denison Cotton Mill at 701 West Rice was one of the largest mills west of the Mississippi, operating 15,284 spindles and 386 looms handling 6,000 bales of cotton a year, all purchased in the Denison area.

During 1937, the mill produced 4.2 million yards of cotton duck material ranging from 19 to 72 inches wide. The cloth was marketed throughout the U.S. under the brands of Great Mallard, Dreadnaught and Pacific Ducks. About 225 people were employed there in 1939. The Cotton Mill closed in 1977.

Flour was processed here in the early days by the Denison Mill and Grain Co., with the Lone Star Mills, built in 1874 having a capacity of 250 barrels of flour a day to provide processed wheat for the surrounding area.

Figure 111 The Denison Cotton Mill, ca. 1940.

Brick was manufactured for home building. The bricks were said to be of superior quality and in the early days were shipped to Sherman, McKinney and farther south. Possibly some of them still are around in buildings here.

The Gate City Hosiery Mill, first knitting mill built in the state, could manufacture 100 dozen men's hose, 100 dozen ladies' hose and 100 dozen children's hose every day. That mill moved here in the 1890s because of the availability of cotton that was used in producing the hose. The American Cotton Oil Co. had a $400,000 plant with a daily capacity for 150 tons of seed.

A foundry, shoe factory, mattress factory, planing mill, two machine shops, candy factory and bottling works, soap factory, broom factory and other smaller industries were in operation at the turn of the century.

A $100,000 ice plant not only supplied ice for Denison and other places but furnished the MK&T with all the ice it needed for its shops, trains, engines and refilling of refrigerator cars.

Then along came such industries as Jacques Power Saw, a post hole digging and small all-purpose tractor manufacturer, and peanut, pecan and soybean processing plants.

W.J. Smith Wood Treating plant was established in Denison after a survey proved that local weather conditions were ideal for the seasoning of lumber. The plant shipped 6,000 carloads of creosoted lumber annually, according to a 1948 report. At that time, it employed 180 people.

The Peanut Processing Company manufactured peanut butter, oils and dairy feeds, as well as processed pecans, handling around 7,500 pounds daily in season with almost all the work done by mechanical machinery.

Figure 112 The Levi Straus factory was originally located on Houston Avenue.

These are only a few of the industries that made Denison their home in the early years of the 1900s through the early 1940s. Ballard Biscuit Company became a part of Pillsbury and Levi Straus started on Houston Avenue, then moved to a new plant on Highway 84. Johns-Manville came to town, as did Standard Brands and more.

Industries now occupy some of the buildings and others now stand empty. Denison is proud of the industry it now has and owes a debt of gratitude to many of these earlier industries that no longer are with us but brought new citizens to town and added to the economy while they were here.

Let's not forget the potato chips that I mentioned in the beginning of this article. I've been told there was a plant here but have not been able to locate the information. Any help would be appreciated.

Ranch Style Beans
By Brian C. Hander

The Waples-Platter Grocery Company is one of the few companies founded before the city of Denison came into existence. The company began in 1871 as a commissary that served the M, K, &T railroad workers as they extended the rail line into Texas.

The commissary was located in a tent at Chickasaw Ben Colbert's Ferry along the Red River where it was suspected the MKT Railroad would be coming through and was begun by Sam Hanna and Joe Owens. Samuel McAfee Hanna Sr. was born in Shelby County Kentucky and made his way towards Texas and the Wild West frontier in the 1870's. Little is known about Joe Owens.

The commissary was stocked with bags of coffee beans, a cracker barrel, bulk sugar, and barrels of lard, and was housed in a tent for six to seven months to provide hunters and ranchers with food as well as much-needed ammunition.

Once the fledgling city of Denison had been plotted and lots sold in September of 1872, the two enterprising men moved their firm known as Hanna, Owens & Co. four miles to the south and became the first wholesale grocery company to arrive in the newly formed city. The firm set up shop in a 25 ft. by 80 ft. building in the 100 block of East Main in 1873, directly across the street from the railroad depot.

The primitive operation included the handling of buffalo hides brought in by hunters from the prairies and the shipment of provisions by ox team into the Indian Territory and other surrounding areas. Freighters would commonly haul hides from Fort Griffin to Denison and return with supplies for cattle ranchers, hunters, and merchants.

Andrew Fox (A.F.) Platter, a dry goods clerk in Missouri, came to Denison in 1877 to visit his sister and was thoroughly impressed by the potential of the frontier town. He returned in 1878 to become a bookkeeper for the Hanna and Owens, and bought Owens' interest in 1882. With Platter's purchase, the firm became known as Hanna, Platter & Co. with the name quickly changing to Hanna, Platter & Lingo with the addition of Edward Henry (E.H.) Lingo to the partnership in the same year.

In 1883 A.F. Platter married a woman by the name of Fannie Waples and together they encouraged her father E.B. Waples and her brothers, Paul and John, to buy major interests in the business. Several years later the company went through yet another name change, as it became Hanna, Platter & Waples when Edward Bridell (E.B.) Waples bought an interest in the company in 1885.

E.B. Waples was also named president of the firm in 1885 and became very active in the city; the Waples Memorial United Methodist Church in Denison bears his name for his contributions to the church. This same year in 1885, a large, elegant warehouse and headquarter building was constructed at 104 E. Main in Denison.

The new warehouse and headquarters was an architectural marvel designed by architect P. Lelardoux of Muskogee, Ok, and was a two-story structure with cast iron pilasters in the facade; cast iron lions head statues, keystones and segmented arch openings. The building was meant to symbolize the company's prominence in Denison, and the large brick edifice did just that for 128 years before it was demolished in 2013.

Figure 113 The Waples-Platter building shortly after completion.

The company's line of grocery products known as the White Swan line was introduced in 1886 to symbolize the company's quality in packaging. The white swan floating on pure water was an image chosen to represent the high standards that Waples-Platter required of their food products. Shortly afterward in 1887 Sam Hanna sold his interest in the company to the sons of Waples, Paul (February 4, 1850- November 16, 1916) and John Waples (April 28, 1848- January 3, 1912) and the firm became known as Waples-Platter & Company.

In 1891 the company was officially incorporated as Waples-Platter Grocer Company and Paul Waples succeeded his father as president before the end of the year. Paul would eventually move to Fort Worth with the company, where in 1906 he became the founder of the Fort

Worth Star that would later become the famed Fort Worth Star-Telegram.

With the success of the company came the need for growth and expansion, which occurred with the opening of the first branch house at Gainesville in 1890 and the establishment of the company at Fort Worth in 1893. Fort Worth would play a crucial role in the company's development eventually becoming the site of the Waples-Platter headquarters. In 1897 the firm's Wapco brand was originated and branches were opened at Bowie and Dublin. In 1898 the Concho line was added, giving the company its third private label.

The year 1902 saw the beginning of operations in Dallas with 1905 bringing branch houses at Greenville and Ada, Oklahoma. In 1907, the Federal Food and Drug Act became effective, but no re-adjustment of company standards was necessary due to the high-quality policies already practiced by Waples-Platter.

The company also came into the manufacturing business beginning in 1906 with the construction of a coffee roasting plant inside an historic building at 110-112 S. Houston Ave. in Denison. The "Roasting Ovens" at the plant were eight-foot cylinders, which the employees fired by hand with coke.

The coffee roasting plant was followed shortly afterwards with a food processing division at Fort Worth in 1913. The year 1913 also marked the birth of the Waples-Platter Canning Plant, later known as Ranch Style, Inc.

Figure 114 The Waples-Platter Grocery building as it appeared ca. 1930.

In 1930 it was agreed to drop the sale of "tobacco and kindred products" and to add a blend coffee to the market as a replacement. The thirties would also bring about another new product that would endure long after the company was no longer in existence, that product would be Ranch Style Beans.

While the famous Ranch Style Beans were already being sold in some form or fashion in the 1870's they did not become a household name until 1935 when they were introduced to the public after three years of extensive research.

It wasn't too long before celebrities such as Elizabeth Taylor, Humphrey Bogart, and Grace Kelly began ordering them. They were even served at President Lyndon Johnson's ranch on many occasions.

Edward McKee is credited with concocting the recipe with a "secret sauce" while working for the Waples-Platter Co. in Denison, he struck gold in the 1930's when he developed the perfect ratio of sauce to beans that would remain popular throughout the Depression.

The beans were released under the White Swan label in 1932, then reintroduced three years later as Ranch Style Beans in the familiar, red-banded black label that was designed by McKee's father, Lloyd McKee. This is one of the only remaining products created by the Waples-Platter Co., and a true Denison-made product, to still be in existence to this day.

Figure 115 The logo for Ranch Style Beans still has the same font set as the original Waples-Platter logo.

Denison's Role in Texas Groundwater Law

The Saga of East v. Houston and Texas Central Railway

By Jimmie Mathews
DHS class of 1965

As the twentieth century dawned, the City of Denison was a young and thriving community with a population of more than 10,000 and a stopping point for more than ten railways. One of Denison's enterprising residents at the time was William Alexander East who had come to Denison in 1883 and went on to serve on the City's police force for more than forty years.

In 1900 Mr. East purchased four lots "on the waters of Paw Paw Creek" in Cook's First Addition to the City of Denison. East's property was located on the south side of East Owings Street near its intersection with South Lamar Avenue. East, along with his wife, Emma Dixon Owen East, lived on one of their lots and rented out residences on the others. East's property included a hand dug well approximately 5 feet in diameter and 33 feet deep. This well provided the Easts and their tenants what he described as "practically an inexhaustible supply of well water . . . that was almost impossible to secure in the markets".

The Houston and Texas Central Railway (H & TC) had arrived in Denison in 1873 when it extended its lines into the City in order to connect with the Missouri Kansas and Texas Railroad (the Katy) which had played a major role in Denison's creation and incorporation in 1872. By 1901, the H & TC determined that it needed a new source of water to power and service its locomotives and machine shops in Denison. In July 1901, H & TC sent its representatives to investigate potential water sources in the area where it owned several lots near East's property.

Perhaps not knowing that he was about to embark on a legal odyssey that would establish the bedrock principle of Texas groundwater law for over a century, Mr. East consented to the H & TC representatives' request to inspect his well.

Based on its investigation H & TC was confident that it had found a reliable water source for its operations. By August 1901 H & TC had dug a well on its property approximately 100 to 250 feet from the East's well. H & TC's well was 20 feet in diameter and 66 feet deep. Equipped with a steam pump, the well began producing 25,000 gallons of water per day for H&TC's use. (Documents prepared by the Texas Water Development Board attached at the end of this article provide a map showing location of H & TC's well and the East's property;

photos showing the location and some remnants of the H & TC pumphouse foundation; and a schematic comparing the size of the East and H & TC's wells.)

Shortly after H & TC began pumping its well, the East's well went dry. Mr. East, frustrated at losing his reliable water supply, focused his attention on H & TC and its new large well. East retained the Denison law firm of Mossley and Eppstein and filed suit against H & TC in in state district court in March 1902 seeking damages of $1,100 for the loss of his well (This is equivalent to $35,551 in 2022).

East's lawsuit alleged that the water in his well came from subterranean streams, or, in the alternative, from percolation of water through his land. He claimed that H & TC's well, because of its size and pumping capacity, drew all the water from under his land and the surrounding territory, and that H & TC's use of the water to supply its "entire . . .railroad company tributary to Denison" was an unreasonable use that cut off the water supply to his well and would continue to do so.

East's case was tried to the court without a jury. H & TC was represented at trial by Head and Dillard, another Grayson County law firm. On December 28, 1902, Judge Rice Maxey of the 15th District court issued his findings of fact, conclusions of law and a judgment. Judge Maxey ruled in favor of H&TC finding:

- The water from the East and H & TC wells is percolating groundwater and not underground from an underground stream;
- The H & TC well was dug without any intention of injuring East's well;
- That East's well had always supplied an adequate supply of water for domestic use;
- The damage East has sustained to his land is $206.25 (The equivalent of $6,665.90 in 2022);
- That H & TC's use of the water from its well was not a reasonable use of H & TC's property as land, and *if* the reasonable use doctrine applicable to defined streams applied in this case H&TC's use would be unreasonable (emphasis added);
- No correlative right exists to underground percolating waters which do not run in a confined channel;
- The H & TC has no liability based on the facts of this case.

Undaunted by this setback, Mr. East appealed to the Dallas Court of Appeals. His appeal apparently garnered attention within H & TC because it chose to supplement its legal team with the Houston law firm that served as its general counsel: Baker, Botts, Baker and Lovett (now known as Baker Botts). The Dallas Court of Appeals, in an opinion by

Justice John Bookhout, relied upon the factual findings of the trial court, but reached the opposite conclusion on the law. The court noted the 1843 English law case of *Acton v. Blundell* which held that digging a well that drains neighboring land would not result in liability unless it was done maliciously had been followed by some American states but concluded that application of the *Acton* rule in East's case "would shock our sense of justice". Instead, the Dallas Court of Appeals chose to rely on an 1862 case from the Supreme Court of New Hampshire which recognized the correlative rights of a landowner in groundwater as a basis to apply a "reasonable use" standard. Because the trial court had found that H & TC's use of its land was unreasonable, the Court of Appeals reversed the trial court and rendered judgment for Mr. East in the amount of $206.25.

H & TC petitioned the Texas Supreme Court to review the judgment of the Dallas Court of Appeals. By any standards—todays or those of the early 1900's—the Supreme Court moved quickly to decide this case. Within six weeks following the Court's acceptance of H & TC's petition, the Court issued a unanimous opinion reversing the Dallas Court of Appeals and affirming the original judgment of the trial court. The Supreme Court relied primarily on the 1843 *Acton* case from the English courts stating that this case had been recognized and followed "probably by all the courts of last resort before which the question has come, except the Supreme Court of New Hampshire" (which the Dallas Court of Appeals had relied on).

Through this case the Texas Supreme Court established the "rule of capture" as a bedrock principle of Texas law concerning groundwater: A landowner has a right to produce groundwater found under his land, and if that production causes interference with the well of a neighbor, this is an injury for which damages are not recognize by the law. The Court stated two policy reasons for its decisions: (1) the origin and movement of groundwater is "so secret, occult and concealed" that setting legal rules for it would involve "hopeless uncertainty" and (2) the recognition of correlative rights would "interfere to the detriment of the commonwealth" with [economic development]. The Court did, however, impose some limitations on its holding. First it noted that its finding of no correlative right between landowners with regard to groundwater was subject to modification by contract or legislation. Secondly it noted that its finding that the limitation on liability for producing groundwater on an owner's property that injured another would not apply if the water production is done wantonly or maliciously to harm the other party.

The significance of the East case is indicated by the extent to which it has been relied on and followed. Since the Court's decision in 1904 the East case has been cited and followed by appellate courts in 51 cases including 10 subsequent Texas Supreme Court cases. Although Texas has effectively mitigated the potential for harm resulting from a strict application of the rule of capture through legislation authorizing the creation of groundwater conservation districts that can impose spacing and production limits through permits, the rule of capture is still recognized in Texas law today.

William Alexander East may have lost his legal battle with the Houston & TC Railway but has left his mark on history. His case is known to all who are familiar with groundwater issues in Texas as the "East case", rather than the "Houston & TC Railway" case.

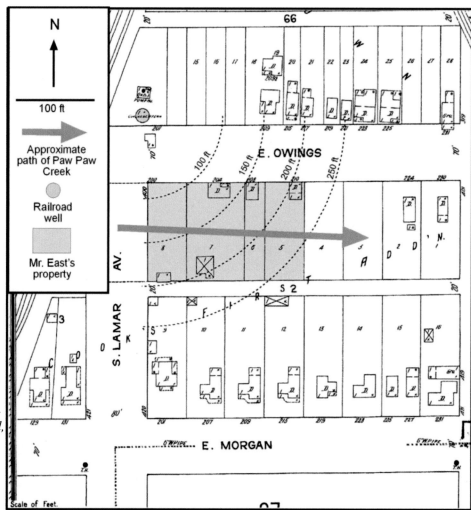

Figure 116 A detail of the 1914 Sanborn fire insurance map of Denison showing the location of the Houston and Texas Central Railroad Company well sunk near the intersection of Owings Street and Lamar Avenue. We have highlighted the location of the well, the properties owned by Mr. East in 1901, the modern approximate location of Paw Paw Creek, and radii of distances from the railroad well.

Figure 117 Photographs taken on January 16, 2004 near Owings Street and Lamar Avenue, including (a) the probable location of the pumphouse for the Railroad well with pieces of foundation cement circled; (b) view to the east while standing on Lamar Avenue, with Pawpaw Creek in the foreground (the creek is channeled beneath Lamar Avenue), Owings Street to the left visible between the trees, and the probable location of the East well between the creek and Owings Street; and (c) looking north at the intersection of Owings Street and Lamar Avenue with the probable location of the Railroad well circled. Photographs by authors.

The Official Denison Flag
By Brian C. Hander

Nothing could boast the community's "Made in Denison" pride quite like the official flag that was designed by our pioneering ancestors. Nearly lost, the design of the flag has a unique story and meaning that still resonates today.

Denison's flag was officially adopted by the City Council early in the city's history in 1872. However, the design was soon lost to time and wasn't uncovered until 1936. At this time, Jack R. Maguire, a Denison student, was interviewing pioneer citizens and found that Denison did indeed have its very own flag.

A drawing was found by Maguire quite by accident some ten years later in an historical display in Fort Worth. The information was relayed back to Denison officials and in 1968 Dr. Rene Gerard, a member of the City Council, promoted the idea of adopting the flag officially once more. Members of the Denison Girls Club, in great secrecy, assembled the first model of the flag and presented it to the council for adoption on November 14, 1968.

The upper half of the flag is green in color and the lower half is white. The two halves are separated by a solid red stripe with a black stripe crossed in the middle with a star in the very center.

The green color represents the green

Figure 118 The Denison flag.

grass of the Indian Territory, the white represents the snowy cotton fields of Texas, divided by the red stripe, the Red River, and crossed by the black stripe, the Katy Railroad. The star is the City of Denison, a jewel at the crossing of a great river and at the interweaving of two great parts of the country.

The flag remains an important part of Denison and is flown at many city facilities.

CHAPTER 7

Untold Denison Firsts

"People who end up as 'first' don't actually set out to be first. The set out to do something they love."

-Condoleeza Rice

To be first, truly first at something, is not incredibly common in today's society. It is often mentioned that anything or any idea worth pursuing had already been done, leaving nothing for future generations to attain. Yet nothing could be further from the truth, and the men and women of Denison, Texas continue to prove that striving to be the community of choice can create many unique firsts.

There are dozens and dozens of stories of individuals who excelled to become the first at something in our community. Likewise, there are some firsts that were completely unplanned and probably not something the individuals are too proud of-would anyone really be proud of being the first to wreck a car in Denison? However, these stories are so unique and worthy of being told so that future generations know firsts have happened in our community, firsts will continue to happen, and that they can be part of these firsts with a little creativity and a dash of determination.

Denison's "Firsts"
By Donna Hord Hunt

Sometime when I am looking for something special, I find the most interesting thing. Such was the case of today's column. This town has had some interesting characters and happenings and while it was not the first town in Texas, its reputation is right up there among the leaders, and it sometimes has been called a "city of firsts." I have always thought it would make a good subject for a movie — even a documentary.

Several years ago, a program for the Newcomers' Club here was about "Denison Firsts." There were a lot of them. As Denison grew into the city it is today, Denisonians have recorded "first" after "first." Some are documented and others have been passed along by word of mouth.

First thing that comes into my mind is the ice cream soda that I have written about numerous times. That is a semi-documented happening. Joseph A. Euper who operated a confectionery in the street level Security building, has been given credit for the first ice cream soda.

Euper not only was a confectioner, he was a city councilman, street railway system builder and an ice cream lover at heart. He probably devised his ice cream soda in desperation trying to meet the "stiff competition" of saloons up and down Main Street in the late 1870s. Pardon the pun in that last statement.

The claim has been challenged a couple of times in magazine articles, giving the credit to someone in another part of the state. But Denisonians know that Euper came up with the recipe. Written reports tell how merchants and other friends were his taste testers and brushed aside their handlebar mustaches to sample his creations.

On May 7, 1873, the Denison City Council officially selected the location of what was to become Texas' first free public graded school here, known as the Washington School, and also the Educational Institute. When a location on Main Street was chosen, the citizens went into an uproar because the 700 block was considered "too far from town" to be accessible to the majority of school children.

Figure 119 The first free public graded school in Texas as it appeared ca. 1900

McDaniel Junior High later occupied the 1914 school that housed Denison High School that replaced the Educational Institute abandoned at the closing of the school year because the school had outlived its usefulness. The school building was demolished in 2007. The grounds have been vacant since then except for a few events, but who knows what eventually might occupy the 700 block of Main that now stands empty just waiting for what might be in the future.

Mavis Anne Bryant and I wrote a book, "Two Schools on Main Street; The Pride of Denison, Texas, 1873-2007," in 2007 that is a history of the high school that included all 11 grades up until 1914.

Sam Houston School was the first white elementary school built in 1886, but in 1874, Denison opened its first black public school, Langston. The last black school, Terrell, was closed in 1967 when the local school system was totally integrated. Terrell now operates as an elementary school.

An electric refrigerator sent ice wagons to the barn here when a Denison company pioneered the shipping of fresh beef across the country in refrigerated railroad cars.

The first session of court was held in Grayson County in 1846 on property near Iron Ore Creek, southwest of Denison near Loy Lake Park, several years before Denison was established in 1872. A log cabin, that may have been a small stable beside a huge oak tree, was the scene when the first court case was against a man for allowing his stock to stray. He pleaded guilty and was fined $8.12.

Harrison Tone, founder of Tone Abstract Co., at his own expense, opened the first post office in Denison in 1872 and served as postmaster for the first year at a salary of $1.

In 1876, Denison acquired an ice factory, the Crystal Ice Co., first in North Texas.

In 1880, the first baseball team was organized and a streetcar line was built to the ballpark in what now is the 1200 block West Bond Street.

In 1890, an event happened that is no secret to any of us living today. On that date, Dwight D. Eisenhower was born here. Our native son was first a five-star general during World War II, then several years after he retired, he was elected president of the United Sates. He visited the town of his birth three times, the last in 1965 after he had served his term as president.

The same day Ike was born, a group of Denison women organized the XXI Club, second oldest women's literary club in Texas that later built the first women's clubhouse in the state.

Figure 120 The XXI Club Building, 1910.

In 1905, President Teddy Roosevelt got his first welcome to Texas here when he stopped briefly while en route to a Rough Riders' Reunion and encampment in San Antonio.

Denisonians got their first glimpse of a flying machine on Oct. 11, 1911, when the Vin Fiz, a box-kite aircraft passed over town and became the first airplane to do so. If you are a regular reader of this column, you read about the Vin Fiz last week.

Figure 121 The Vin Fiz Flyer as it started its cross-country journey.

I'm running out of room, but want to mention briefly a few more firsts.

The Annie P was the first steamboat to navigate the Red River, stopping at Riverside Park just north of Denison in 1890.

The first cattle trail driven out of Grayson County toward Kansas City was headed up the old Preston Trail to where the herd forded the Red River.

Denison was the first town in Texas to be built by the arrival of the MK&T Railroad during its extension to the south in 1872. A community known as Red River City sprang up near the river, but gradually shut down or was absorbed by Denison as the Katy settled down here.

The first electric interurban to be built in Texas ran from Denison to Sherman in 1901. It was in 1896 that J.P. Crearer purchased the mule streetcar line of both Denison and Sherman then installed electric cars to inaugurate his interurban.

One of the first public parks in the state was Forest Park, which still stands in the center of town and is home to Munson Stadium where the Denison Yellow Jackets and other athletic groups play.

We probably could go on and on if we gave it some more thought, but that's enough for today.

First African American Property Owner

The first known property owner of color in Denison was Mr. Joseph Davis. He was born a slave in Louisiana and came to Denison in 1872 when the town was just forming.

After being freed, he worked as a riverman, in a lumber yard, and as a Cowboy in Texas before coming to Denison. He and his wife, Matilda, were married at Baton Rouge, Louisiana, in 1866. They had fourteen children and were Baptists.

Davis purchased a plot of ground bounded by Washington and Elm Streets and Lamar and Houston Avenues. He also owned some 120 acres along the Big Mineral creek.

Davis worked for the Houston and Texas Central Railroad for about twenty-five years before he and his family moved in 1900 to Platter, Oklahoma. There he died on January 14, 1922, at the age of 82. His wife, a few years his junior, lived until 1932.

Two of his descendants remained in the area following the death of their parents: George Davis and William "Dock" Davis. The original Davis property is now owned by the Terrell High School Alumni Association.

First Automobile Accident

The first automobile accident in Denison took place on the evening of August 11, 1907, roughly four miles west of the city. The automobile driven by a Dr. James ran off a high bump and turned completely over. The occupants were John Suggs, along with his wife and baby, Elmer E. Davis, and Dr. James, with his wife and child.

The baby of Mr. and Mrs. Suggs had its nose broken but was otherwise unharmed, Mr. Suggs was considerably bruised and Dr. James sustained a fracture of the left rib. The worst injured was Mr. Davis who suffered a badly wrenched back.

Figure 122 John Suggs, one of the passengers in the first automobile accident in Denison.

First Denison Club

In October of 1924, Denison students attending Austin College came together to form the first Denison Club ever established at the institution. The group originally consisted of eighteen students with the following officers: Charles M. Hill; President, Lenore Hanks; Vice President, and Lola May Hensley; Secretary-Treasurer.

The purpose of the club was to promote the general welfare of the college, and especially that of the Denison students, and to provide an organization through which the Denison students could work harmoniously and with effect.

The first official meeting of the group was held at Denison's newly opened Hotel Simpson on October 14, 1924. Denison High School Principal B. McDaniel addressed the club along educational lines. Those in attendance included Mary Carroll, Wilma Carroll, Venita Carroll, Effie Newland, Lenore Hanks, Aline Smith, Helen Fisk, Dorothy Woods, Alice Wilson, Anzo Anderson, Daugherty Collins, B. McDaniel, Joe Dixon, Harold Williford, Charles McGregor, Ralph Hightower, Fred Lee McFadden, Charles M. Hill, Howard Badgett, Girard French, F. Martin, and a Mrs. McCaughey.

Figure 123 Principal B. McDaniel, first speaker at the Denison Club.

The club continued into 1925 with Ralph Hightower as President, Aline Smith as Vice President, and Fred McFadden as Secretary-Treasurer. Those in attendance for this meeting included Charles M. Hill, Aline Smith, Gladys Lewin, Anzo Anderson, Edwin Dean, Ralph Hightower, Fred McFadden, Asa Person, Charles M. McGregor, Ellen Crook, Lora Adams, Frances Irving, Ruth Davis, Lola Teas, Rayburn Thompson, Charles Bruno, Clyde Houck, James Morris, James Mathis, and Yate Phillips.

While the club held on for these two years, there is no mention of them in further newspaper articles. Speculation leads us to believe that many members graduated and as they left the school so did the desire to keep the club alive.

First Bicycle in Denison

Dr. Alexander W. Acheson was the first resident of Denison to own a bicycle. Acheson received his bike on June 5, 1879 and it was described as a machine that had one big wheel at the front that perched the rider six feet up into the air. The doctor was reported to have had a skinned nose after just a few riding sessions and sadly, broke the bicycle before he even had it a week. Thus ended the streak of the first bicycle to roam Denison.

First Building in Denison

The first frame structure of any kind in Denison was erected in 1872 on the northeast corner of Forest Park. The building was used by the Denison Town Company, responsible for laying out and selling lots in the fledgling town and was later used as a place for general information, much like a visitor's center.

First Dial Telephone
Found by James K. Sears

LAWRENCE HORN, employee of the Southwestern Bell Telephone Company, hands Mayor Harry Glidden the first dial telephone to be installed in Denison as City Commissioners Clarence Weideman and Walter Lebrecht look on. The dial telephone was installed in the City Council room at City Hall at 9:30 a.m., Monday, May 23, 1955.

Photo by Press Staff Photographer

The Denison (TX) Press
Vol. 26, No. 48, Ed. 1 Friday, May 27, 1955, Page 1

First African American Graduate
Found by James K. Sears

Mamie Dossey marked her spot in Denison history in June of 1908 when she became the first African American pupil to graduate from Denison. The exercises were held at the Hopewell Baptist Church, and it was reported that the church was at max capacity.

The church had been ornamented with purple and gold decorations, the class colors, and white, representing the class flower, a carnation. A program was carried out that included singing, recitations, and the reading of Mamie's essay on "Time, an Agent". Superintendent F. B. Hughes, accompanied by the entire school board of trustees, presented Miss Dossey with her diploma.

First African American Woman on City Council

Lee Alyce McGrew was born on October 24, 1925, in Dallas, Texas to Ross Lee Sheppard and Alyce Rubio. Lee Alyce attended public schools and graduated from Prairie View A & M University. An avid learner, Lee Alyce also attended UCLA Los Angeles, Cal Lutheran, Thousand Oaks, Calif., Southeastern Oklahoma State University, Durant, Oklahoma, East Texas State, North Texas State and the University of Texas at Dallas.

Lee Alyce began teaching in 1956 locally before returning to California in 1960. There she taught at Compton until 1962 before going to work for the Los Angeles County Probation Department from 1962-1969, and then went to work for the Los Angeles Unified School District from 1971-1978. She arrived in Denison in March of 1979, finding a position with the Sherman Independent School District. She would serve at this post until her retirement in 2003.

Lee Alyce made her mark on history when she was elected to the Denison City Council. She served six years on the Council and was highly regarded for her desire to move the community forward for all. She was also a member of the Sherman BPW, the Grayson County NAACP, and served as a director of Teaching Teachers to Teach. She was also appointed by then Governor George W. Bush to serve on the Continuing Advisory Committee for Special Education.

Described as a mover and shaker in the community, Lee Alyce passed away on August 17, 2005, at the age of 79. She left behind a legacy of community service and exemplified the meaning of a servant leader.

First African American Principal & First African American City Councilmember

Figure 124 Mr. D.D. McKnight's staff photo from the 1957 Terrell High School Yearbook.

Mr. Drewey D. (D.D.) McKnight made history when he became the first African American administrator at Hyde Park Elementary following desegregation at Denison ISD. Mr. McKnight grew up in a segregated Denison school system, attending Terrell High School and graduating at the age of sixteen

He attended Prairie View A&M but had a two-year intermission when he served in the Navy during World War II. He completed his degree upon his return and became a math teacher at Terrell High School in Denison for nineteen years until many of the teachers were sent to different schools following desegregation laws.

He remained in the Denison education system and was appointed as principal of Hyde Park Elementary. He also holds the title of the first African American elected to the Denison City Council.

First Bale of Cotton Bought

On May 9, 1895, *The Dallas Morning News* published the following tidbit in its Denison news condensation: "Denison, Tex., May 8. – J. S. Searcey, the oldest resident of Grayson County was in the city today from Bonham in the interests of the Protective Association, which looks after stolen horses. Capt. Searcey came here fifty years ago. He was the first to locate in Denison and purchased the first bale of cotton ever bought on the streets."

First Woman to Ride in an Automobile

In August of 1900 an automobile traveled to Denison from Sherman and attracted a great deal of attention. It took fifty minutes for it to make the trip from one city to another and cost a whopping $1,300. Miss Birdie McLynn took a ride in the horseless carriage and cemented her place in history as the first lady in Denison to ride in an automobile.

YMCA Firsts

G.C. Freeman, the first Secretary of the Denison YMCA, set aside $30 of his $75 per month salary for the upkeep of the YMCA building. Mr. Freeman held his position for eighteen years until his death in 1911.

On August 1, 1911, Gamaliel C. Freeman was murdered by gunshot near Armstrong, Oklahoma while surveying for a location for a new boys' camp. His killers were never caught. On July 2, 1913, a memorial tablet was installed in the sidewalk at the northeast corner of Main Street and Mirick Avenue in Denison in honor of all he did for the community. The marker remains in place today.

The first large sum of money paid toward the YMCA building fund was given by Mrs. Sarah. C. Acheson, who sold her diamonds in order that the work could be carried on. Mrs. Acheson was very active in local charitable and temperance work throughout the state. She served three years of active service in the Women's Christian Temperance Union and was hailed as one of Denison's finest citizens.

Figure 125 Sarah Cooke Acheson, noted philanthropist and active Temperance Union member.

Firsts in Religion

Figure 126 The First Presbyterian Church as it appeared in 1874.

The first church organization to erect a building in Denison was the Presbyterian denomination. The first minister was Rev. Josiah Milligan, and the first Sunday School Superintendent was Dr. Alex A. Acheson. The first choir leader was his wife, Sarah Acheson.

The first sermon preached within Denison was by Rev. Josiah Milligan, the second by Rev. Holman, and the third by Rev. E.Q. Gillian, the Episcopal Rector. Although the Presbyterians had the first church building, all churches combined initially to use one building known as the Union Church. This structure was later moved to the intersection of Walker Street and Austin Avenue.

First Business to have Electric Fans

Wilfred A. Hallenbeck, a confectionary and bakery owner, was the first businessman in Denison to introduce electric fans in the city. In 1895, Hallenbeck had the fans installed in his building at 309 West Main Street. The hope was that other business owners in Denison would embrace the delightfully cool technology for their patrons as well.

Figure 127 An interior view of Hallenbeck & St. John, caterers, ca. 1909.

First Jewish Rites of Marriage Performed

On January 1, 1879 Mr. Isaac Lowenthal of Dallas and Miss Emma Carr, daughter of Mr. and Mrs. L. Carr, of Denison, were united in marriage at the resdience of the bride's parents on Gandy Street. Rabbi Suhler performed the ceremony, making it the first marriage ceremony according to the Jewish Rites ever performed in Denison.

First School in Denison to have a Cafeteria

The first educational building in Denison to have a cafeteria was the Central Ward school. In 1925, carpenters and painters were finishing up work on the space that was equipped to care for 125 students at one time. The idea was spearheaded by the Parent-Teacher Association of the school and was initially operated by volunteers from the association. Ten and fifteen cent meals would be served throughout the entire school term and made available for all students.

Figure 128 The original rendering of Denison's Central Ward School, from the collection of the Denison Alumni Museum.

First Female Bootlegger Sentenced

Mrs. Simmie Combs, a 5'1" unassuming 32-year-old housekeeper, was found guilty of manufacturing intoxicating liquor and sentenced to one year in the state penitentiary on Friday, April 10, 1925. Mrs. Combs was the first woman convicted of manufacturing liquor in Grayson County following the passage of the Dean Act which made the offense a felony. Mrs. Combs attempted to prove in defense testimony that she had employed the still, which was found in her home on West Morton Street, in preparing prune juice for her four children, who are said to be afflicted with tuberculosis, and also that whiskey had been prescribed by a physician for her children. Arresting officers testified that they found a still in operation and approximately 350 gallons of fermented mash in her home. Mrs. Combs remained in in the Texas State Penitentiary at Huntsville, Texas until her release on November 5, 1926.

First Electric Elevator

Hibbard Brothers wholesale and retail grocery, owned by W.S. Hibbard and F.P. Hibbard was the first mercantile house in Denison to put it an elevator run by electricity. The firm added the elevator in 1896 and invited the general public to their site at the corner of Main Street and Houston Avenue to see how smoothly the new innovation could operate.

Figure 129 Hibbard Brothers, ca. 1890.

First Ordained Priest from Denison
Found by James K. Sears

Raymond Harvey, a Denison boy who attended St. Patrick's Parochial School and Denison High School, received his ordination to the priesthood in St. Louis in June of 1921. Harvey grew up with his aunt, Miss Hattie Veith, at 1612 West Bond Street in Denison. Upon graduation from DHS the young man entered St. Mary's Seminary at Perryville, Mo. where he took four years of theological studies.

The Archbishop John J. Glennon of St. Louis would lead the ordination and Harvey was expected to return to Denison shortly to celebrate his first mass at St. Patrick's Church. The date of his first mass was set for

July 3, 1921, and many newly ordained priests were expected to attend as well as early schoolmates of the Denison lad.

The Denison Herald announced that Raymond Harvey was the first Denison boy to be ordained to the Catholic priesthood, stating there would be tears in the eyes of those seeing the Reverend Harvey in his priestly robes.

First Woman Juror to Serve in a Justice of the Peace Court

In 1955, Ellen M. Schirmer, an employee of the Grayson County Health Department, was the first woman juror to serve in a jury trial in Denison. *The Denison Press* reported that Mrs. Schirmer was running an errand when she passed Justice of the Peace C.B. Carroll's office at 120 West Main Street.

The judge called her in and asked her to serve on a six-member jury. The paper stated, "She, believing that every privilege in life carries along with is a responsibility, accepted the judge's invitation and reported afterward that she thought it was her duty to serve her government, city, state, or national, whenever it was possible."

Figure 130 Ellen Schirmer, the first female to serve as a juror in Denison.

The trial involved a Denison man charged with being drunk in public and disturbing the peace. The man demanded a jury trial and was found guilty and assessed a fine of $60.00. Mrs. Schirmer said she was glad to have the experience but did add that she never did get to finish the errand she started out to do.

Denison's First Mascot

Prior to 1908, the mascot for Denison High School was the raven. On November 24, 1908, the student body decided a change was in order. In the first edition ever printed of *The Yellow Jacket*, the school publication stated, "The Raven was considered very inappropriate as the bird of that name is such a croaking creature. Our name now, The Yellow Jacket, is much more appropriate. This little fellow is very lively and makes himself felt in the world, as we wish to do." From that point forward, Denison has been known as the Fighting Yellow Jackets with countless numbers of alumni making themselves felt in this world and our community.

Figure 131 One of the many renditions of the Fighting Yellow Jacket since the student body elected the creature as their mascot.

The First Female Bowler

1st Lieutenant Emily Goodwin made local history in September of 1959 when she became the first woman to make a man's bowling squad at Perrin Air Force Base when she turned in a 209-210-129 series. Her 210-line featured four strikes in a row, a double, and the rest spares, with the exception of one open frame.

First Train Ticket Sold
Found by James K. Sears

The Sherman Democrat reported on April 1, 1911, that Denison's new Union Station was officially in service. The first ticket sold from the new station was to New York City on the Katy and Pennsylvania rail lines. The ticket holder was R. T. Grimes of 520 West 183rd Street in New York City.

First Architect

Mr. Q. Green was the first architect to establish an office in Denison. He made a specialty of bridge building and was awarded many contracts throughout the area. His shop and office were located near the intersection of Crawford Street at Houston Avenue, next to an early day hotel by the name of the Cameron House.

First African American in Denison

A man known as "Gimp" Cummings touted the claim as the first African American to locate in Denison. He came to the city in August of 1872, one month prior to the sale of the first lots. He arrived with O.B. Gunn who surveyed and laid out Denison.

Denison's First State Football Championship

While many consider 1984 to be Denison's historic State Championship title, it was actually nearly half a century earlier that the first State Football Title was claimed. In 1947, The Terrell High School Dragons, under the coaching of educator Evans T. (E.T.) Hardeman were crowned co-champions with Taylor Price High School after a tie game of 6 to 6.

The following year, Terrell would go on to win the championship against Orange Wallace High School outright with a score of 13 to 0. The game was held at Denison's Munson Stadium on Christmas Day and remains one of the greatest achievements in Denison athletic history.

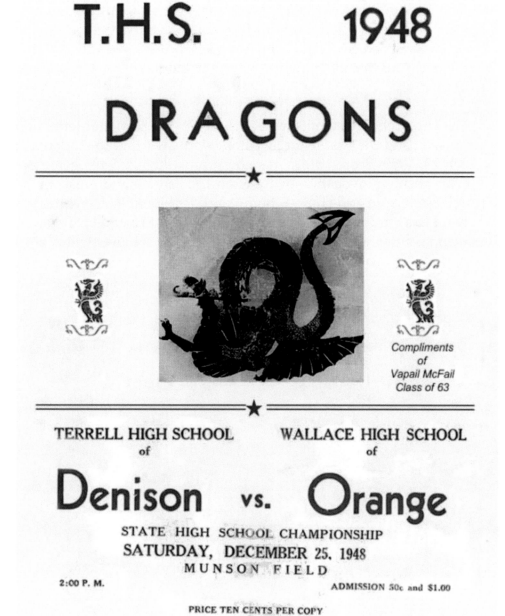

T.H.S. 1948
DRAGONS

★

Compliments
of
Vapail McFail
Class of 63

★

TERRELL HIGH SCHOOL
of

WALLACE HIGH SCHOOL
of

Denison vs. Orange

STATE HIGH SCHOOL CHAMPIONSHIP
SATURDAY, DECEMBER 25, 1948
MUNSON FIELD

2:00 P. M.

ADMISSION 50c and $1.00

PRICE TEN CENTS PER COPY

Figure 132 A copy of the T.H.S. State Championship football program from the Anderson-Terrell Alumni Association records.

First Academic Letters in the U.S.

Denison was the first school district in the entire nation to honor students with letters in academics. Prior to this, all school districts across the country acknowledged athletics as worthy of a letter, but not academics and other organizations.

This was such a momentous accomplishment that in 1958 letters were received from across the U.S. and all the way to Germany asking about the program. NBC asked for rights to film the awarding of the first letter jackets and President Eisenhower sent a letter of congratulations. This bold move by the leaders of Denison cemented the fact that all students were valued. That all students deserved recognition for their excellence. And that all students had the potential to excel in different areas of study.

Terrell High School students were included in the academic letter honors as well and the first letter sweaters were awarded to students on March 23, 1959. Scores of interested citizens attended the ceremony with an opening invocation by Revered J.T. Fennell and music by the Terrell High band and choir. School Board President W.E. Winter was on hand to award the sweaters alongside Terrell Principal E.T. Hardeman and commended all of the winners on their achievements.

Figure 133 The first Terrell High students to earn their academic letters were Frankie Brown-Math, Obie L. Greenleaf-Chemistry, Thomas Wrenn-History, Tommy Hilliard-Math, Cecelia Hardeman-English, Jo Ann Tucker-Biology, Joyce Jones-English, and Barbara Mitchell-History. The group was pictured in The Texas Standard in the May-June 1959 issue.

Parade Magazine ran an article covering Denison High School's letterman in October of 1961. Superintendent of Schools Horace W. Goodgion stated, "We felt a letter was a prestige symbol, and we felt it was high time a good student was given some prestige." The magazine stated that within just a few years over 100 school districts had adopted a similar plan with many of them sending observers to Denison to learn the full process. The awarding of "prestige" continues today with students earning letters in sports, academics, and extracurricular activities. Students may choose from letter jackets, letter sweaters, and letter blankets.

First Female to Serve as Mayor

Janet Gott, a lifelong resident of Denison, was elected the first female Mayor of the City of Denison in 2018. Janet was born and raised in Denison and graduated from Denison High School. Late in life she attended Southeastern Oklahoma State University, earning a degree in industrial management.

She would later return to school in pursuit of industrial engineering studies. She worked for the Johns-Manville plant in Denison for thirteen years until it closed in the 1980's. She would later join BAG Corp where she served as Vice President of Global Affairs and remained there until her retirement in 2010. Janet was re-elected to her position on May 1, 2021, with one of the largest margins of victory ever recorded in a Denison election bringing in 83% of the votes.

Figure 134 Mayor Janet Gott's official city portrait.

First Gentleman of Denison

Just as Mayor Gott was a trailblazer for women in a leadership role, so too was her husband as Denison's first official Gentleman. Jackson "Jack" Gott gained his title in 2018 following his wife's election to the seat of Mayor. He was in the fire service for over 38 years with twelve of those years as Fire Chief of Sherman, Texas.

Jack attended many social functions alongside Janet and filled his role with integrity and respect, much as he did in anything he pursued. Described as brave, resourceful, and courageous, Jack ultimately passed away during his wife's second term during the COVID-19 pandemic.

Figure 135 Jack Gott, the First Gentleman of Denison.

First Female President of the Denison NAACP

Mrs. Jerlean Fennell Coffey became the first woman President of the Denison Chapter of the NAACP, following in the footsteps of her father, the Reverend J.T. Fennell, former pastor of Mt. Olive, New Hope, Iron Ore and Victory Baptist churches in Denison.

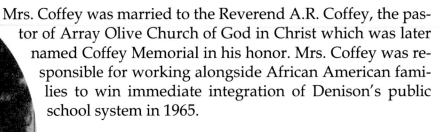

Mrs. Coffey was married to the Reverend A.R. Coffey, the pastor of Array Olive Church of God in Christ which was later named Coffey Memorial in his honor. Mrs. Coffey was responsible for working alongside African American families to win immediate integration of Denison's public school system in 1965.

First Knitting Mill in Texas

The Gate City Hosiery Company erected the first knitting mill in Texas between the summer and fall of 1900. The mill had the capacity to produce 300 pairs of hose per day and employed fifty people. The company was composed of local capitalists from the Denison Commercial Club along with F.J. and C.A. Depuy of Atlanta, Georgia.

Figure 136 Mrs. Jerlean Coffey, trailblazing President of Denison's NAACP Chapter.

The mill was constructed of stone and was located at Owings Street and Chandler Avenue due to its proximity to the Katy Railroad tracks. The building was completely destroyed by fire in the early morning hours of January 30, 1904. Tragically, the company was never able to financially recover from the fire and by 1907 the site was home to the Denison Mattress Factory which still stands to this day.

Figure 137 The Gate City Hosiery Company, ca. 1900.

First Male Principals Appointed
Found by James K. Sears

Three new school principals were assigned by the Denison School Board in June of 1939, marking the first instance that men were named as principals of Denison schools. Francis L. Jones of Denison, a graduate of Denton High and North Texas State Teachers College, was assigned Lamar School. T. B. Livingston, a graduate of Waxahachie High

School and North Texas Teachers College, was assigned Raynal School. The final candidate was widely known in school circles, Mason B. Frazier, a graduate of Samuel Houston College at Austin, was assigned the combined principalship of Anderson School and Terrell High School.

The First Ministerial Alliance

Denison's first Minister's Association consisted of Reverend T.E. Sherwood, pastor of the Methodist Episcopal Church, South, Reverend L.J. Adams Jr., pastor of the First Presbyterian Church, Reverend T.H. Corkill, pastor of the First Methodist Episcopal Church, North, and Reverend W.E. Tynes, pastor of the First Baptist Church. This association, now greatly expanded, still exists to this day and is a vital part of the Denison community.

Figure 138 Denison's first Ministerial Alliance.

First African American to Run for School Board

Mrs. W.M. Groce, a housewife, den mother, and partner with her husband in his Groce Grocery and Market at 720 North Mirick Avenue filed as a candidate for trustee of Denison's public schools in March of 1960. Mrs. Groce was not victorious in her run, receiving 315 votes in the April 1960 election, however she began the conversation and opened the door for people of color to enter political races in Denison.

Figure 139 An advertisement for Groce's Grocery from the Terrell High School Yearbook.

First Mayor and Council under Council-Manager Charter

In 1956 the City of Denison approved a charter resolution that created a Council-Manager form of government. Prior to this, the elected Mayor served as the official Manager of the City and conducted all duties necessary for the day-to-day operations of the community. The first council under the new form of government included Albert Martin, Ralph Porter, Mayor E. J. Lilley, B. McDaniel, Carl Flanery, Walter Lebrecht, and C. Weideman.

Figure 140 The first City Council members of the new Council-Manager form of government are sworn in.

First Female Chamber of Commerce Director

Figure 141 Elayne Meador's photo from the 1930 Denison High Yearbook.

Miss Elayne Meador, daughter of Mr. and Mrs. Grover Meador, 615 West Gandy, and manager of the Edna Freel's Clothing Store, was appointed a director of the Denison Chamber of Commerce on February 28, 1950. Miss Meador said she thought it was a great honor to be asked to serve on the Board, aside from the fact that she was the first of her sex to be granted that opportunity, and that she sincerely pledged herself, through her participation in their program, to live up to that honor. Miss Meador further stated that a woman's reaction could turn the trick in nearly every situation when decisive action was needed.

First Night Game
Found by James K. Sears

In the first Yellow Jacket home football game played after sunset, Denison's opponent was Dallas Sunset High School. The date was September 28, 1934, and the visiting Bisons won 19-0. The game was played at Forest Park Field, renamed Munson Field in March of 1936 following the death of William B. Munson, Jr. Mr. Munson was School Board President and Director of Athletics during construction of the new field. Officially or not, within a few years of the renaming, Munson Field was being called Munson Stadium.

Figure 142 An early view of Munson Stadium with lights.

First Kite Contest Winner

Jim Patillo, an Eagle Scout, won first place in the inaugural Scout Kite Contest on April 15, 1935 at Denison's Gray Field. Events included high flying, one-eight and one-quarter mile dashes, fancy kites, flight challenges, and a battle royale. Patillo was awarded a scout handbook for his efforts. No other reports can be found if the kite competition became an annual event or not.

Figure 143 Sam Patillo's photo from the 1937 Denison High School Yearbook.

First African American Boy Scout Troop

According to an article published in 1998, Denison was the first city in Texas to support an African American Boy Scout Troop. This occurred following the integration of the National Organization in the late 1920's.

The Troop, registered as number 403, grew to include both a Pack and Post as well. All three of these scouting groups were sponsored by the Terrell School with many of the teachers volunteering to serve as leaders.

Figure 144 Denison's African American Boy Scout Troop, seen with leader D.D. McKnight in 1957.

First Female President of the Denison Chamber of Commerce

Diana Kerbow Williams made long-awaited history in 2002 when she was elected as the first President of Denison's 90-year-old Chamber of Commerce. Williams had been involved with the Chamber for a number of years and had served well in every role she was appointed to. She would not remain the first for long though as the second female, Deborah Magourik, was elected to the post in 2007.

First President of the Denison Alumni Association

Miss Carrie Johnson, an 1888 graduate of Denison High School, was the first President of the Denison Alumni Association. The class of 1888 was the first to hold graduation ceremonies, but Mrs. Grace Clifford Knaur was considered the first graduate, having earned her diploma in 1885. The original site of the annual Alumni Homecoming was the lawn of T.V. Munson's home, Vinita. The site was eventually changed following the need for more space as the event grew larger.

Figure 145 Carrie Johnson, the first President of the Denison Alumni Association.

First House in Denison

The first house erected in the fledgling town of Denison is said to have been built in the 800 block of West Main Street, then considered incredibly far outside of the community. The home was constructed of logs with clay used to fill in the cracks and mismatched boards used on the roof as they had to be shaped quickly by hand and skilled labor was in short supply.

A fence was added several years later once lumber became more readily available. The home belonged to Dr. Alexander Morrison and was saved by W.M. Esler and moved to his backyard. His hope was to turn it into a museum, but finding no one willing to fund the endeavor he eventually tore it down and burned the logs in his fireplace in the 1930's.

Figure 146 A view of Dr. Morrison's home, believed to be the first constructed in Denison.

CHAPTER 8

Determined Denisonians: Untold Individuals

"There is always light, if only we're brave enough to see it. If only we're brave enough to be it."

-Amanda Gorman
Youngest Inaugural Poet in U.S. History

We've all read of Denison's great Hometown Heroes. T. V. Munson, Dwight D. Eisenhower, and Sully Sullenberger are household names across much of our community. But what if we were to expand the lens of what makes someone a hero? What if we honored individuals who dug deep, who pressed on, who made a positive impact for others?

Not to say our three known heroes deserve any less recognition, for they truly accomplished deeds that many of us could never do. However, in this section we strive to cast a glance upon others either from Denison originally, moved to Denison, or impacted Denison, that may not be as well known. From women who became titans of industry to teachers who made an impact, these are stories that must be told and celebrated so that we may remember these incredible individuals and their crowning achievements.

Mason Steele Frazier Sr.
By Dr. Mavis Anne Bryant

Figure 147 Mason Frazier Sr. as pictured in the Terrell High School yearbook, 1941.

From 1939 until 1952, Mason Steele Frazier Sr. was principal of Terrell High School in Denison, Texas.

Mason Frazier was the grandson of slaves in Stockdale, North Carolina. His father, John Wright Frazier (1864–1949), was a remarkable man who received an early education from white teachers and later schooling at the hands of African American teachers.

In 1880, at the age of 16, John Frazier entered Bennett Seminary (now Bennett College) in Greensboro, North Carolina, graduating in 1886. According to a biography published in 1907 as part of a program celebrating the 25th anniversary of the Metropolitan AME Church in Austin, Texas, John "was a poor boy, worked his way through school by milking, attending the school ground, sawing wood for the kitchen, teaching classes, and other labor of a like nature."

In 1886, Frazier secured a teaching position at Victoria, Texas. After teaching there for 14 years, he was appointed to teach mathematics at the new campus of Samuel Huston College in Austin. Austin City Directories from 1903 to 1907 list him as a librarian as well as mathematics teacher at the college.

Reuben Shannon (R.S.) Lovingood served as the first president of what is now Huston-Tillotson University in Austin, Texas. Huston-Tillotson was formed in 1952 through a merger of two institutions: Tillotson College and Samuel Huston College. Samuel Huston College began operating as a school in 1876. In 1887, Samuel Huston donated property for the college with the request that the institution bear his name. In 1910, the now Samuel Huston College was chartered as a private educational corporation. R. S. Lovinggood was born in 1864 in South Carolina. He graduated from Clark University (Clark Atlanta University) in 1890. Throughout his life, he was a prominent writer, educator, and leader in the Methodist Episcopal Church. He was elected president of Samuel Huston College in 1900 (the same year John Frazier was hired) and throughout his tenure worked to improve the college, grow the student body, and raise money for the institution. He died in 1916.

John Frazier worked closely with President R. S. Lovingood to develop the college, serving the institution for 28 years. Lovingood lived next door to the Fraziers until his death in 1916. The Census of 1910 counted him, wife Mattie, and five children there. After President Lovingood died, Frazier served as the college's interim president until the following year. He served as secretary of the Teachers State Association (the counterpart of the all-white Texas State Teachers Association) for three successive years, and helped bring the association out of a large debt. He also served as a delegate to the General Conference of the Methodist Episcopal Church in 1900 and alternate in 1904. He was the conductor of, or instructor in, more than ten summer normals, short courses which provided an option to many teachers and prospective teachers to prepare for state teacher certification examinations. Frazier's social activities included membership in the Black fraternal organization, Grand United Order of Odd Fellows (GUOOF).

In 1892, Frazier married Laura Allman, age 25, of Bennettsville, South Carolina. She was born on April 6, 1867, and lived until June 17, 1962. She came from a family of planters. In 1903, the Austin City Directory listed her as a teacher in the primary school at Samuel Huston College. The Fraziers had three children: Mason, Lauraine A., and John S. Mason was born in 1904 on the campus of Samuel Huston College.

Lauraine, a boy born in 1909, died as an infant. Information is lacking on John S. Frazier.

Laura Allman Frazier became a founding member of Austin's Frederick Douglass Club in 1906, and of the Hearts East Circle of King's Daughters Organization, a charitable group which cared for the elderly, promoted the development of spiritual life, and stimulated Christian activities.

In 1905, John Frazier purchased a house at 810 East Thirteenth Street in Austin's African American section. It had been built in 1876 by an immigrant stonemason, Joseph Limerick, though he never occupied it. The Frazier family lived there after 1905, and by the 1930s, Mrs. Frazier operated the house as lodging for African American students and travelers who were excluded from white-owned hotels in Austin during the Jim Crow era. From the 1930s to the early 1960s, the Frazier house was listed in travel guides as lodging for "Negroes." As the Limerick-Frasier House, it was designated a local landmark in 1978 by the City of Austin. It was listed on the National Register of Historic Places in October 1990.

John Wright Frazier passed away in Austin on July 2, 1949. His wife continued operating her guest house.

As for his son, Mason Steele Frazier, by 1930 he was teaching in a college (perhaps Samuel Huston) in Austin. Around 1940, he accepted the position of principal and chemistry teacher at Terrell High School in Denison, Texas. Very soon he married Edith Augusta Stone, who took a teaching post at Terrell School also. They had three children: Laurene Clothilde Frazier Smith (born 1943), Mason Steele Frazier Jr. (1948), and John Stone Frazier (1948). Mason and Edith lived at 731 West Johnson Street in Denison and taught together until moving to Los Angeles, California, around 1955. Mason's obituary in the Los Angeles Times says "he was a school administrator for 15 years in Texas and for 18 years with Compton Unified School District [in California]. He retired in 1973." Mason's mother Laura passed away in Los Angeles on June 17, 1962. She was buried next to her husband in Austin's Oakwood Cemetery.

Edith and Mason Frazier were divorced in October 1980. In 1982, she married another school principal, Jerome B. Busby (1911-1995), who had headed the Jack Yates High School, located very near Texas Southern University in the historic Third Ward in Houston, Texas. Mason Frazier died in Los Angeles on October 18, 1990. Edith Augusta Stone Frazier Busby passed away in Los Angeles on September 16, 2001.

Denisonians Made Names for Themselves
By Donna Hord Hunt

While my column was typically a "Yesterday" column, the story I'm about to tell also takes place "Today." One night, I did a program for the Grayson County Historical Society out at Frontier Village. The topic of the program was "Archie Gibbs and other Denisonians who made names for themselves."

Most of them I have talked about in past columns so I was busy finding information for the 31 people I discussed, some more than others.

Some may remember Gibbs, who left Denison to become a Merchant seaman aboard a freighter that was torpedoed by the Germans, only to be rescued before being torpedoed a second time that same day. Then he was "rescued" by a German u-boat that had just torpedoed both ships. I say he was "rescued" because he found himself a prisoner of war and was held for four days aboard the submarine before being released with a promise never to sail in those waters again.

Gibbs' story was taken from a biographical book he wrote in 1943. The book definitely was not a best seller. When Joe and Jerry Bassett told me about the unusual experience of a former Denisonian, I went to Amazon and purchased the last copy — a used one — that was available.

Gibbs' picture is on the cover and he was a nice-looking man, not that that has anything to do with the story.

I feel sure that most readers at least have heard of the second Denisonian who made his mark in the air and on the water. Captain Chesley B. Sullenberger, whose dad, C.B., was a Denison dentist, his mom, Pauline, was a Denison ISD teacher and his grandparents, the Hannas, were prominent in Denison's earlier days.

Sully, as he is now called, is Denison's newest hero, having successfully landed U.S. Airways Flight 1549 on the Hudson River on Jan. 15, 2009, saving the lives of all 155 passengers and crew on board.

Figure 148 Chesley "Sully" Sullenberger from the 1969 Denison High School Yearbook.

As luck would have it for Denison, Sully's 1969 Denison High School class was planning its 40th reunion in June and Denison schools were quick to invite Sully to give the graduation address that same weekend of June 6. Since Sully preferred to share the spotlight, Denison planned a gigantic "Heroes Day" placing the light on Five Star General and 34th President of the U.S. Dwight D. Eisenhower, and the internationally known horticulturist Thomas Volney Munson, who saved the grapes of France.

For a little change of pace, we jazzed up the program just a little by talking about Tommy Loy, a Denison High School graduate who gained fame as the trumpeter who played the National Anthem at all home games for the Dallas Cowboys for many years.

A couple of months ago, Tommy's memory was spotlighted at the Sherman Jazz Museum with a special exhibit of his musical instruments, awards and even his Cell Block uniform he wore when he played with that popular jazz band.

A name that probably is better known today among Denisonians than they were in his day is Edward S. O'Reilly, a colorful internationally famous soldier

Figure 149 Tommy Loy, the Dallas Cowboy's national anthem icon.

of fortune, writer and lecturer was introduced to the Denison Herald 50 years after he was born in 1880.

Tex is said to have ridden a mule from Texarkana to El Paso in 1898, was a drill instructor in the Chinese Imperial Army in 1901 and served as an officer in the Mexican Army in 1913 and 1914. He was a policeman in Shanghai, a soldier in the Philippine Insurrection, the Boxer Rebellion, and in 1911 was one of Madero's Foreign Legionnaires. It was said that he also fought with Poncho Villa and in North Africa. That's a pretty good record for one person. Lowell Thomas wrote "Born to Raise Hell" was about O'Reilly.

I hope some remember Mary Elizabeth Lease, the wife of a Denison druggist, who addressed the newly formed Denison Women's Christian Temperance Union in the 1880s as one of her first moves down the road to national fame as the Populist Party's Joan of Arc.

Phil McDade was born in Denison in 1901 and while he never had a music lesson, became a well-known bandleader in the era when swing was king.

Clora Bryant, Helen Cole and Margarite Bradshaw all graduated from Terrell High School, where they developed a taste for music. Clora played her trumpet with music greats such as

Figure 150 Mary Elizabeth Lease

Louis Armstrong, Carl Perkins and Dexter Gordon. Helen, a drummer had her own band and travelled all over the world and Margarite, who later taught school in the north, played with the Prairie View Co-eds.

Bob Boatright did his first serious fiddle player with the Texas Playboys and in 2002 his name was added to the Western Swing Music Society of the Southwest's Hall of Fame.

At least three or more Denisonians have been recipients of Carnegie Hero Medals and that is a great record for a town the size of Denison.

Hartley Edwards, while in the Army during World War I, was called on to play "Taps" to signal the end of the war.

Figure 151 Bob Boatright, Hall of Fame fiddle player from Denison.

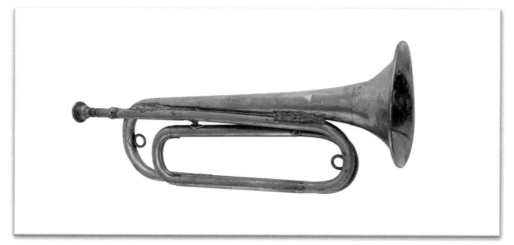

Figure 152 Hartley Edwards' M1892 C.G. Conn bugle now resides in the Smithsonian Museum.

He also played at both President Truman's and President Kennedy's funerals.

The list goes on and on and we may work up another column on some of the other hometown folks who made a name for themselves. I still have a pretty good list that we talked about at the Historical meeting and I am sure there are many more that I either forgot or didn't know about. I would appreciate suggestions to add to my list for my next column. We've had a lot of talented individuals and I'm sure there are more to come.

Carnegie Heroes
By Brian C. Hander

As mentioned in the previous article, Denison has the distinction of three individuals who earned the Carnegie Medal. This high honor is bestowed on those who perform acts of heroism in civilian life in the United States and Canada.

The following history of the Carnegie Hero Fund and Carnegie Medal comes from the Carnegie Hero Fund Commission website at carnegiehero.org.

"We live in a heroic age," Andrew Carnegie wrote in the opening lines of the Carnegie Hero Fund Commission's founding Deed of Trust in 1904. "Not seldom are we thrilled by deeds of heroism where men or women are injured or lose their lives in attempting to preserve or rescue their fellows."

Carnegie's "hero fund," administered by a twenty-one-member commission in Pittsburgh, was charged with honoring whom he called the "heroes of civilization," whose lifesaving actions put them in stark contrast to the "heroes of barbarism, (who) maimed or killed" their fellow man. That the mission of the Hero Fund as set forth by Carnegie is unchanged over more than a century, despite massive upheaval in the social and world order, is testament both to his foresight and to essentially unchanging human nature.

Figure 153 Andrew Carnegie, creator of the famed Carnegie Medal.

The Commission's working definition of a hero as well as its requirements for awarding remain largely those that were approved by the founder. The candidate for an award must be a civilian who voluntarily risks his or her life to an extraordinary degree while saving or attempting to save the life of another person. The rescuer must have no full measure of responsibility for the safety of the victim. There must be conclusive evidence to support the act's occurrence, and the act must be called to the attention of the Commission within two years.

Those who are selected for recognition by the Commission are awarded the Carnegie Medal, and they, or their survivors, become eligible for financial considerations, including one-time grants, scholarship aid, death benefits, and continuing assistance.

To date, more than 10,000 medals have been awarded, the recipients selected from more than 100,000 nominees. About twenty percent of the Medals are awarded posthumously. Awardees are announced four times a year, following meetings of the Commission.

The Carnegie Medal

The Carnegie Medal is a bronze medallion three inches in diameter and is awarded to civilians who risk their lives to an extraordinary degree saving or attempting to save the lives of others.

Andrew Carnegie's profile in relief dominates the obverse of the medal. The reverse carries as background, in low relief, the outline of the United States and Canada, the Commission's field of operation, and the seals of the two countries appear in high relief. The reverse of the medal centers on the cartouche, or inscription plate, which carries an embossed statement naming the rescuer, the rescued, and the place and date of the heroic act.

Figure 154 The Carnegie Hero Medal profile (above) and reverse (bottom right).

The cartouche is adorned with laurel, ivy, oak, and thistle, respectively signifying glory, friendship, strength, and persistence – the attributes of a hero. A verse from the New Testament encircles the outer edge: "Greater love hath no man than this, that a man lay down his life for his friends" (John 15:13).

Early medals awarded by the Commission were struck in bronze, silver, and gold, with distinction of medal grade contingent on the Commission's assessment of the heroic act being recognized. Changes in awarding policies over the years precluded the issuance of gold medals to individuals, and by 1981 the issuance of silver medals was discontinued.

Nineteen gold medals had been awarded to individuals, the last being Charles L. Coe, thirty, of Burkburnett, Texas, who died in a fire rescue act in 1923. The last of the 617 silver medals went to Brian Mervyn Clegg and Robert Stephen Grant for their rescue of three individuals from exposure in a downed airplane in Lake of the Woods, Kenora, Ontario, in 1979.

Henry L. Halliday
Bronze Medal #1105

Henry L. Halliday saved Charles M. Herron from a runaway horse in Denison on June 20, 1913. Charles, three, sitting on a velocipede, was directly in the path of a horse that was running away and galloping at a speed of about thirteen miles per hour. The horse was hitched to a wagon partly loaded with lumber. When the horse was about fifty feet from Charles, who did not realize his danger, Halliday, twenty-nine, baseball player, saw that it would run over the child. He ran about fifty feet, grabbed Charles with one hand and the velocipede with the other when the horse was but two feet from him, and threw the child to a place of safety. Halliday barely escaped being struck by the horse, which passed him at undiminished speed.

Clarence J. Farris
Bronze Medal #2497

Clarence J. Farris saved Gertrude Reynolds from being killed by a train in Denison on May 1, 1929. Gertrude, fourteen months, toddled on a track when the locomotive of a work train was 140 feet from her and approaching at a speed of ten miles per hour. The engineer applied the airbrakes and called to Farris, twenty-seven, locomotive fireman, who was on the locomotive. Farris grasped a handrail and jumped from the cab of the locomotive to the ground. He then ran 128 feet to a point ahead of the locomotive, which was reducing speed, grasped Gertrude around the waist, and jumped off the track. The locomotive was not more than five feet from him when he cleared its path.

Marvin Ray Griffith
Bronze Medal #6364

Marvin Ray Griffith saved Mario S. Escalera from drowning in Denison on March 31, 1978. Escalera, twenty-five, paralyzed from the chest down, was in the driver's seat of a two-door sedan when, with a trailer attached, it rolled into Waterloo Lake. Marvin, sixteen, high-school student, was on the trailer and moved to the open window at the driver's seat, holding to it as the sedan began sinking. Submerging with the automobile, which was in deep water about 120 feet from the bank, Marvin reached into the vehicle and took hold of Escalera. A very large air bubble from inside the sedan then was expelled through the window, aiding Marvin in getting Escalera out. At the surface, Marvin managed to get Escalera into a boat that was at hand, and in it they proceeded to the bank.

Little Known Noteworthy Denison Residents
By Natalie Clountz Bauman

From the book "Quantrill's Raiders in North Texas"

Most people are aware Denison has been home to many famous people, even if briefly; like President Dwight D. Eisenhower, Chesley "Sully" Sullenberger, and Doc Holliday. However, people may not realize there is a group of iconic individuals who have resided in Denison. Former members of Civil War fighters Quantrill's Raiders, the James-Younger "Gang" and some of their families were among Denison's most noteworthy number.

Jesse James

W.A. Eddings, who knew and wrote about Jesse and Frank James, was interviewed by a reporter.

The reporter asked - "Where did you see Jesse James first after the war?"

Eddings - "I saw him right here in Denison. That was in 1875. I came to Denison and found him tending bar here in a Main Street saloon."

Reporter - "Did you recognize him?"

Eddings - "Well, I should say so. Jesse's was a face you would never forget, and I knew him as soon as I saw him. He was going then under the name of Tom Dorr, and I stayed all night with him the time I speak of and we talked over old times. He was in Denison for some time before he went back north."

Figure 155 Jesse James in his 1874 wedding portrait.

Frank and Jesse James in Denison

An interesting milestone occurred in the life of Jesse James in Denison in 1881, though he didn't realize it at the time. A newspaper article was written by W.S. Adair, whose father, B.F. Sala built playhouses in Texas from Galveston to Dallas, was published in 1923 in The Dallas Morning News. Adair recalled the time when Frank and Jesse James stayed at the McDougall Opera House located at 225 West Main. The latter stages of the building of this opera house would have been in 1881 with the opening set for Dec. 15, 1881. "While building an opera house at Denison for J. "John" B. McDougall, he made me sleep on the stage to watch the property. Late one night Mr. McDougall brought two men into the theater and told me to let them sleep on the stage."

"At 4 o'clock in the morning, Mr. McDougall came back, shook me out of my sleep, and told me to drive the two men in his hack to Colbert's Ferry on Red River, four miles north of town. One of the men sat with me and the other occupied the back seat. When we reached the ferry, the man who sat with me said: 'Young man, do you know who I am?' I said, 'No Sir.' Then he put a stick of dynamite under me by saying: 'I am Jesse James,' and immediately added, 'This is my brother, Frank.' He then handed me a brass cavalry spur, saying, 'You have won your spurs tonight.'"

Figure 156 The McDougall Opera House in the 200 block of Denison's Main Street.

Frank and Jesse James often hid out in Murphy's barn on East Main Street in Denison when in town. McDougall would furnish them with supplies. He was rumored to be called "Colonel" as he was a Confederate sympathizer and possibly an officer in the Knights of the Golden Circle (along with the James Brothers) who were trying to revive the old Confederacy after the Civil War.

Adair further stated: "In 1885 when Frank James came to Dallas to live, he became my neighbor on Race Street. I called on him at his home one night, and, showing him the spur, which I had kept, and still keep, asked him if he remembered it. **'Perfectly,' he said and added with emotion, 'that was the last time my brother was ever in Texas.'"** So when Jesse James left Denison and crossed the Red River out of Texas in 1881, never to return. He proceeded to St. Joseph, Missouri where on April 3, 1882, he was shot and killed by his own partner, Bob Ford.

Cole Younger's Sisters Lived in Denison

The Younger family were intelligent, educated, prominent members of their northwestern Missouri community before the war. Cole Younger's father opposed secession, although he was by principle a states' rights man, and knew Abraham Lincoln personally. He was brutally ambushed, robbed, and murdered by Kansas pro-Union Redlegs, who also burned their farm, killed or maimed some of his sisters, and left the rest of his family homeless in the harsh winter. This induced the remaining Younger sons to join Quantrill under the black flag. Cole Younger was a prominent member of Quantrill's Raiders during the Civil War and what was dubbed the James-Younger Gang after the war; a group who participated in bank and train robberies. After the war, Quantrill's Raiders, being a guerilla organization and not an official regiment in the Confederate army, was not offered a pardon. This automatically made them technically outlaws unable to engage in a legitimate business. Since they were considered outlaws anyway, they behaved as outlaws to make a living.

Being no longer welcome in Missouri, the Younger sisters came to friendlier territory in Texas. In the 1887 Denison City Directory, Cole's sister Henrietta Younger is listed as a teacher and is living in the same household with her sister Martha Ann Younger Jones and her husband Lycurgas Jones. Martha Ann was a teacher also.

Young William R., engr Mo. Pac. Ry, r. 519 W. Morgan.
Young William W., machinist Mo. Pac. Ry shops, h. W. R. Young.
Younger David (c), porter Mo. Pac. Ry, r. 715 W. Bond.
Younger Henrietta Miss, teacher, h. Lycurgus Jones.
Younger Thomas (c), porter, r. 713 W. Bond.

Figure 157 An early day Denison City Directory listing Miss Henrietta Younger.

The Youngers were very religious people, active in the Christian Church in Denison. The Younger sisters' religious activities are mentioned in Denison newspapers: The Sunday Gazetteer October 28, 1888 - "'The Christian Spark' is the name of a new religious paper about to be published in Denison. **Miss Henrietta Younger, of 319 Barrett Avenue, is managing it."**

Henrietta Younger along with the family of her sister, Martha Ann Younger Jones, attended the Christian Church of Denison. In *The Sunday Gazetteer*, February 10, 1889, pg.4 reported - "A very pleasant entertainment under the auspices of the Christian Church Sunday School took place at the church edifice, on Armstrong Avenue, Monday night, the principal features of the performance being contributed by the "White Buds" - a little mite of a literary society connected with the Sunday school, and presided over by **Miss Retta (Henrietta) Younger.**"

The Sunday Gazetteer (April 7, 1889, pg.4) reported that **Miss Retta Younger** had left that week for Independence, Missouri where she would teach in the public schools. In the summer of 1889, Miss Henrietta spent time in Stillwater, Minnesota, as she wrote a letter dated July 17, 1889, to "My Dear Little White Buds", little girls from her literary society in Denison. The letter was printed in the July 28th issue of The Sunday Gazetteer as it describes the weather and scenery of the area as well as her trip on an excursion boat and the lumber companies in the area. In the summer of 1889, a petition was being circulated to the Governor of Minnesota to pardon the Younger brothers as "imprisonment was for reform, not punishment...." (The Sunday Gazetteer - Denison, Texas, June 30, 1889).

During her brother Bob Younger's illness in prison, Henrietta was permitted to act as his nurse. However, still in prison at Stillwater, Henrietta's brother Bob, just four years older than herself, contracted tuberculosis and died on September 16, 1889. The Denison Sunday Gazetteer of September 29, 1889, reprinted the account of Bob's death and remarks made by the prison chaplain, taken from the Prison Mirror. The chaplain, "Mr. Albert then addressed a few words of comfort directly to Miss Retta Younger, and her brothers, Cole and Jim, and closed by reading the 23rd Psalm."

Henrietta Younger became the wife of A.B. Rawlins on Sunday, April 1, 1894, at Gainesville, Cooke Co., Texas; **the bride had taught school for many years in Denison** and the groom was a practicing attorney in Cooke County - Sunday Gazetteer, April 1, 1894. According to the 1900 Federal census they were living in Oak Cliff, Dallas Co., Texas at 314 Ninth St. along with five children from his previous marriage; A.B. was Deputy County Clerk. By spring 1910 A.B. & Henrietta Rawlins are renting a home at 723 C Street in Ardmore, Carter Co., Oklahoma along with A.B.'s youngest son, Fisher Younger Rawlins.

Figure 158 Below: Robert Younger, Henrietta Younger, Cole Younger, and James Younger, September 1889. Courtesy of the Library of Congress.

LEE MCMURTRY, QUANTRILL RAIDER, PIONEER SETTLER OF DENISON
Levi Boone "Lee" McMurtry

LEE McMURTRY.   T. F. MAUPIN.

Figure 159 A view of Lee McMurtry from John Edwards' book, Noted Guerrillas.

Lee McMurtry was also one of Quantrill's Raiders and went to Kentucky with Quantrill in 1865. Quantrill was killed and McMurtry was captured in Nelson County, KY, and was one of the few Raiders pardoned on July 26, 1865. After the war, he went to Las Vegas, N.M. where he was engaged in merchandising for the next two years. In this he prospered, but closed his business out and again returned to his native State and located in Jackson County, Mo. where he began handling cattle and continued until 1871 when he came down to the Choctaw Nation and then to Denison, Texas, continuing in the same business and prospered. In 1883 he moved to Wichita Falls, Texas, Wichita County, where he resided and engaged in the cattle business and became sheriff there.

Figure 160 Lee McMurtry on the right, about 1866.

The Fort Worth Telegram on June 22, 1908, printed an excellent summary and tribute to Lee McMurtry upon his death: "Lee B. McMurtry, 66 years old, died Sunday in Ft. Worth and with his passing, one of the most remarkable characters of the early days of the southwest goes to his final reward. McMurtry was a personal friend of Jesse James in the days of his career in Missouri. He has told many listeners how he was with Bill Quantrill when he was shot toward the close of the civil war and last fall at Wichita Falls met Cole Younger for the first time in 36 years. McMurtry was present at the famous massacre at Lawrence, Kansas when the entire city was shot up and burned. Once with a few comrades, when surrounded by Colorado troops, he cut his way through the military cordon and in his flight that day had three horses shot from under him. In New Mexico, he freighted for years. **McMurtry was a pioneer settler of Denison, Texas, after the war, being a cattleman there.**

Next, he moved further west, became a peace officer, and was made sheriff of Wichita County. At Wichita Falls he made the best sheriff thereabouts had ever known. He was absolutely fearless and enforced the law to the letter. It is told of him that when he was a member of the Quantrill guerrilla band during the civil war, he once saved the life of Senator Stephen B. Elkins, who was a school friend of his. McMurtry, who cast his lot with the Quantrill band, often told how he came to join that organization.

The company he always explained was raised of fearless and daring men on the frontier who were accustomed to ride and shoot and was intended as a light horse attachment of the Confederate army. Their recklessness led them into trouble with the leaders of the Confederacy and before they were aware of it, they were declared outlaws and both the federal and the Confederate governments were against them. 'I fought under the black flag for two years,' said McMurtry to a Telegram reporter last fall at Wichita Falls, 'And I tell you it's a mighty dangerous business.'

Last fall when Cole Younger was with his (Wild West) show company, the meeting of the two men at Wichita Falls was touching. Younger had only a short time before been released from a long term in the penitentiary as a result of his many expeditions in the early days of bandit operations. The two men recognized each other after a separation of thirty-six years and Younger was taken to McMurtry's home, where they spent hours telling their reminiscences of the days when the only law was the law of the gun. The death of McMurtry came very suddenly Sunday. He was visiting at the home of his daughter in Fort Worth at 1514 Lawrence Avenue when he was suddenly stricken and died. Interment was made at Wichita Falls, Texas."

The Wichita Daily Times (Wichita Falls, Texas) on July 7, 1908, added some further details: "**Regarding the Late Mr. McMurtry -** The following is a true biographical sketch of the late Levi B. McMurtry of whom such an erroneous statement was published upon his death, stating 'he was with the James boys in their outlaw days and fleeing into old Mexico and a price being placed on his head later, returned, stood trial and was cleared.' He was never guilty of having to be brought to the bar of justice in answer for a crime of any kind. Levi

Boone McMurtry was born in Calloway County, Missouri September 25, 1841. He was educated in Missouri, leaving school when 17 years of age. His first employment was in the freighting business as a driver of a mule team, and he continued at this business until the outbreak of the civil war in 1861. With his brothers, he entered the Confederate service and was with Quantrill and other leaders principally in the States of Kansas, Missouri, and Arkansas, but was transferred to the eastern side of the Mississippi River in the last year of the war and was in Nelson County, Kentucky when hostilities ceased.

Lee was wounded under the eye in the same battle in September 1864 in Fayette, MO. in which one of his brothers, George, was killed. Returning to his western home, he shortly afterward moved to Las Vegas, N.M. where he was engaged in merchandising for the next two years. In this, he prospered, but closed his business out and again returned to his native State of Missouri and located in Jackson County where he began handling cattle and continued until 1871 when he came down to the Choctaw Nation continuing in the same business and prospering. **He also lived in Denison, Texas until 1883 (also engaged in the cattle business there).**

In 1883 he moved to Wichita Falls, Texas, Wichita County, where he resided and engaged in the cattle business until his death, which occurred June 21, 1908, while at his daughter's in Fort Worth. He was sheriff of Wichita County for four years. He was a Royal Arch Mason and a member of Wichita Lodge No. 202. On January 8, 1867, he was united in marriage to Catherine H. Burns at Independence, Mo. To this union, three children were born - Grizzelle, Cosette, and Avon."

Crime and Calamity Strike the McMurtry's in Denison

Some interesting occurrences in the life of Lee McMurtry in the last year of his residence in Denison were reported in Denison's Sunday Gazetteer newspaper. He was up to any challenge, however, having faced, and survived many potentially deadly situations so far.

On May 20, 1883, an unwelcome guest came calling on the McMurtry house in Denison – a tornado. The article stated for a town to be well advertised, it must be visited by some sort of disaster like this tornado. (It's true that in those days, bad news like this was often reprinted in newspapers all over the country, making potential immigrants aware of its existence.) I'm sure the McMurtrys could have done without the publicity! About 9:30 in the morning on May 17th two heavy clouds approached, one from the southwest and the other from the southeast. They met over the city of Denison, spinning up a terrific tornado that struck the southwestern part of town.

A tree was blown down on Sears Street, which struck the residence of Lee McMurtry, throwing down the wall on that side. Mrs. McMurtry and her mother, Mrs. Burns, who were in the house, were partially buried in the debris. Mrs. McMurtry received a severe scalp wound, caused by falling timber. The wound was about twelve inches wide in the shape of a semi-circle. Dr. Hanna dressed the wound, which was painful, but she was not dangerously hurt. Mrs. Burns also suffered injuries, but not of a serious nature.

An article on July 1, 1883, reported just a month after the tornado, at the end of June on a Friday night about midnight, another unwelcome guest dared to invade the sanctity of Lee McMurtry's home. This invader found more than he bargained for there, but with Lee McMurtry, AND his neighbors! He messed with the wrong people!

Someone attempted to enter the residence of Lee McMurtry by the back door. Miss McMurtry was the first to give the alarm, and the man was then seen retreating from the house, no doubt in terror of the enraged ex-Quantrill man about to aerate his body with lead projectiles! But then he was seen by the neighbor Mr. Boggs, who came out and fired two pistol shots at the hastily retreating man.

G. G. Randall, whose residence was on the opposite side of the street, was attracted by the sounds of the pistol shots. Randall fired three shots himself, but no one knew if the bullets hit the man as he continued to run. The burglar then fired two shots at Mr. Randell, who fired four more shots in return, but it was so dark he could not aim properly and make them effective. Needless to say, their burglary problems came to an end. Chalk one up for neighborhood watch.

This is not a complete list by any means of noteworthy Denison residents, even among former Quantrill men. Denison can be proud of its rich history!

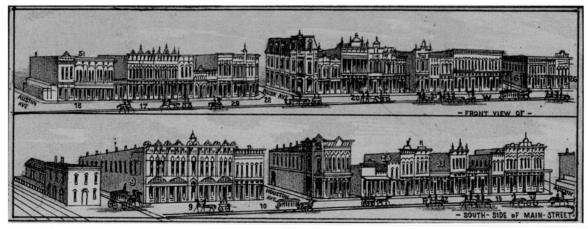

Figure 161 A view of Denison's Main Street from the 1886 Bird's Eye View Map.

Clora Bryant
By Donna Hord Hunt

Sherman has its own Jazz Museum and if this was the 1940s maybe the Queen of Jazz and some of her fellow musicians could make an appearance close to their hometown. The Prairie View Coeds, a group of jazzy musicians, five of which hailed from Denison, all appeared in the 1940s while attending the all-black Prairie View A&M University in Houston.

Perhaps the best known of the five musicians was Clora Bryant, who as a child was a member of the choir at her Baptist church. When her brother joined the military, he left his trumpet behind and Clora learned how to play it. At Terrell High School, she played in the marching band and turned down scholarships from two other colleges to attend Prairie View, where she was a member of the Prairie View Coeds Jazz Band that toured in Texas and performed at the Apollo Theater in New York City in 1944.

It was at the Apollo that Clora became a hit when she played "I Had the Craziest Dream" on her version of a solo by trumpeter Harry James.

I didn't know anything about Clora until a few years ago when as I was looking for a Christmas gift for my husband that would suit his love of jazz. I found a great one in a discount bookstore that made a big hit, although I didn't know what I was getting. It looked like something that would come in handy for a jazz lover.

Figure 162 Clora Bryant in an early publicity photo by James J. Kriegsmann.

If you want to know most anything about any great jazz entertainer, "The Biographical Encyclopedia of Jazz" by Leonard Feather and Ira Gitler probably holds the answer.

And wouldn't you know it, as soon as I started thumbing through the book, I found the name of a female musician who was born in Denison, Texas.

I learned about Bryant a couple of years earlier when Marguerite Bradshaw told me how she, Clora, Helen Cole, Elizabeth Thomas Smith and Alice Marie Jones Grubbs played with the Prairie View Coeds and how they had been honored at the university during the 2002 Founders' Day and Honors Recognition Convocation there.

Figure 163 Clora Bryant's photo from the 1941 Terrell High School Yearbook.

These five women, all graduates of Terrell High in Denison during the days of segregation, all went to Prairie View in early 1943. When the honors program recognized their accomplishments, they were among the ten surviving members of the all-girl orchestra.

While Coeds, they traveled from Texas to New York, playing at dance halls, military bases, stage shows and best of all at the Apollo Theater serving as goodwill ambassadors for the school and as one of the first African American college women's bands during World War II.

After completing their education at Prairie View, all went on to make names for themselves in their chosen career fields. Clora and Helen Cole, who became well known as a drummer with her own band, were the only two who retained music as their career.

Marguerite, who moved back to Denison after she retired, was an assistant principal and principal and did the pilot project for decentralization of New York City schools in the office of the superintendent.

Helen, who also moved back to Denison after she retired, completed her major in business and worked at the Citizens National Bank until she retired from Bank One here.

Elizabeth Thomas Smith, who lived in New York City, retired as food manager over baking at one of the top New York restaurants, then operated her own catering business there.

Alice Grubbs, who lived in Philadelphia, helped her daughter raise twins after she retired.

Clora, who was born on May 30, 1927, moved to Los Angeles after she retired, traveled all over the world and played trumpet as a sit-in with the country's most famous bands. She was honored in May 2002 at the Kennedy Center as the Mary Lou Williams Jazz Woman of the Year, an honor she described as "awesome." She was the first woman jazz player to go to Russia when Gorbachev was in power.

Clora grew up listening to the good big bands that her father, Charles Bryant, loved. These included Count Basie, Duke Ellington, Glen Miller, Lionel Hampton, Harry James and others. When Clora was three years old her mother, Eulila, died and she and her brothers, Frederick and Melvin, were raised by their father. His love of jazz and blues was passed to his children.

After attending Prairie View, Clora and her dad moved to Los Angeles in 1945 for her to be "discovered." Once in L.A., Bryant joined the celebrated International Sweethearts of Rhythm band as a featured soloist. She transferred to UCLA and became active in the Central Avenue jazz scene and recorded her first album, "Gal with a Horn," in 1957.

She played Las Vegas in the 1960s and had a role in the only movie of her career, "Pepe," starring the Mexican matinee idol, Cantinflas. She appeared as the only female in the big orchestra behind Sammy Davis Jr.

Figure 164 Clora Bryant plays the trumpet with the Dixieland band in Hermosa Beach, Ca.

In 1951, she worked in Los Angeles as a trumpeter for Josephine Baker and Billie Holiday. Two years later, she moved to New York City. That year she performed with the Queens of Swing as the Hollywood Sepia Tones in a variety program. They were the first women's jazz group to appear on television.

In 1988, Bryant wrote to Soviet President Mikhail Gorbachev suggesting she might be "the first lady horn player to be invited to your country to perform". Remarkably, Gorbachev issued a formal invitation and Clora was able to tour Soviet Russia with her sons to great acclaim.

Following a quadruple bypass surgery in 1996, Clora ceased playing the trumpet and began focusing on lecturing on jazz history in local colleges and grade schools.

Clora was honored in 2002 by the Denison Alumni Association as a Distinguished Alumni. Unfortunately, she was ill and couldn't make the trip to accept the honor, but her close school friend Marguerite Bradshaw stepped in and accepted the award for her.

When interviewed several years ago, Clora was emphatic in making it known that she had a wonderful father, Charles Bryant, who gave her an appreciation for the music that led to a career that took her to places she never imagined and earned high honors for her outstanding talent. She was featured in the 2014 film, "The Girls in the Band" and was highlighted in the 1989 documentary "Trumpetistically, Clora Bryant." Clora died on August 25, 2019, at the age of 92.

Terrell High School Song

I

Dear Terrell we hail thee, all praise to thy name. Thy banners unfurl to thy breeze, Thy children salute thee
and pledge to thy fame, Like soldiers who drink to the lees.

II

All around thee arise the first temples of God. Lifting high, leafy arms to the sky. While we pledge to thee daily to cherish and guard - All the lessons we've learned in thy halls.

III

To the youth of our town, to the youth of our race. Thou art ever a tower of strength, and in years of the future in hours of strife. We shall draw from thee wisdom and grace.

IV

Thou art more a than a name, Thou art more than cold stone, Thou art spirit and beauty and light - And the standards we raised in the years 'neath thy dome. Are the standards

Bill Anoatubby
By Brian C. Hander

Bill Anoatubby, the youngest of six children, was born in Denison, Texas on November 8, 1945. His father died before Bill's third birthday, and his widowed mother, Opal, moved him and his five siblings to Tishomingo, Oklahoma, the capital city of the Chickasaw Nation. Anoatubby graduated from Tishomingo High School in 1964 where he played football and was active in student government.

He attended Murray State College in Tishomingo before transferring to East Central University in Ada, Oklahoma, where he earned a bachelor's degree in accounting. Anoatubby would go on to undertake additional studies in business and finance at East Central and Southeastern Oklahoma State University in Durant, Oklahoma.

Figure 165 Governor Anoatubby's official Chickasaw Governor portrait.

Anoatubby married Janice Lamon in 1967 and would later have two sons, Chris and Brian. Throughout his college years he served in the Oklahoma National Guard, attaining the rank of staff sergeant and command of a light truck platoon before his honorable discharge in 1971.

In his early career, Bill was employed as an office manager for the American Plating Company and then went on to serve the Little Giant Corporation in Oklahoma City as the company's Chief Accountant.

In July of 1975, Anoatubby began employment with the Chickasaw Nation as Director of Tribal Health Services where he managed health programs in a 13-county region in South Central Oklahoma. He would move from this position to Director of Tribal Accounting and in 1978 was appointed as a special assistant to the Chickasaw Governor and Controller. In 1979, Anoatubby was elected as the first Lieutenant Governor of the Chickasaw Nation, serving alongside Governor Overton James.

Figure 166 Bill Anoatubby is sworn in as the 30th Governor of the Chickasaw Nation. Photo courtesy of anoatubby.com

In 1987 Anoatubby was elected as the 30th Governor of the Chickasaw Nation and has served 9 consecutive terms in office since that time. The Chickasaw Nation has 15,000 employees and offers more than 200 tribal programs and series. Under Governor Anoatubby's leadership, tribal assets have grown 200-fold alongside tremendous financial growth.

Chickasaw Nation Statistics

Constitution: August 30, 1856 (Ratified in 1983)

Capital: Tishomingo, Oklahoma

Members: 70,000

Area: 7,648 square miles encompassing 13 counties

Number of Employees: 13,500

12th largest federally recognized tribe in the United States

Chickasaw Nation Lighthorse Police Department founded on October 1, 2004.

Net Assets grew from $9.2 million in 1987 to $3.3 billion in 2019.

Viola Edna Beck van Katwijk
By Brian C. Hander

Viola Beck van Katwijk was born on February 26, 1894, in Denison, Texas to German immigrants from Saxony, Max Oswald Beck and Mina (Frank) Beck. The family moved to Dallas in 1911 where a young Viola began teaching piano lessons. She and her sister Irma became quite proficient and studied piano in Berlin with Richard Burmeister, a former pupil of Franz Liszt. Viola would go on to study under Percy Grainger as well.

Viola, at age twenty, made her solo debut as a pianist with the St. Louis Symphony Orchestra. She and her violinist brother, Curt, toured as part of The Beck-Allen Trio for several years prior to her marriage. In 1920 she won the national Mu Phi Epsilon composition contest, an honor she would repeat in 1930.

Viola began to perform throughout Dallas music circles alongside other composers and musicians such as pianist Paul van Katwijk, Dean of the School of Music at Southern Methodist University. They married on July 15, 1922, and Viola accepted a position on the faculty at SMU as a professor of music in September of 1922. She remained with the university until she retired in 1955.

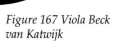

Figure 167 Viola Beck van Katwijk

Viola van Katwijk had an incredible career and was the composer of such works as "Dusk on a Texas Prairie", "The Jester", and "Gamelan". She was a charter member of the Dallas Music Teachers Association as well as a charter member of the Mu Chi Chapter of the Mu Phi Epsilon music fraternity.

Viola passed away in Dallas, Texas on December 25, 1980, at the age of eighty-six. She was preceded in death by her husband and the couple is buried in Hillcrest Memorial Park in Dallas.

The Paul and Viola van Katwijk Collection is archived at Southern Methodist University. The collection includes over 100 letters and manuscripts from well-known composers such as Debussy, Mahler, Rachmaninoff, and Rossini. Additionally, three manuscripts of Viola's compositions are archived at the Texas Women's University Library in Denton, Texas.

Booker Telleferro Ervin II
By Brian C. Hander

Booker Telleferro Ervin II was born on October 31, 1930, in Denison, Texas. He learned to play the trombone at a young age and was taught by his father, who played the instrument with Buddy Tate. After Ervin graduated from Terrell High School in the class of 1947, he joined the United States Air Force and was stationed in Okinawa.

It was at this site during the Korean War that he taught himself to play tenor saxophone. With his service complete in 1953, he went to Boston to study at the Berklee College of Music. He moved to Tulsa in 1954 where he played in a band with Ernie Fields.

Ervin would travel to several locations including Denver and Pittsburgh before arriving in New York City in the spring of 1958. He joined Charles Mingus from 1958 to 1960, then played in different groups until the autumn of 1964, when he left for Europe. There he would play gigs in France, Spain, Italy, Germany, Norway, Sweden, Denmark, and The Netherlands.

He even received a guest spot at the 1965 Berlin Jazz Festival, during which he performed a twenty-five-minute improvisation. Upon his return, Ervin led his own quartet that recorded for Prestige Records. The group included pianist Jaki Byard, bassist Richard Davis, and drummer Alan Dawson.

Figure 168 A photo of Booker Ervin II in his early thirties.

Ervin's final recorded appearance occurred in January of 1969 where he was a guest on a Prestige album headed by Eric Kloss. In his career,

Ervin played with the likes of Eric Dolphy, Horace Parlan, and Randy Weston. He recorded for Savoy, Candid, Bethlehem, Pacific Jazz, and Blue Notes in addition to his work with Prestige.

The most memorable moments from his career were nine albums he recorded for the Prestige Record Label that included The Blues Book, The Space Book, The Freedom Book, The Song Book, Setting, The Pace, The Trance, and Exultation. Popular recordings included "Largo", "Little Jane", "Git It", "That's It", "Up & Down", "Happy Frame of Mind", "Tex Book Tenor", and "The Book Cooks."

Ervin died of kidney disease in New York City on August 31, 1970, at the age of thirty-nine. His gravestone is in The National Cemetery, East Farmingdale, New York.

Figure 169 Booker Ervin's Junior photo from the 1947 Terrell High Yearbook

Figure 170 Terrell High School, constructed in 1927 and demolished in 2000. Terrell Elementary School, located just west of the former high school site, still bears the name of August H. Terrell.

Major Jewel Barton Butler, Sr.
By Brian C. Hander

Jewel Butler was born in Denison, Texas on June 6, 1922, to Edward Arthur Butler and Louise Hill Stewart Butler. Jewel was one of eleven children and grew up at 324 East Herron Street, which had been purchased by his father in 1919 and consisted of just over ¾ of an acre. This site is a mere five blocks away from the birthplace of Dwight David Eisenhower, the man who would serve as President of the United States while Jewel was in the service.

Figure 171 Jewel Butler's graduation photo from the Tuskegee Institute. Courtesy of the Butler family.

Edward Butler Sr. worked an average of 56 hours per week with the Katy Railroad and supported his family on his earnings of $102 per month. Many of the Butler children first attended Denison's Anderson School for elementary education and then Terrell High School for their secondary education, and according to the 1940 U.S. Census all were able to read and write by the time they were five.

Jewel played defensive end for the Terrell Dragons, hailed as one the of the best football teams in the state and title holders of the first State Championship in Denison when they tied in 1947, and then turned around in 1948 for an all-around defeat of Orange Wallace High to win yet another State Championship. He graduated from Terrell High School on May 29, 1940 and entered the Army as an enlisted soldier in August 1942, began active duty in June 1943, and then started training at Tuskegee in December of 1944.

He graduated from the Tuskegee Institute on September 11, 1945, as a Second Lieutenant and was assigned to the 99 Fighter Squadron, just missing action in WWII. Major Butler was part of the Red Tails, sometimes referred to at the Schwartze Vogelmenshen (Black Birdmen) by the Germans, and flew missions in North Africa, Sicily, and Europe.

Two of the aircraft he flew while in service include the P47 and P51. He served in the Army before he was transferred to the Air Force to become part of the first integrated units that served in the Korean War.

The Black Airmen that composed this elite unit returned home with 150 Distinguished Flying Crosses, Legions of Merit, and the Red Star of Yugoslavia. With the magnificent war record of these individuals and the unparalleled skills they were able to offer, the U.S. War Department led a review of their racial policies.

Major Butler served for more than twenty years in the Air Force and was awarded numerous medals for his efforts.

Kurt Cichowski helped provide the following information regarding the medals accrued by Major Butler during his time in the Army Air Service and the Air Force:

I.   The Air Medal with two oak leaf clusters. This means he was thrice recognized for meritorious or heroic action while engaged in aerial flight

II.   The American Campaign Service Ribbon for having served at least one year in the military from Pearl Harbor Day until March 2, 1946. Major Butler's enlisted time, as well as his efforts in flight school, qualified him for this.

III. The World War II Victory Ribbon given to those who carried out military duties from Pearl Harbor Day until Dec 31, 1946. His time flying at Lockbourne qualified him for this award.

IV.   The National Defense Service ribbon is awarded to those who serve in the military during times of conflict. Major Butler was in the Army, and/or the Air Force, for World War II, Korea, and Vietnam.

V.   The Korean Service Medal with three campaign stars. This means Major Butler conducted operations in Korea for three of the ten military campaigns recognized for having occurred in that conflict.

VI.   The Air Force Longevity Service Award, with four oak leaf clusters, depicting that Major Butler was in the Air Force for at least 20 years. He was in the military, including his Army time, for 22 years, 2 months, and 12 days.

VII.   The Armed Forces Reserve Medal recognizing those military members who served in the Reserve Component; Major Butler was in the Air Force Reserves.

VIII.   The United Nations Service Medal, an international award, is awarded to those military members, from any country, who served more than 30 days in that conflict.

Major Butler retired from the Air Force on November 1, 1963, at Sheppard Air Force Base in Wichita Falls, Texas. He passed away on December 13, 1992, in Houston, Texas.

Figure 172 Major Jewel Butler Sr. shortly before his retirement. Courtesy of the Butler family.

On March 28, 2022, a mural was unveiled and dedicated to Major Butler with the largest crowd ever in attendance for a public art dedication in Denison. Major Butler has officially been proclaimed a Denison Hometown Hero and has become the first, yet certainly not last, person of color to be featured in a mural in downtown Denison.

May his story inspire the endless pursuit of service above self, of dedication to a higher calling, and unwavering pride in who we are and where we come from.

Figure 173 Above, the newly completed Major Jewel Butler mural in downtown Denison, completed by Denison graduate and muralist Steven Bohall. Below, Major Butler's family pose for a photo after the dedication ceremony on March 26, 2022.

TERRELL GRADUATE WAS A GREAT DEBATER
By James K. Sears

It is relatively common knowledge locally that the Denison High School boys' and girls' debate teams won state championships on the same day in Austin in 1937. But probably no one in town knows that two years earlier a recent graduate of Denison's Terrell High School was a member of little Wiley College's three-man team that would inspire Oprah Winfrey and Denzel Washington to make the 2007 movie "The Great Debaters."

Figure 174 The Wiley College 1934-1935 debate team. Daniel Willis Ford, Denison debater, is pictured at left front in this photo.

The movie grew out of a 1997 article of the same title in the magazine AMERICAN LEGACY. Because the article appeared 62 years after the fact, and because documentation of the story is sparse, hard to find, and inconsistent, some details that emerged in the magazine are contradicted by other sources.

The article identifies the three debaters from Wiley who outargued the reigning national champions from the University of Southern California as Hobart Jarrett, Henry Heights, and James Farmer. Although those three did compose the team that beat USC in a rematch the following year, Jarrett's two teammates in the spring of 1935 were identified in contemporaneous newspaper reports as Cleveland Gay of Gary, Indiana, and Daniel Ford of Denison, Texas.

Daniel Willis Ford was born in Denison in 1915. The 1920 Census lists his father George as a widowed hotel cook. Daniel and his younger brother Melvin were raised with the help of their grandmother, Josie Ford, at 613 South Crockett Avenue, beside a Texas & Pacific Railroad crossing. In the 1930 Census Josie is listed as a laundress.

Not long after Daniel went off to Marshall, Texas, for college in the early 1930s, the rest of the Ford family left Denison, too. Josie does not appear in any Denison city directories after 1934. George and Melvin were living in Dallas in 1937 when Melvin, a dishwasher, died of appendicitis at the age of 20.

After he finished at Wiley College, Daniel moved to Oakland, California, and started a business that sold novelty pens by mail. He died in Los Angeles in 1993. Few other details of his life survive in public records, but his legacy of helping to advance race relations in the 1930s through his participation in Wiley College's historic interracial debates is one that will endure for generations.

Figure 175 Denison's Anderson School served African American students in elementary education before it was combined with Terrell. This school is where Daniel Willis Ford would have attended before going to Terrell for his secondary education. The building was demolished in 1966.

Joseph Theodore (J.T.) Munson
By Brian C. Hander

Joseph Theodore (J.T.) Munson was born in Fulton County, Illinois on September 30, 1841, to William and Maria Linley Munson. J.T. attended Abbington College followed by the University of Kentucky and finished his education at Bethany College in Virginia.

Following school, he enlisted in the army in 1864 and remained in the service until the surrender the following year. Munson, along with his parents, traveled to Denison in 1876 to make his home with them at the corner of North Houston Avenue and Parnell Street.

Shortly after his arrival in Denison, J.T. partnered with Harrison Tone to form the Tone & Munson Real Estate and Abstracts Firm. While this business would prove short-lived, it gave both men great experience with Denison's business elite and new developers looking to enter the community.

Figure 176 J.T. Munson as a young man.

J.T.'s achievements were numerous but one of his most notable was the surveying of land in West Texas to help pay for the design and construction of a new Texas State Capitol building. How he came about this ambitious task is a rather unique story in itself. In the early years of their entry into Texas the Munson brothers, including J.T., W.B., and T.V., became well tied to Governor Oran M. Roberts.

Under legislation passed in 1879, a five-member Capitol Board was established and headed by Governor Roberts. The first order of business for the Board was to award a surveying job on the basis of sealed bids to help subdivide the state's vast land holdings in West Texas into tracts of one league (4,428 acres) each.

Munson had become quite proficient as a surveyor through his work with real estate, and was awarded the job of surveying the nearly three million acres with a winning bid of $7,440. He was paid by the state from the sale of 50,000 additional acres of the West Texas land that he helped survey. The requirement was that he have the job completed by the last day of September 1880, and true to his word, the survey was completed early on September 8, 1880.

The final report of the 739 leagues, including field notes and sketches, was filed in the Land Commissioner's office at Austin. The land sale, much of which became the famed XIT Ranch, enabled by J.T. Munson's survey, yielded $3,224,593.45 to the state to pay for the new capitol building that was dedicated eight years later in 1888.

J.T. returned to Denison and engaged in the real estate business with his brother, W.B. Munson. A new venture was begun when Jot Gunter, J.T. Munson, and W.B. Munson Sr., as partners, surveyed large portions of the rest of North Texas during the period of railroad building into Texas in the 1870's and 1880's.

By February of 1885 Munson went into business with the First National Bank of Denison, along with his brothers and sisters as stockholders. He also became quite proficient in mule raising, breeding over 300 mares that became prized throughout North Texas.

In 1890, J.T. became the principal backer of the Denison Cotton Manufacturing Company, a venture that came with a $500,000 price tag and produced the largest cotton processing building in Texas upon completion. The company was located at 701 West Rice on the southern edge of Denison, very near his brother, T.V.'s home and vineyard, Vinita.

The mill would become Denison's largest employer with over 300 workers, some spending their entire lives working and living within the vicinity of the large building. The firm was so successful that in 1898 Denison's Commercial Club sent J.T. to Atlanta, Georgia to convince outside investors to open a hosiery mill in Texas. The Cotton Mill would supply the needs of the Georgian company in exchange for their relocation.

The trip proved successful, and the Gate City Hosiery Mill was formed, manufacturing 300 dozen pairs of hose daily each of women's, men's, and children's stockings. While the future looked bright, by 1900 the Cotton Mill was in serious financial trouble. Needing advice and capitol, J.T. called upon his brother Ben.

Figure 177 The Gate City Hosiery Mill, the first of its kind in the State of Texas.

Figure 178 The Denison Cotton Mill, ca. 1900.

On August 5, 1905, Ben Munson Sr. incorporated the Denison Cotton Mill with new capitol and served as its President until his death. The capital stock was fixed at $150,000 and J.T. Munson remained a minority stockholder in the company. This action retained Denison's industry that was a vital part of the economy and livelihoods of many of her citizens.

The Munson brothers joined forces once again in Ben's Nueces Land & Livestock Company that was organized on July 16, 1909 with original incorporators Ben Munson, J.T. Munson, L.B. Moore, M.T. Mathes, C.J. O'Maley, T.L. Clark, and E.C. Sturgis. The land controlled by this company totaled nearly 73,000 acres across Lasalle, McMullen, and Duval Counties which proved quite profitable through oil leases, royalties, and grazing leases.

J.T. Munson was a noted reader and acquired an extensive library that surpassed any within the city, and with this quest for knowledge came an incredible donation to the citizens of Denison. J.T. Munson was the financial founder and sponsor of the XXI Club of Denison. This was the second ladies club organized in Texas and the first in the state to own their own clubhouse. Munson generously donated the lots and most of the funds needed to build the clubhouse, which would house the city's first public library.

He donated a 130-acre park to the City of Denison in 1908 which we today know as Munson Park. Some sources claim he also donated land surrounding Waterloo Lake for use as a park.

Figure 179 J.T. Munson's tombstone in Denison's Fairview Cemetery.

Much like his brother T.V., J.T. was also described as being fond of horticulture and could often be found tending the trees and foliage around St. Luke's Church across the street from his home. He served as an exalted ruler of the Denison Lodge No. 238 Elks Club and held a life membership in the program.

J.T., W. B., and W.B. Munson Jr. organized and incorporated the Munson Realty Company, previously operating as the Munson Brothers Realty Company, on February 5, 1915. Each of the brothers held 747 shares of stock with Ben Jr. holding six shares. J.T. served as the first President until he was succeeded by his brother on January 1, 1918.

Joseph Theodore Munson died on June 9, 1919, at his apartment at 515 West Woodard Street. The 76-year-old bachelor had been in failing health for several months yet still attempted to complete his works at the Munson Real Estate firm.

A special resolution was passed by the members of the Munson Realty Company shortly after Munson's death and read as follows:

In Memoriam

At a meeting of the Board of Directors of The Munson Realty Company held in Denison, Texas, June 23rd, 1919, the following testimonial to the memory of the deceased Director and Vice-President, Mr. J.T. Munson, was unanimously adopted:

Since the last meeting of this Board, death has invaded its circle and claimed one of its most esteemed members.

After a brief illness Mr. J.T. Munson of Denison, Texas, departed this life on June 9th, 1919.

Mr. Munson was born near Astoria, Fulton County, Illinois, Sept. 30th, 1841, his parents being William and Maria Linley Munson. He was reared on a farm and attended district school in the community when he was not engaged in farm work. Later he attended Abbington College, Illinois, following which he took a course at the University of Kentucky, his education being finished at Bethany College, Virginia.

Coming out of college he enlisted in the Confederate cause in 1864 and remained in the service until surrender the year following. In 1878 he left Illinois in company with his parents and located in Denison and made his home with them until their death in 1890 in the homestead which still stands on North Houston Avenue and Parnell Street.

Being a practical, as well as skilled surveyor, soon after coming to Texas Mr. Munson was employed to survey the State Capitol lands in the Panhandle, following which he returned to Denison and engaged in the real estate business on his own account, later forming a partnership with H. Tone, Sr., which connection continued until he associated himself with his brother, W. B.

Munson, under the firm name of Munson & Bro., which was afterword incorporated as The Munson Realty Company, of which he was Vice-President. He was also Vice-President of The Denison Cotton Mill Company.

He was at one time President and General Manager of the Galveston, Houston & Northern Ry. Company, a line operated between Galveston and Houston.

Because he knew, understood, and fully appreciated the benefits of educational advancement along proper scientific lines, he became the founder and was the benefactor of the XXI Club, the first ladies' club to be organized in Texas. He donated the lots on which the building now stands and furnished most of the funds that went into its construction.

Also believing that out of doors recreation is a necessary adjunct to the happiness and general well-being of the people, he donated to the City 130 acres of land lying adjacent to the corporate limits of Denison for public park purposes.

Mr. Munson was a Past Exalted Ruler of the Benevolent and Protective Order of Elks, holding a life membership in the Denison Lodge No. 238, under whose auspices his funeral was held from the home of his brother, W. B. Munson.

He is survived by the following relatives: One brother, W. B. Munson of Denison, Texas; three sisters, Mrs. Louisa E. Douglas of Tecumseh, Nebraska, and Misses T.M. and M.G. Munson of Point Loma, California.

Mr. Munson was a gentleman of sterling integrity and a high sense of honor, as well as a scholar of deep research, possessing a wide range of scientific knowledge.

We express our deepest sympathy and sincerest condolence to his brother, sisters, nieces, and nephews, and direct that this Memorial be spread upon the records of the Company and a copy of the same be transmitted to them.

Figure 180 The XXI Club that was built with a generous endowment from J.T. Munson. The cornerstone, now at the Denison Public Library, still bears Munson's name.

Eloise Munson
By Brian C. Hander

Eloise Munson was the youngest of numerous children born to William Benjamin (W.B. or Ben) Munson Sr. (1846–1930) and Mary Ella Newton Munson (1852–1951). Ben and his two brothers, J. T. and Thomas Volney, had come to Denison in the town's earliest years, acquired large tracts of land, and became leaders of the new community. The first Munson home was a brick structure at 302 West Gandy Street, built in the early 1870's for W.B. and his new bride.

Eloise was born on September 20, 1888, and according to Munson family legend was the only of Ben's children who he himself did not name. One of his wife's closest friends, Louise Perry, suggested a name combination that would honor both mother and friend. Put Ella and Louise together and you got Eloise, which went over very well with Mr. Munson.

Figure 181 A portrait of Eloise Munson when she was a young girl.

Eloise graduated from Denison's Educational Institute (the first Denison High School) in the Class of 1905. The Educational Institute was the first free, graded public school in Texas. Eloise attended the University of Texas, graduating in 1909 with a Bachelor of Arts degree in Fine Arts. Her sister Linley Munson Tonkin, ten years older, was a noted artist in the Southwest.

Immediately after graduating, Eloise lived in Denison and traveled to Canada and possibly Europe before she was drafted for work in her father's office. Her obituary in *The Denison Herald* on March 30, 1969, stated that she began to work at her family's Denison businesses during World War I.

The 1920 census listed her occupation as stenographer at Munson Realty Company. The 1927 Denison City Directory listed her as secretary-treasurer of Munson Realty Company alongside her father who served as President. Donald Joseph, author of the book "Ten Million Acres", a biography of Eloise's father, described her as an important part of a business "triumvirate with her father and Ben, Jr."

Around 1912, Eloise's parents had built a large home at 1127 West Morton Street. As she never married, she continued to live with them. They deeded the home to her in 1921, maintaining the right to live there with the understanding that Eloise would agree to handle all up-keep and expenses for the remainder of their natural lives.

When Ben Sr. died in 1930, Eloise's brother, William Benjamin Munson Jr., the only male among Ben and Ella's children, took over leadership of the family's businesses. Unfortunately, Ben Jr. died of a heart attack six years later, in 1936, at the age of 50. At that time, Eloise took charge.

Figure 182 The Munson home on West Morton Street where Eloise resided for the majority of her life.

From 1936 to 1955, she served as President and General Manager of the Munson Realty Company and President of the Denison Cotton Mill. The Cotton Mill was one of the largest employers in Denison for many years with continuous shifts throughout the day and night. It is said that Eloise always signed her name "E. Munson" during her years as President, and commonly conducted business with firms who were never aware that they were dealing with a woman.

Aubrey Lockett, the President of The National Cotton Congress did business with "E. Munson" for ten years before he discovered she was a woman. Lockett would later recall, "Miss Munson had earned the respect of every man she did business with long before they discovered she was a woman. There is little doubt that had it been generally known at the outset that she was a woman, it would have altered business relations."

Following her tremendous career as a titan of industry herself, Miss Eloise decided to step away from the limelight and turned over her duties to members of the family. Upon her retirement the Realty Company was headed by Curtis McKinney and the Cotton Mill was headed by W.B. Munson III.

Although semiretired from business activities, Miss Eloise maintained a desk in the same building where she started her business career, in the historic Munson Blook in the 300 block of West Woodard. Miss Munson was also a director of the Citizens National Bank from 1936 until her death in 1969. She served on the executive committee during construction of the bank's new home and was crucial in enlisting architect Donald Mayes to design the structure.

One unique recreational past time that Miss Eloise delighted in was golf. She excelled in this area, amongst other sports, and it is said that the family home contained many of her cups and trophies that had been won in tournaments over the years.

Eloise and her mother occupied the Morton Street home together until Ella's death in 1951, at age 99. A nurse also lived in the home during the later years.

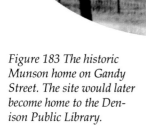

Eloise was a staunch supporter of the Denison Public Library, which opened in November 1935. She served as chairman of the Denison Public Library's Board of Trustees from the library's inception until her death. She also allowed the library to use the original Munson home on Gandy Street rent-free for two years, later donating the building to the city.

Miss Munson created the W. B. Munson Foundation in 1943, naming the philanthropic fund after her pioneering father. In 1957, this foundation donated $200,000 toward the construction of a new brick building specifically to house a public library.

Figure 183 The historic Munson home on Gandy Street. The site would later become home to the Denison Public Library.

The foundation financed the construction of a new wing at Denison's Madonna Hospital and was amongst the heaviest donors towards the new Memorial Hospital drive. Miss Eloise served as a charter member of the Memorial Hospital board and gave liberally to this project.

Funds were also used for the construction of the Munson Baseball Field at Denison's Senior High, three public parks and playgrounds, and Little League Ball fields in East Denison and on West Woodard.

Countless other gifts were made by Miss Eloise throughout the years, however not even immediate family members knew the full extent of her donations to various projects, large and small, as she frequently insisted on complete anonymity.

Upon her death on March 28, 1969, Eloise left an estate valued at some $3.5 million dollars. She left the Morton Street house and the majority of her money to the Munson Foundation. That foundation, governed by a board of directors containing two direct Munson descendants, has since given many millions of dollars to fund scholarships, health programs, educational pursuits, and other projects that benefit the city of Denison, Grayson County, and the entire Texoma region.

The historic Munson home on Morton Street was eventually purchased by Munson descendants in 1976 and remains in the possession of the family to this day. The home was restored by John Munson and was awarded an official Texas Historic Marker by the Texas Historical Commission in 2013.

Figure 184 Miss Eloise Munson, seen here in the Denison Public Library which she helped establish.

Projects funded by the W.B. Munson Foundation following the death of Miss Eloise included the building and equipment needed in the Eloise Munson Radiation Center at the Memorial Hospital; paid for one-half of the cost of the library expansion in the 1970's; and provided funding for the T.V. Munson Memorial Vineyard at the Grayson County Junior College Campus.

Miss Eloise is buried in her family's plot at Fairview Cemetery, Denison, Texas.

Figure 185 The historic W.B. Munson Block where Eloise Munson maintained her offices as she worked to continue the family's business enterprise. This building, constructed in 1888, is still owned by Munson descendants and continues to house their family businesses alongside other Denison professional offices.

W.B. Munson, Jr.

By Brian C. Hander

William Benjamin Munson, Jr., was born on January 1, 1886, to William Benjamin Munson Sr. and Mary Ella Newton Munson. He was born in the historic Munson home at the corner of Gandy Street and Rusk Avenue, one of the first brick residences erected in Denison and later the site of the Denison Public Library.

After receiving his elementary instruction at the Stevens School, Mr. Munson graduated from Denison High School, the first free public graded school in Texas, and later entered the University of Texas to spend four years specializing in Mining Engineering.

Completing his university work in 1906, Mr. Munson returned to Denison and surrendered his ambition of becoming a Mining Engineer to assume, while still in his youth, the management of the Denison Cotton Mill which had been constructed largely through the efforts of his father and uncle.

Munson married Miss Betsy Kerr of a prominent Sherman family on June 16, 1914, to which union five children were born. The couple made their home at 1130 West Bond, directly behind the home of W.B. Munson Sr. and Mary Ella Munson. One son, John Kerr Munson, died tragically on April 16, 1927, after being struck by a passing automobile near his home on Bond Street. The young lad remained in a coma for twelve hours before death took its grim toll. The funeral was held at Denison's First Presbyterian Church where a stained-glass window was later dedicated in his memory.

Figure 186 William Benjamin Munson, Jr.

After operating the mill for several years in the capacity of Secretary-Treasurer, Mr. Munson became President of the organization after the death of his father in 1930, becoming formally elected by the Board of Directors on January 7, 1931. He received national recognition in textile circles, serving as President of the Duck Manufacturers' National Organization and as Vice President of the Texas State Manufacturers' Association.

Mr. Munson went on to serve as a director of the Cotton Textile Institute of New York and held the chairmanship of several of the organization's important committees.

Recognized by authorities as one of the state's outstanding bankers, Mr. Munson wrote a brilliant chapter for the history of North Texas banking through his organization of the Citizens National Bank which he served as President until January of 1936 when he yielded this post to become Chairman of the Board. The bank would remain a Denison institution, serving generations of North Texans for decades.

Figure 187 The Citizens National Bank, ca. 1900.

Those associated with him in the banking business described his judgement and foresight in all matters pertaining to finances as phenomenally sound. He was also linked with Sherman banking interests through the Merchants and Planters National Bank.

Other business connections included the Presidency of the Munson Realty Company and the Nueces Land and Livestock Company, a directorship in the Texas Electric Company handed down to him by his father, a builder of the interurban line, and the owner of considerable property, including farmland near Denison, ranch holdings in South Texas, and vast acreage throughout cities in Grayson County.

A director of the Chamber of Commerce since its organization, Mr. Munson served two terms as President and was particularly active in highway promotion and the Good Roads Movement. He was an outstanding advocate of Grayson County's concrete highway system adopted in the early 1930's and joined many committees on trips to Austin for conferences on highway matters.

Mr. Munson's climaxing civic service was as President of the Denison School Board, a position he held for twelve years, activated by an absorbing interest in the educational institutions of the city. Few persons of Mr. Munson's manifold business responsibilities had ever given the time and thought to schoolwork that made his administration as School Board President so brilliant an achievement.

During his tenure Denison saw more expansion and improvement in school facilities and organization than ever before in the city's history, including the erection of new buildings for Raynal and Peabody and the construction of additions at the High School and Central Ward. He was instrumental in the erection of the Cotton Mill School, later known as Golden Rule, in 1922. Munson served on the advisory board for the school alongside E.H. Hughes, E.C. Everett, W.W. Clark, and M.S. Magee.

The 1930's WPA program to enlarge Peabody Elementary and Terrell High School was instituted under the leadership of Munson. An ardent patron of school athletics, Mr. Munson was almost individually responsible for the construction of a football stadium at Forest Park, contributing not only his time and services, but personal funds as well.

Figure 188 Raynal School, ca. 1925. W.B. Munson Jr. was instrumental in obtaining new schools such as this for Denison students.

Although doomed for failure, the Y.M.C.A.'s struggle to survive in Denison found an able champion in Mr. Munson who served as a board member in charge of finance and again supplemented his efforts by liberal monetary contributions. He was a member of the state YMCA Executive Committee in an effort to help gain further notoriety and hopefully funding for the Denison institution.

During several terms as President of the Denison Rod and Gun Club, he was in charge of the construction of the golf course, the renovations of the old club home, and finally the erection of a new building to serve the club.

W.B. Munson, Jr. passed away on February 26, 1936, at 8:08 o'clock at the Wilson N. Jones Hospital in Sherman after suffering a heart attack the week prior.

Mr. Munson was en route to Dallas to attend a meeting of the Texas State Manufacturers' Association, of which he was Vice President, when stricken by his fatal illness. He was Chairman of the Resolutions

Committee for the meeting of the Texas Manufacturers' Association, and while illness prevented his attending the Dallas Convention his proposed resolutions dealing with economic policies were adopted.

First taken to a Dallas clinical hospital, he was removed to the Sherman hospital after apparently showing some improvement. However, this improvement would not last and Munson passed just days after arriving at the hospital.

An editorial in *The Denison Press* described Mr. Munson eloquently when it published, "Ben as his friends called him, was human to the core, and through that seemingly impenetrable outside there looked one of the most compassionate set of eyes. What some took to be indifference and cold reaction was only the misunderstood Ben. Really, he was a fine soul. He had his weakness like all men, but at heart Ben Munson was a lover of the welfare of the city in which he lived and his love for the best interests of youth was a consuming passion. He wished for all children what he himself would give his own."

All business houses in Denison closed from 3:15 to 4:15 on February 27th to honor the memory of the Denison pioneer. Services were conducted at the First Presbyterian Church under the direction of Rev. S.L. Terry and the body was placed in the Sherman mausoleum. Pall bearers were H.G. Edmiston, H. Bodkin, Ford Seale, W.L. Peterson, R.B. Hutcheson, David Platter, J.T. Suggs, O.O. Touchstone, and H. P. Burney.

The Forest Park Athletic Field was officially renamed Munson Field on March 14, 1936, in memory of W.B. Munson, Jr. for his tenure as School Board President and Director of Athletics. He was responsible for much of the funding of the new field and gave personal supervision to much of the construction work. The motion passed unanimously by the City Council and remains so named to this day.

Figure 189 A postcard image of Denison's Munson Stadium, ca. 1940.

Betsy Kerr Munson
By Brian C. Hander

Betsy Ella Kerr was born on November 9, 1891, in Sherman, Texas to John S. Kerr, a prominent horticulturist, and Amelia Rutherford Kerr. She was a graduate of Sherman High School and Kidd-Key College and spent a year in New York at the Comstock School for Girls.

She was married June 16, 1914, to W. B. Munson Jr., son of one of the founding fathers of Denison. The marriage ceremony was performed by the bride's uncle, Reverend R.E. Vinson of Austin, who was assisted by Dr. T.W. Wharton of Sherman. Misses Eloise Munson, Berta Maxey, Pauline Thompson, and Helen Hardy served as bridesmaids and Miss Ruth Kerr, sister of the bride, was the maid of honor.

Groomsmen for Mr. Munson were John A. Haven, Franz Kohfeldt, Paul Platter, and a Mr. Spotts. Mr. William Sims served as best man. The happy couple traveled on an extended honeymoon in the golden west with September 1st as their date of return where they would make their home in Denison.

Figure 190 Mrs. Betsy Kerr Munson.

While other members of the Munson family played key roles in the business affairs of the family, including Miss Eloise Munson, Mrs. W.B. Munson Jr. was a tireless volunteer worker in the community. Some of her largest accomplishments came from her service in organizations such as the First Presbyterian Church and numerous community projects, including the Girls Reserve, Red Cross and Denison Service League.

She organized the Girls Reserve, a Christian organization for young high school girls, under the auspices of the YWCA in 1930 and remained its sponsor for many years.

For more than thirty years she was a member of the Grayson County Red Cross Board as well as Chairman of the Red Cross Building Committee which was responsible for erecting a structure used by the organization for many years. Another phase of her Red Cross work was her service as a Gray Lady at the McKinney Veterans Hospital.

In 1955, noting a need for a volunteer service group of women in Denison, she directed the creation of the Denison Service League and served as its first President. Mrs. Munson would remain as a member of the board following her presidency and devoted countless hours towards the success of the organization.

She had a keen interest in the Denison Parks and Recreation program and served on this committee for many years. She worked zealously on a city-wide bond issue to make sure it included the construction of two municipal swimming pools. One, constructed near Waterloo Lake, still remains in use today.

When Denison merchants completed a new Main Street serpentine project in the late 1960's, Mrs. Munson culminated another of her incredible community accomplishments when she led the city in the creation of an eternal flame as a memorial to the men and women in the Armed Services. The flame remains in downtown Denison and is now located in the beautiful Katy Plaza in the 100 block of East Main Street.

Figure 191 The eternal flame placed in downtown Denison, ca. 1968.

Mrs. Munson served for many years on the Building and Grounds Committee of the First Presbyterian Church. She was a Sunday School teacher for thirty years and helped form a new building committee that led to the construction of a modern sanctuary, dedicated in 1967.She was an active elder on the church board at the time of her death.

Mrs. Munson was also active in the Denison Rod & Gun Club, and again served on many of the committees that led to the major remodeling of the club. She was a member of the House Committee of the club for many years. In this role, Mrs. Munson was able to direct to the operations of the Club, including making recommendations for clubhouse rules, improvements, needed repairs, and alterations of structures owned by the Denison Rod & Gun Club.

Betsy Munson died on January 1, 1970, at Denison's Memorial Hospital after suffering from heart disease for several years.

A plaque honoring Mrs. Betsy Kerr Munson was placed in the First Presbyterian Church. Reverend Samuel J. Wylie presided over the dedication, and Mrs. W.E. Wilcox, daughter of the late Mrs. Munson, unveiled the plaque. Mrs. Wilcox then tendered a check for $15,000 from her mothers' estate to the church.

The plaque read "In memory of Besty Kerr Munson (1891-1970) for unselfish gifts of her talent and her time to this church. We gratefully dedicate this plaque."

The bronze plaque was placed in the foyer of the new sanctuary, which Mrs. Munson worked so hard to achieve during the later years of her life. The memorial remains today as a lasting legacy to the high ideals of Mrs. Munson.

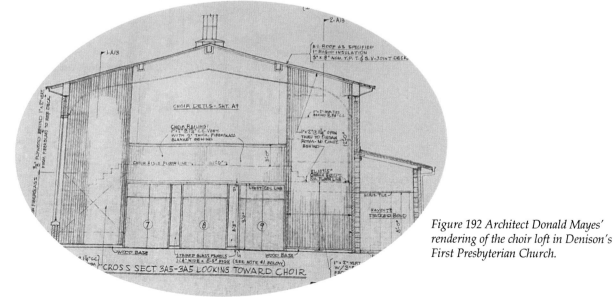

Figure 192 Architect Donald Mayes' rendering of the choir loft in Denison's First Presbyterian Church.

W.B. Munson III

By Brian C. Hander

William Benjamin Munson III was born to William Benjamin Munson Jr. and Betsy Kerr Munson on August 3, 1915. He was the eldest of five children born to the couple. Mr. Munson was raised in Denison, attended Denison's schools, and graduated from Denison High School in the class of 1933.

He attended Davidson College in North Carolina, the University of Texas at Austin, and studied textile engineering at Georgia Tech University. He was a member of the Alpha Tau Omega social fraternity, Sigma Iota Epsilon honorary management fraternity, and Phi Psi honorary textile fraternity.

Munson married Miss Martha Mann de Golian, an Atlanta socialite from a prominent family, on February 25, 1941, at the Cathedral of Christ the King. The couple made their home in Denison following the marriage.

Figure 193 William Benjamin Munson III

Munson was active in Boy Scouts as a youth, earning his Eagle rank, and with five sons and two daughters, he continued to be active in Scouting as an adult, serving as a National Council Representative for the Texoma Valley Council of Boy Scouts. For his tireless efforts to advance the ideals of Scouting including community service, self-sacrifice, and dedication, Munson was awarded the Silver Beaver.

Mr. Munson was also very active in church affairs in Denison, serving in numerous capacities at the historic St. Patrick's Catholic Church.

Mr. Munson was head of the Denison Cotton Mill from 1937 until its closure in 1977. Ben III was head of the mill following Pearl Harbor when all cotton millers rolled up their sleeves and committed to a 100% war production schedule. This show of patriotism would earn the mill the Army-Navy "E" Award for Excellence on March 26, 1945, the only Denison industry to earn such an honor. The Denison Cotton Mill also held the distinction of being the first mill west of the Mississippi to be honored with the award.

The hard duty of closing the mill fell upon Ben III. By January of 1977 the firm employed 330 people with three different shifts. In a statement to employees Munson said, "You, and those employees before you, have made the Denison Cotton Mill Company outstanding in the industry since 1905. Close cooperation between our employees, management, stockholders and customers enabled us to withstand the flood of imports that closed every other textile mill in the Southwest producing comparable fabrics during the last 10 years."

"Foreign textile producers benefit from very cheap labor, low living standards and subsidy payments by their governments on various exports to such countries as the United States. These conditions result in imported fabrics comparable to our material selling some 40 percent below the price of cloth manufactured in the United States. Our government has not seen fit to place any effective limits on the ever-increasing volume of these imports."

"In appreciation to those who remain on our payroll until released by this company, a final extra payment will be made of at least $100 less required deductions. This payment will be based on a formula of one day's pay for each 12 continuous months since the last date of employment. It will provide much higher payments for our employees with considerable seniority."

It was expected the mill would require about two months to work out their present stock and meet orders that had been placed. The Denison Cotton Mill was the only surviving producer of cotton duck west of the Mississippi River at that time, and had been in continuous operation for more than 70 years.

Munson's statement to employees closed with; "Our individual association in many cases extends over nearly half a century, and I deeply regret these circumstances. My most sincere good wishes to each one of you." The 168,000 square foot building on a 15-acre site would be made available for industrial development shortly after it was closed.

Mr. Munson was Chairman of the Board of Citizen's National Bank, the very institution his father established, officer and Director of Munson Realty, Nueces Land and Livestock Company, Capital Southwest Corporation, and the Texas Manufacturers' Association.

Figure 194 A 1960's aerial view of the Denison Cotton Mill complex.

Mr. Munson also served as President of the Texas Cotton Manufacturers Association, Denison Chamber of Commerce, Denison School Board, Rotary Club and the Denison Charter Commission. He was a member of the Denison City Council and director of the W.B. Munson Foundation, which was created by his Aunt Eloise Munson.

Mr. Munson was on the Board of Regents of Austin College in Sherman, Texas and was instrumental in several projects completed at the campus. In 1981 he was named by Gov. Bill Clements to the Board of Regents of East Texas State University, in Commerce, Texas. This institution would later be known as Texas A&M-Commerce.

One unique project that Mr. Munson was passionate about was a broader recognition and understanding of Thomas Volney Munson, his great-uncle, who is credited with saving the European vineyards from phylloxera. He worked closely with Grayson County College toward the completion of the T. V. Munson Memorial Vineyard which included the Munson Enology Center and Museum. The Enology Center and Museum were dedicated with a celebration marking the 100th anniversary of T.V. Munson's acceptance of the French Legion of Honor Chevalier du Mérite Agricole.

Figure 195 The Munson Memorial Vineyard at the Grayson College West Campus

While the early Munson's donated land for public use, Munson III headed the family foundation begun by his Aunt Eloise that was a major contributor to many educational and health projects in Denison. He was described as a kind, caring, gentle man, who seldom raised his voice and who often avoided the spotlight in everything he did.

William Benjamin Munson III passed away at the age of 73 on May 19, 1989, in a hospital in Monroe, Louisiana following a prolonged illness. A requiem mass was read at St. Patrick's Catholic Church under the direction of Reverend Emil Slovecek. Mr. Munson was buried in Fairview Cemetery in Denison.

The Munson Memorial Garden

One final memorial that remains to both Ben and Martha de Golian Munson is the Munson Memorial Garden at the site of the former Texoma Medical Center at 1000 Memorial Drive in Denison.

The garden contains a plaque that reads as follows:

The Ben III and Martha Munson Memorial Garden is constructed of pieces of history from the Munson Family and the birth of Denison, Texas.

Stone Pillars of the Pergola

The stones used to create the pillars were the foundation of St. Francis Xavier Academy built in 1900-1901 by the Sisters of St. Mary of Nemur, Belgium. Initial letters of the Sisters of St. Mary's motto "Ad Majorem Del Gloriam" (For the Greater Glory of God) are among the inscriptions on the stone. St. Francis Xavier's Academy was founded in Denison in 1876 by the Belgium Sisters who came to the United States in 1819 following the Napoleonic Era. Each stone weighs approximately 4,000 lbs. and was cut in half by hand to form the columns for this pergola.

Waterfall

The source of water coming from underneath the pergola has been copied from an original railroad bed culvert that still exists in perfect condition north of Denison. These culverts were approximately 20' to 30' long and built by stacking huge boulders to make the walls of the culvert and laying large solid rocks on top to support the railroad above it. This occurred in 1875 just as the nuns were beginning construction of St. Xavier's.

Grape Vines

In 1876, W. B. Munson's brother, T.V. Munson, brought his nursery business to Denison and established one of the most famous vineyards in the South. Several of the vines that he introduced into the American Grape Culture are planted at the base of the columns under the pergola. Also, the garden contains flowering plum trees, a variety developed by T.V. Munson and still found thriving in areas around Denison.

Brick Pavers

The brick pavers that make up the floor of the pergola were the pavers used in the original streets of Denison. Thanks to Mr. Wilcox who captured pavers as they were resurfacing Gandy and Sears Streets. These pavers were probably laid in Denison during its development in 1876-1877.

Figure 196 Photos of the Munson Memorial Garden as it appeared in 2022.

Dr. Claude Organ
By Donna Hord Hunt

Dr. Claude Organ was born on October 16, 1926 in Marshall, Texas, and grew up in Denison and attended the city's segregated Anderson Elementary School and Terrell High School. His mother was a teacher and his father worked for the Postal Service after serving in World War II, then finished school at Lincoln University in Missouri.

Both of his parents held college degrees and instilled a sense of self-worth in Claude. They also emphasized the importance of education and encouraged the pursuit of higher education. Claude was the middle of three children that the couple had.

After high school graduation in 1943, he first went to Xavier College in New Orleans, graduating cum laude in 1948. Then he was named Chairman of the Board of the school for six years. It was at Xavier that he met his wife, Betty, although the two weren't married until fate brought them together once more in the future.

Figure 197 Claude Organ's Sophomore photo from the 1941 Terrell High School Yearbook.

Betty had gone to nursing school in Boston while Claude was in medical school. Five years after initially meeting, the couple ran into each other in Houston and were married two years later.

He was turned down at the University of Texas in Austin because he was black, so he began medical school at the age of 20 at Creighton University in Omaha, NE. There he became the first black student to attend the school, where he was treated the same as all other students and found no patient refusal.

He received his medical degree from Creighton and remained at the school to complete his internship and residency. His educational journey and the lengths he went to receive his education inspired Dr. Organ to become an advocate to opening doors for other minority and women surgeons.

Following a brief time in the U.S. Navy as a surgeon at Camp Pendleton, Dr. Organ returned to Creighton, where he would work his way up to become the first African American chair of the surgery department. From this post he would go to the University of Oklahoma to serve as a surgery professor.

Later he went back to Howard University where he had once been rejected as a young student, but this time to give a speech as president of the American College of Surgeons. In fact, Dr. Organ had the distinction of being only the second African American to serve as president of the American College of Surgeons and chairman of the American Board of Surgery.

By 1988, Dr. Organ had moved to the East Bay to lead the establishment of the University of California Davis-East Bay Department of Surgery, now known as the UCSF-East Bay Department of Surgery. He would remain at this facility until he retired in 2003.

Figure 198 Dr. Claude Organ

His honors were many; he lectured often and authored more than 250 scientific articles and book chapters; primarily on general and endocrine surgery. He authored or co-authored five books and lectured worldwide for many years and was editor of the *"Archives of Surgery,"* that was distributed in 85 countries to 33,000 surgeons.

He was dedicated to opening doors for other minorities and women surgeons.

Dr. Organ was named a Distinguished Alumni by the Denison Alumni Association in 2004 for his many contributions to minorities and the field of surgery.

Dr. Organ died on June 18, 2005, in Berkley, CA following heart-related problems. Together with Betty, the Organ's had seven children, all incredibly successful in their chosen fields, and ten grandchildren.

Figure 199 Claude Organ, Sr., father of Dr. Organ, was the President of the Terrell Dad's Club in 1946. His photo appeared in the Terrell Yearbook where he was described as reliable, fair, courteous, and willing to help anyone in any way. His thoughtful and imaginative leadership was instilled in his children as well.

Denison's Little Rascals
By James K. Sears

When Denison celebrated its fiftieth anniversary on September 23, 1922, the first *Our Gang* comedy short had been in movie theaters for less than two weeks. The popularity of the series, produced by Hal Roach Studios in Culver City, California, was such that it lasted until 1944. In 1955 it was syndicated for television under the title *The Little Rascals*. In its original two-decade run the series totaled 221 films, featuring more than forty child actors. A surprising number of those actors had connections of one sort or another to Denison, Texas.

Figure 200 Our Gang in 1929.

In late August 1922, Joe Cobb, soon to be six years old, traveled on vacation with his father from their home in Wewoka, Oklahoma, to Los Angeles, where they made the rounds of the movie studios. Arriving at Hal Roach's just as the noon whistle blew, they were taken to lunch by the casting department. Joe so impressed them that after lunch he was taken immediately to the wardrobe department and put to work on a film. The director, who was also the supervising director for *Our Gang*, installed him in the Gang upon completion of the film. The following spring the first *Our Gang* short that featured Joe "Fatty" Cobb opened in theaters. The films usually included at least one little girl, a tough kid, a fat kid, a smart kid, and a minority kid. Cobb was the first of four actors to play the fat kid.

Although Joe was not born in Denison, his mother was. Flossie Jewel McComas (1888-1929), daughter of Katy engineer Frank McComas (1850-1928) and his first wife Lettie (1853-1904), graduated from Denison High School in 1908. She married James Hardin Cobb (1888-1959), son of a Denison cabinetmaker, on the day after Christmas in 1913. The ceremony took place in Flossie's parents' house at 1000 West Main Street, recently demolished but still visible on Google Street View as of September 2021. Joe's other grandparents, J. B. (1847-1927) and Lizzie (1855-1930) Cobb, lived at 521 West Crawford Street in a house that is also no longer there.

The newlyweds made their home in Wewoka, where James practiced law and Flossie taught music in the public schools. Joe, the second of their three children and only son, was born a short distance up the road in Shawnee on the morning of Election Day, Tuesday, November 7, 1916. Two days later *The Wewoka Democrat* reported that the baby born to J. H. Cobb and wife was named Woodrow Wilson Cobb. How long he remained a namesake of the reelected President is unknown. By the time he signed his contract with Hal Roach in 1922 he had changed his name to Joe Frank Cobb.

Cobb was one of the stars of the *Our Gang* series' silent years, extending from 1922 to 1929. *The Denison Herald* was aware of his local connection and mentioned it more than once during that time. The minor detail of his Oklahoma birth did not keep *The Denison Press* from claiming him as "a Denison boy" in 1932. He appeared in eighty-six shorts before being replaced at age twelve by Norman "Chubby"Chaney. After Cobb's acting career ended in the early 1940s, he took a job as an aircraft assembler in a defense plant. His congenial personality is on display in a three-minute biography on YouTube.

Kendall McComas was born nine days before Joe Cobb. Whether the two were related is uncertain. They may have been distant cousins. Flossie McComas' parents came to Denison in late 1879 or early 1880 from Pottawatomie County in Northeast Kansas. Kendall was born in adjacent Jackson County more than thirty-five years later. Only twenty miles separated the small communities where the two McComas families lived. If they were not related, it is a remarkable coincidence that they both had the same surname and both produced an *Our Gang* cast member.

Although Kendall was a few days older than Joe, he did not appear in an *Our Gang* film until three years after Joe had aged out of his role. Joe was a big kid at twelve when he retired in 1929. Kendall was small for his fifteen years in 1932, when he joined the cast as a lad whom the other kids called "Breezy." His mother on screen addressed him as "Brisbane." He appeared in eight *Our Gang* shorts, all of them released in 1932.

Figure 201 Kendall McComas

After he retired from acting, Kendall worked in the defense industry as an electrical engineer. Both he and Joe were scheduled to retire on their sixty-fifth birthdays in 1981. Joe would live twenty more years until his death in 2002. Sadly, Kendall would commit suicide two weeks before his retirement was to begin.

The only *Our Gang* actor born in Denison was Harold Eugene Wertz, Jr. According to his birth certificate, on file with the Texas Bureau of

Vital Statistics, he entered the world on August 3, 1927, at his grandparents' home in the Sugar Bottom neighborhood. The address was 623 South Armstrong Avenue, next door to the Wertzes' hardware and furniture store. Neither building is still there. His father, also born in Denison and also named Harold (1903-1984), was a 1921 graduate of Denison High School. While the younger Harold was still a baby, the family moved to California and settled in the Los Angeles area, where the older Harold found work as an athletic director with the Long Beach schools. The grandparents, Lewis (1869-1949) and Lura (1869-1956) Wertz, remained in Denison. They are buried in Fairview Cemetery.

In 1931 word reached Thelma Wertz (1907-1988) in Long Beach that Hal Roach was looking for a new fat kid to replace Chubby Chaney, who was outgrowing the role. She sent pictures of her son to Roach, who invited them to come for a screen test. Harold was quickly selected over hundreds of other applicants. In 1932 he was cast as "Bouncy" in three shorts-- "Choo-Choo!," "The Pooch," and "Hook and Ladder." As with many of the other *Our Gang* shorts produced after the advent of sound, they were remakes of earlier silent ones.

Also appearing in Bouncy's three shorts was the newest cast member, George "Spanky" McFarland. Born October 2, 1928, in Methodist Hospital in Dallas, he was only three when he made his film debut in 1932. Spanky stole every scene he was in that year, while four-year-old Bouncy faded into the background with almost no lines to speak. It must have been obvious to studio executives that young McFarland was the future of the part of the fat kid in the gang. After an earthquake in early 1933 shut down production for a time at the studios, they invoked the "act of God" clause in Wertz's contract and declined to renew it.

Figure 202 "The Pooch," 1932. George "Spanky" McFarland is second from left. Harold "Bouncy" Wertz is at far right.

Wertz served in the Merchant Marine in World War II. After the war ended, he founded and operated a steel pipe company in Long Beach. He died in 1999 and is buried along with his wife and his parents in Forest Lawn Memorial Park in Cypress, California.

It may have been after *The Little Rascals* began to air on television in the 1950s when word started to circulate in Denison that Spanky

McFarland was a hometown boy. Perhaps someone's parent or grandparent remarked, "One of those kids was born in Denison. I think it was the fat one." Or maybe it began even earlier than that. In any case, it's not hard to imagine how the mistake became accepted fact. Spanky was the best known of the four fat kids in the series. Of the three who preceded him, two were from Denison.

To this day there are those who swear they can remember old-timers recounting specifics of Spanky's visits to family and friends in Denison. Some say he grew up there and attended Denison schools, although he actually moved to California when he was only three. Associations of Spanky with Denison have been published in books, newspapers, and magazines for decades. As recently as May 2017, his biography on the internet site Wikipedia said he was born in Denison. All the evidence for that, though, is thus far anecdotal, unverified, and contrary to the documentary evidence.

George McFarland worked at a variety of jobs after his retirement from show business. He died in Grapevine, Texas, in 1993 at age sixty-four. The legend of his Denison roots is too firmly entrenched to fade away anytime soon. Perhaps the easiest way to come to terms with it is to welcome him as an honorary member of the Denison Little Rascals Club and to carve or paint Spanky's name on the imaginary clubhouse door along with those of Fatty Cobb, Breezy McComas, and Bouncy Wertz.

Figure 203 From the 1932 Our Gang short "Hook and Ladder."

Frances Cameron
By Brian C. Hander

Frances Marilyn McCloud Cameron was born on July 19, 1936, to Neil and Duressie Amelia Smith McCloud. Frances graduated from Denison's Terrell High School in 1954 as the Valedictorian and went on to attend Prairie View A&M University in Prairie View, Texas where she graduated with a Masters in Music and Education.

She returned to Denison and married Mr. Leo Samuel Cameron Jr. on April 6, 1963, and had two sons, Reginald and Derrick.

Prior to integration Cameron taught the third and fourth grade at Langston Elementary School for five years. From 1964 to 1973, she taught at Layne Elementary School before finishing her career at Houston Elementary School in 1993.

Frances made history in 1997 when she was appointed to fill a vacancy on the Denison School Board. She claimed her spot as the first African American to serve on the Board, representing students, families, and citizens of Ward 1.

At her retirement, Cameron was the longest serving board member in the history of the Denison Independent School District with 18 years of service and was the only woman on the board for many of her years of service.

When asked about her service upon her resignation from the board, Cameron stated, "We did what's best for our kids so that they become productive citizens then they will make the right decisions when they become eligible to run for the Board. They are proud to be Yellow Jackets."

Figure 204 Mrs. Frances Cameron, ca. 1985.

Cameron resigned from the School Board in 2015 following the illness of her mother. Other accomplishments throughout her life included nine years of service as a board member for the Texoma Educators Federal Credit Union, a State of Texas Dream Maker Award winner from the Business & Professional Women's Club, and Texas Teacher of the Year.

Frances was also a lifelong member of the Hopewell Baptist Church in Denison where she served in the church choir and as a pianist and Director of Music. Mrs. Cameron passed away on October 10, 2020 and was buried in Denison's historic Oakwood Cemetery.

Clara Blackford Smith
By Brian C. Hander

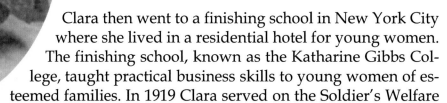

Clara Godwin Blackford was born on April 9, 1893 to Godwin Lewis Blackford and Eugenia B. "Gene" Rue. Her father served as the longtime President of the State National Bank in Denison and was an investor in many of Denison's leading establishments. Clara attended classes at Denison's Burleson School then went on to attend the Educational Institute (the first iteration of Denison High School) where she graduated in May of 1907. Immediately following graduation Clara was enrolled at St. Mary's College, an Episcopalian school for women in Dallas, Texas.

Clara then went to a finishing school in New York City where she lived in a residential hotel for young women. The finishing school, known as the Katharine Gibbs College, taught practical business skills to young women of esteemed families. In 1919 Clara served on the Soldier's Welfare Committee of the Denison Red Cross alongside Mr. E.J. Smith, Mrs. W.B. Munson Jr., Mrs. P.J. Brennan, Mrs. George Williams, Mr. Tom Dollarhide Jr., and Mrs. R.M. Doak.

Figure 205 Clara Blackford as a young girl.

Clara married Allen Jerome Reed, a well-known silk manufacturer of New York and New Jersey, on January 27, 1922 in a small ceremony inside her parents' home at 1200 West Sears in Denison. Reverend Dr. J.E. Aubrey officiated the ceremony, and afterwards the couple honeymooned to the Bermuda Islands before returning to New York.

Allen died suddenly in January of 1925, just three short years after their wedding. Clara would return to Denison following her husband's death where she would meet William Aubrey Smith.

William was born on January 29, 1893 to Erwin Jesse Smith, a prominent local attorney, and Nannie Weir Smith. He attended Denison schools and graduated from Denison High School. From there he attended Highland Falls Prep School in New York and Texas A&M University. During World War I, Aubrey served as Captain in the 36th Division in the Machine Gun Corp.

Figure 206 The Read family's silk mill, ca. 1915.

Clara and Aubrey were married in 1930 and lived in Houston, occupying an opulent apartment in the fashionable Warwick Hotel near Rice University. Aubrey was in the oil business, serving as Secretary of Smith & Gaes and Secretary-Treasurer of the Houston Royalty Company. During this time Clara became incredibly active as a philanthropist and social worker.

Figure 207 The Warwick Hotel, ca. 1929.

Around 1953, the Smith's returned to Denison and occupied Clara's family home at 1200 West Sears. Clara maintained an office above the State National Bank while Aubrey was listed as lawyer in city directories. In the mid-1950's, Clara established the annual Blackford Memorial lecture series at Denison's Memorial Hospital that focused on cancer and similar diseases. The first lecture was held at the Hotel Denison with the chief of M.D. Anderson coming to speak on his research.

She further set aside an endowment fund for the treatment of cancer as a memorial to her father who had died suddenly when Clara was only 29 years old. His obituary stated he had traveled extensively for the benefit of his health which had been failing for several years prior to his death. It is assumed that he had cancer, and that this is what sparked her philanthropic giving for the lectures and the M.D. Anderson Clinic.

Figure 208 Clara Blackford Smith, ca. 1924.

Aubrey passed away on December 5, 1977 at the age of 84. Services were officiated by Reverend Harrison Lee of the Christ Episcopal Church of Dallas with the burial taking place in Denison's Fairview Cemetery. Shortly thereafter, Clara established the Clara Blackford Smith and W. Aubrey Smith Charitable Foundation in 1978. The foundation was dedicated to promoting quality education, healthcare, and human services programming for underserved populations in Texas.

Clara Blackford Smith passed away on August 2, 1983 at the age of 90. She was a member of the American Cancer Society board of directors, as well as a member of the St. Luke's Episcopal Church, Denison Rod and Gun Club, Texoma Medical Center board of directors, Interfirst Bank board of directors, and a director of the North Texas Loan and Trust Company.

The M.D. Anderson Cancer Center in Houston established the Clara B. Smith Training Center within their Social Work Department in 1986 as a memorial to Mrs. Smith. Clara was a longtime friend and benefactor of the department, frequently contributing financial support for indigent patients and training institutes for social workers throughout Texas.

The center's Department of Social Work utilizes the program to offer field placement opportunities for Bachelor of Social Work and second-year Master of Social Work students. The educational goal of the program is to provide the highest quality hands-on learning experience to students to prepare them to enter the social work profession with confidence in their skills and knowledge.

The Smith Foundation has been a major part of Denison for many decades and has made substantial gifts that have helped move our community forward. Many of the grants throughout recent years include; a large donation to Denison ISD to fund the construction of the Smith Tennis Center, a large amount of academic scholarships for local students to pursue higher education, Denison's Music on Main program, the Denison 4th of July Fireworks Show, a $1 million gift to Denison ISD to fund the Smith Center for the Performing Arts, among many others. As of this writing, the Smith Foundation has granted nearly $27 million to various projects and organizations in our community.

The Smith Foundation became more widely known in 2019 following a legal dispute between former foundation board members and Bank of America, the financial institution in charge of the trust fund. Bank of America fired the local Board of Trustees of the foundation and there was fear that the fund established by Mrs. Smith may not be used the way she intended.

Local community advocates Ronnie Cole, Sherry Christie, and Kris McKinney worked diligently to help regain local control of the funds. In 2020, the Smith Foundation came back under local leadership and a new Board of Trustees was established. The agreement reached with Bank of America ensures local control over any decisions made regarding grants. This monumental victory retained the Smith Foundation as a vital part of Denison's future.

Figure 209 Above, the Blackford-Smith home at 1200 West Sears Street. This home is a stunning example of the Craftsman design and is the home of Mr. and Mrs. Jerry Hatfield.

At left, the State National Bank as it appeared during its 75th Anniversary celebration.

Pierre Lelardoux
By Mavis Anne Bryant

Pierre "Peter" Lelardoux (1843–1910) was generally recognized as Denison's leading architect between 1877 and 1904. Born in France in 1843 and presumably trained there in the Beaux Arts tradition, he came to the United States in 1870 with his wife Marguritte (1840–1894) and young daughter Marie (1869–1912).

Going to Chicago after the Great Fire in 1871, Pierre partnered with J. Austin and later with M. Patterson of Decatur, Illinois. He is known to have designed, in 1875, a six-story apartment building at the southwest corner of Michigan Avenue and Peck Court, though it was never constructed. On October 27 of that same year, Lelardoux became a naturalized citizen of the United States. Naturalization records said that he had lived in Illinois, Indiana, Wisconsin, and Iowa.

There is much that we do not know about Lelardoux, since many of his records and buildings have been lost. We cannot say, for example, what caused him to leave France and seek the United States. However, in surviving photographs, maps, and old newspapers, we can still find remnants of his Denison designs that were erected and later demolished. In their soaring levels, mastery of stone and brick; in their breathtaking arches, towers, asymmetry, and ornate surface decoration, we can glimpse what Denison's ambitious elite saw he had to offer their emerging frontier community.

Figure 210 Sherburne House 1103 West Gandy Street, Denison, Grayson, Texas, USA Spring 1880

Demonstrating versatility as well as necessity, the architect initially seems to have taken on any project he was offered. On October 14, 1877, the Denison Daily News reported that, though Pierre was new in town, he was designing "several fine two-story brick business houses on Main Street." In January 1880, the same paper found him drawing plans to convert the basement of the Grayson County Courthouse into a jail for county convicts. In April 1880, shoe-store owner Manly Hardy Sherburne engaged him to design a house at 1103 West Gandy Street, at the corner of North Tone Avenue.

Pierre Lelardoux, architect, designed the home for Manly Hardy Sherburne (1843 - 1901) and his wife, Marie Augusta Mason Sherburne (1849 - 1925) at 1103 West Gandy St. The house was built in the spring of 1880. The house was listed as vacant in 1940 according to the Denison City Directory and not listed in the City Directories from 1946 forward. Probably burned or was demolished.

In July 1880, the Denison Daily News wrote that Lelardoux was designing the McDougall Opera House at 221–223 West Main Street, for John B. McDougall and druggist Francis R. Guiteau. Before the opera house was constructed, however, Guiteau's family funding fell through when his first cousin, Charles Julius Guiteau, assassinated U.S. President James Garfield on July 2, 1881.

Figure 211 M.H. Sherburne. Source: Donna Hunt, "Information on Pioneers Found in Old Newspaper," Herald Democrat, June 10, 2012. Originally published in Denison TX Daily Herald, January 1, 1879.

McDougall continued with the project on his own, but it is not clear that Lelardoux was still involved. Denison's other leading architect at the time, Joseph Schott, later advertised the opera house as one of his products. Located on the second and third floors of the building, the opera house opened on January 12, 1882. Including the furnishings, it cost McDougall $28,000. The Guiteau and Waldron Drug Store moved into the ground floor.

To emphasize his skills, Lelardoux advertised in Denison's Sunday Gazetteer in 1883: "P. Lelardoux, Architect, Denison, Texas: Will furnish Plans, Details, and Specifications at Regular Rates, and will be responsible for all Architectural Defects. Will take charge of, or superintend, all kinds of buildings on percentage. Will take Contracts for Fine work."

In 1884, as Denison entered a phase of major economic expansion, town leaders decided to mount a major exhibit at the 1884–1885 International Exhibition at New Orleans. This massive exhibit, "The Denison Gate," echoed Denison's nickname, "The Gate City," so called because Denison was the first town reached as the Katy railroad built south into Texas.

Lelardoux was tapped to design the large exhibit; he engaged a Mr. Willoughby of Chicago to carve the dark wood structure. Local women contributed fine needlework, embroidery, and paintings, while photographer Paul Verkin (later of Galveston) produced a set of large photos of Denison scenes. Construction supervisor was Otto Schumacher.

Figure 212 McDougall Opera House, 221-223 West Main, 1883. Source: One of a set of stereoscope views of "Scenes in Texas," issued by "Hardesty & Dean, Portrait and Landscape Photographers, of St. Louis, 1883."

Figure 213 "Denison Gate." Exhibit mounted by Denison, Texas, "The Gate City," at 1884-1885 International Cotton Exhibition at New Orleans. Architect of the "Gate" was Pierre Lelardoux. Construction supervisor, Otto Schumacher. Carving done by Mr. Willoughby of Chicago. Photos by Paul Verkin of Denison. Source: Stereoview by Edward L. Wilson.

After its stay in New Orleans, the big "Gate" moved to the Dallas State Fair in fall of 1887. Then it was transferred to Denison's Exposition Hall. Opened around 1889, the Exposition Hall was built near the Denison Cotton Mill at 926 Star Street, corner of College Boulevard. The timber-frame hall, a social hub owned by the Denison Land and Investment Company, sat in a park-like setting surrounded by the firm's

Figure 214 Exposition Hall, Denison, Texas. Source: Denison Bird's-Eye Map, 1891: Amon Carter Museum: Texas Bird's Eye Views.

"Boulevard Addition," a fancy residential development in the southwestern part of Denison. The Exposition Hall, and the much-admired "Gate" with it, burned in a great conflagration on August 20, 1893.

Also in 1884, the Missouri, Kansas and Texas Railroad engaged Lelardoux to design buildings in Muskogee, Indian Territory (Oklahoma). One source says that he lived there when he took on the large Waples-Platter Grocer's headquarters and warehouse at 104 East Main Street (on the Katy tracks) in Denison. According to a Texas Historical Marker, the building was completed in 1885, when E. B. Waples bought interest in the company and was named its president. The structure "was a two-story building with cast-iron pilasters in the façade, terra cotta lions-head statues, keystones, and segmented arch

Figure 215 Waples-Platter Grocer Company, 104 East Main Street. Demolished 2013. Source: "Art Work of Grayson County," 1895. See Hunt & Bryant, IMAGES OF AMERICA: DENISON(Arcadia,2011), page 14.

openings. The elegant building was meant to symbolize the company's prominence in Denison and survived for 128 years until it was demolished in 2013."

In a long article, "The Work of P. Lelardoux," Denison's Sunday Gazetteer on September 27, 1885, detailed the architect's recent accomplishments. At 300 West Main Street, a little more than two blocks west of the Waples-Platter Building, the State National Bank had asked Lelardoux to erect a fine new bank of brick and stone. The three-story structure, 25 x 65 feet, had a fire-proof vault and a front door on an angle, facing the corner of Rusk Avenue and Main Street.

Large windows flooded the first floor with light, good for business. The second floor was "divided into suits of rooms and offices." The third floor was "fitted up for a Masonic lodge." The building cost $15,000. It remained largely intact for many years, though taking in another building on the west. In the 1970s, banking changed, with larger banks purchasing small ones nationwide. In 1970-1971, Interfirst Bank purchased the State National, demolishing the ornate original building and replacing it with a large two-story white marble structure. Today it houses Denison's city government.

Figure 216 State National Bank. 300 West Main Street, Denison, Grayson, Texas, USA, about 1890. Source: Enlarged half of a Verkin & Enos stereograph in SMU's digital collection. The strange conical object that looks like it is on the roof is actually an arc light hanging in the intersection.

According to the same 1885 article, Lelardoux had designed two Main Street buildings 25 x 100 feet, though it did not give exact addresses. Each cost $5,500. One belonged to Dr. D. Alphonso Cook; the 1887 Denison City Directory listed him as a physician and surgeon practicing at Guiteau and Waldron's drug store, at 223 West Main Street.

The other building, at 200 West Main, belonged to Millie A. Peterson Chichet, a widow preparing to marry Edward C. Harbison. Her lot had been the first one sold at Denison's initial public auction in 1872. Then the Grand Southern Saloon occupied the lot. Millie's husband, Martin Chichet, operated the saloon until he died in 1883, leaving her as owner. The saloon had burned to the ground on August 4, 1884. The Sunday Gazetteer noted that Millie's new building designed by Lelardoux had a "coquettish air."

* * * * *

Pierre did not neglect residential construction during this busy period, being engaged by two of the town's leading couples to build new homes in 1885.

Robert Coleman "Cole" Foster Jr. (1834–1910) was one of those able, experienced men that the MK&T Railroad recruited to Denison in the town's earliest days. Born in Kentucky, Foster had moved to Kansas in 1856, briefly attended the U.S. Naval Academy at Annapolis, Maryland, and studied law in Tennessee. Back in Leavenworth, Kansas, he practiced law and was elected to the Kansas House of Representatives and then the state Senate during the Civil War. In 1871 he married Amanda "Mandy" Harrelson (1842–1916); they came to Denison in 1875. In addition to serving in the Texas Legislature for three terms, he invested in numerous enterprises and operated a dairy farm where he raised prize-winning Jersey cattle. He was a leading attorney specializing in railroad matters.

According to his 1910 obituary in the Sunday Gazetteer, "Every member of the bar respected, admired and loved him—respected him for his integrity, admired him for his ability and wisdom, and loved him because he was a man full of the milk of human kindness." Cole organized the Denison Young Men's Christian Association in 1891 and served as YMCA president for many years. He was active in Baptist church activities. He also was one of a small group of men who spearheaded the conversion of Denison's National Commercial College, at 500 West Main Street, into the first Denison Hotel. It opened as a first-rate hotel in September 1902.

In 1885, Cole and Amanda engaged Lelardoux to plan and supervise construction of a Colonial-style home in the center of a full city block at 1107 West Sears Street (northwest corner of Tone Avenue). The site previously had been occupied by a horse-racing track, according to Sarah Cooke Acheson's obituary for her horse George in Denison's Sunday Gazetteer on December 13, 1891.

The Foster house, which cost $8,500, was a two-story and attic frame structure on a brick basement and stone foundation. The ground floor enjoyed a large wraparound porch, and several small porches adorned the second floor. The Sunday Gazetteer's 1885 article made much of the irregular shape of the house, which produced a breeze in every room. On November 10, 1936, the Dallas Morning News celebrated the home's fiftieth anniversary, noting its 12-foot ceilings, white pine woodwork, plastered walls, and several fireplaces, one with a solid cherry mantel, hand-carved and fitted with tile imported from England. A sizable barn stood behind the house. The spacious grounds were planted with elm and live-oak trees ordered from South Texas.

RESIDENCE OF R. C. FOSTER, ESQ., DENISON.

Figure 217 Home of Robert Coleman "Cole" Foster Jr. 1886. 1107 West Sears Street at Tone Avenue, Denison TX. Source: Handbook of Northern Texas, 1886, C.S. Burch Publishing Co. (via Portal to Texas History)

After the Fosters' deaths in 1910 and 1916, their home was acquired by Charles H. Jones (1861–1924), owner of a local furniture store, who in 1902 had married Minnie M. Marsh (1868–1953). As a brilliant and beautiful young woman, Minnie had won prizes and acclaim for her speaking ability and scholarly attainments. She served as principal of Denison High School for several years, then taught English and American Literature at the North Texas State Normal School (now University of North Texas) in Denton. After marrying, she gave up fulltime teaching and public speaking. Beginning in 1907, she served on the Denison School Board. When her husband died, Minnie's eulogy was printed in full in the Sunday Gazetteer. She called the house "his idea of heaven."

The spacious Foster home, full of light, books, and music, must have been a comfort to the widow. Neighborhood children loved to visit her, and she taught private classes there. Minnie took over Charles's real estate business and operated it successfully for years. She donated a full block to the City of Denison to create Jones Park in southwest Denison. Then, when she passed away in 1953, her will bequeathed the big house to the Denison Public Library for use as a branch library. However, by the time legal wrangling over the will ended, the house at 1107 West Sears was long gone. It had been demolished in the fall of 1963 to make way for an apartment house.

Figure 218 Minnie Marsh Jones. In 1897-98, Marsh was Federation Secretary of Denison's XXI Club. This is an undated poster suggesting that she was running for some office (perhaps a national Federation of Women's Clubs) and was "endorsed by the Texas Federation [of] Women's Clubs."

* * * * *

The Sunday Gazetteer's 1885 article devoted much print to the "three-story building over a light habitable cellar or basement" that Lelardoux had designed for Dr. Alexander W. "Sandie" Acheson (1842–1934) and his wife Sarah Cooke Acheson (1844–1899) on a full city block west of downtown. A reporter called it "the finest mansion north of Dallas."

Figure 219 Home of Dr. A.W. Acheson and His Wife Sarah Cooke Acheson. 1419 West Woodard Street, ca. 1886. View looking to northwest. Detail from Henry Wellge's 1886 Birds-Eye Map of Denison, on website from the Amon Carter Museum.

Both Achesons had grown up in Washington, county seat of Washington County in southwestern Pennsylvania, where they had been raised as staunch Presbyterians and had attended the best schools in their hometown. Sarah had a beautiful singing voice and studied music. At the onset of the Civil War, Sandie entered the Union Army as a private in the 13th Regiment Pennsylvania Volunteers. Eventually he became a captain in the 140th Pennsylvania Infantry and was injured at Spotsylvania, Virginia. He married Sarah while home recuperating.

After the war, he studied medicine, graduating at the University of Pennsylvania in Philadelphia. In 1872, the Missouri, Kansas & Texas Railroad hired Dr. Acheson as its surgeon in Denison, making him the town's first trained doctor. Other railroads hired him, too. In his long life, there was hardly any public health issue, business enterprise, or governmental or political matter in which Dr. Acheson did not contribute his interest, talent, and scientific knowledge. He was a skilled orator.

Figure 220 Another view of the Acheson Home. 1419 West Woodard Street, 1886. This sketch from the Handbook of Northern Texas (Chicago: C.S. Burch Pub. Co., 1886) shows part of the grounds, including a tennis court on the lawn.

Figure 221 Portrait of Dr. A.W. "Sandie" Acheson, 1928. Photo by Walter P. Lebrecht.

Sarah Acheson was her husband's full partner. As her 1899 obituary put it, "She was the leader in the organization of literary and musical societies, in fact no plan for the improvement of the people of the city—socially, morally, and religiously—but was given her hearty aid and cooperation." The couple was among the twelve charter members of Denison's First Presbyterian Church. Later they helped found a Congregational church. Living in a town awash with saloons, Mrs. Acheson could not avoid seeing the devastation caused by addiction to alcohol.

By 1886, she was president of the Women's Christian Temperance Union (WCTU) for Grayson and Cooke counties. In 1888 she was unanimously elected president of the Texas WCTU. For three years, Sarah traveled and lectured throughout the state at her own expense, donating her salary back to the organization. Sarah became increasingly sensitized to discrimination against women and to their victimization. She helped organize and served as first president of the Denison Equal Rights Association, the first woman's suffrage club in Texas. She signed the call for a statewide suffrage convention that resulted in the formation of the Texas Equal Rights Association (TERA) in 1893. In spring 1893, Sarah was one of those helping to organize a Texas branch of the National American Suffrage Association.

The Achesons' 1885 Italianate house at 1419 West Woodard Street was designed to accommodate all their interests and activities. The ground floor, with its welcoming front door, octagonal hallway with tiled fireplace, wide interior spaces, and outdoor views, easily hosted fundraisers, committee meetings, musical performances, and charitable clothing drives. The second floor had four comfortable bedrooms, each with a fireplace. Speaking tubes and trumpets, as well as gas lights, functioned throughout the building.

*Figure 222 Portrait of Sarah Cooke Acheson, 1896. Source: Elizabeth Brooks, "Prominent Women of Texas" (Akron, Ohio: Manufactured by the Werner Company, 1896), pp. 149*151. Online through HathiTrust Digital Library*

To facilitate 360-degree views of the surrounding area, a spiral staircase led to an octagonal observatory, with a periscope sticking up above. Dr. Acheson had a laboratory in the basement, with a human skeleton and scientific paraphernalia where he could perform chemical tests, carry out experiments, compound medicines, and tinker with inventions. On at least one occasion, the doctor had a critically ill patient stay at his house for days, so he could keep continuous watch over him.

Sadly, Sarah passed away in 1899, and in 1934 Sandie died alone, with a caretaker, in his big house. He was 91 years old and had driven his own automobile until two weeks earlier. At the time, he was one of the oldest practicing physicians in Texas. He was said to be the oldest living member of the Grand Army of the Republic nationwide. His will divided the doctor's assets among his four living descendants— daughter Alice and her three children. As for the house, rumor says that lightning struck the periscope, causing a fire that destroyed the house. No one could verify just when the house burned, though perhaps it was before the Acheson heirs sold the property to H. B. Perryman and C. W. Pierpont on November 8, 1935. Perryman was a real estate developer.

It is said that Tom Suggs, judge of the 39th District Court, used the materials remaining after the fire—brick and stone—to build a house at 1431 West Woodard Street. He left Denison in 1944 as general counsel of the Texas & Pacific Railroad and became president of that railroad in 1958. In the late 1940s, Fred Zuercher owned the house. Around 1955, Col. John H. Anderson and Dorothy Kohfeldt Anderson acquired it and commissioned a major remodeling by architect Donald Mayes. The house remained in the Anderson family for many decades. Indeed, the north side of the 1400 block of West Woodard Street, which never had an alley and faces a park-like median strip, has remained one of Denison's most attractive residential blocks. In the years after Dr. Acheson's death, several beautiful houses came to occupy the Acheson homesite.

*****

Lelardoux's next major project emerged from the fertile minds of the Leeper brothers, Edward and John, hardware merchants, and their partner, J. T. or "Tom" Boldrick, owner of a Denison shoe store. According to Calvin Mauldin's story, "The Rise and Fall of the Security Building," published in the Denison Herald on April 26, 1992, "The structure would be a showcase for their hardware business when completed." Construction ran into problems early on, hitting hard rock a few feet into the soil, and financial trouble ensued. The foundation alone cost $65,000, according to Leroy Anderson's interview with Edward D. Leeper in the Denison Press, March 5, 1955.

Initially planned to encompass six or seven stories, the building eventually was built with five. The corner at 331 West Main Street was topped by a turret, and many plate-glass windows faced both Main Street and Burnet Avenue. Above the ornate front door sat "Old Stoneface," made from a two-ton stone brought from East Main Street and chiseled by an itinerant French sculptor who happened into town one day. During construction, crowds came from as far away as Dallas to see the structure publicized as "Texas' first skyscraper."

Figure 223 The Leeper-Boldrick Building, located at 331 West Main Street in Denison, TX, was designed by French architect Pierre Lelardoux and constructed in 1891. It was a project of Thomas Boldrick and Edward and John B. Leeper. Later it was called "the Security Building." Photo as originally built. Source of photo: Art Work of Grayson County (1895).

The building was partially completed and ready for occupants by 1891. A Sunday Gazetteer advertisement from November 22, 1891, depicted the new building, with the Leeper Hardware Company boasting, "We are now located in our new quarters." According to the 1891 Denison City Directory, the firm had been incorporated on January 1, 1890, with capital stock worth $51,000. Edward D. Leeper was president; Levi Lingo vice-president; John B. Leeper secretary and treasurer; and Paul Leeper a clerk. The company was described as wholesale "jobbers in hardware, stoves, tinware, agricultural implements, carriage and wagon wood work."

Soon thereafter, the three partners sold their interest in the structure. "As a supposed safety measure, the fifth floor and hipped roof were removed by the new owners," Mauldin wrote. The alteration detracted considerably from Lelardoux's elegant design. By 1914 or 1915, the now-four- story building was renamed the "Security Building," after the Security Bank briefly occupied part of the first floor. With the onset of the Great Depression, the edifice became a "professional building" hosting most of Denison's doctors, lawyers, and dentists. On December 3, 1952, the City of Denison issued a demolition notice on grounds of safety. The process took five months of hard labor.

* * * * *

Having completed so much work in the 1880s and early 1890s, perhaps Pierre Lelardoux was exhausted. In 1891, he was living on the east side of North Mirick Avenue between West Johnson and West Elm streets. This area had been his neighborhood for many years. Pierre had created the Lelardoux Addition, a residential development running north and south near downtown. Around this time, he created Lelardoux Park at the corner of Mirick Avenue and Elm Street. On August 2, 1891, the Sunday Gazetteer noted that a German organization, the Widukind Lodge, Sons of Herman, would celebrate its first anniversary with a sumptuous picnic in the park.

The early 1890s were years of financial hardship in Denison, as hopes of industrial development proved unrealistic and many investors lost money. The nationwide Panic of 1893 heightened economic worries. Lelardoux's reputation may have suffered from the big LeeperBoldrick or "Security" building's construction and financial troubles. Architectural fashions, too, were moving away from the ornate styles in which he excelled. Perhaps his wife also was ill and required care, as she would pass away on October 29, 1894, and be buried in Calvary Cemetery.

Thus, on September 18, 1892, Pierre published a notice in the Sunday Gazetteer: "For fourteen years I have labored amongst you as a professional architect.... On account of health and for other reasons, I have determined to engage in the real estate and insurance business." He also began to secure patents for inventions: a "press-box for horizontal oil-presses" (May 1895), an "automatic [train] car switching system" (March 1896), and a "roller press for extracting oil from cotton seed, etc." (December 1897). Despite Pierre's intention to abandon architecture, the Sunday Gazetteer of January 7, 1894, reported that Denison's city council had allowed Lelardoux $253 for "drawing plans for a three-room school building for the Fourth ward." It is not known if the school was erected, or even designed.

At the end of the century, John Bue McDougall (1819–1920) asked Lelardoux to design a house at 412 West Morton Street. It was an offer he couldn't refuse. McDougall was one of Denison's wealthiest citizens; he and his wife were dedicated supporters of St. Patrick's Catholic Church. Like Lelardoux's wife, both would be buried at Calvary Cemetery. Their three-story Queen Anne Victorian–style mansion would be constructed in 1900.

Figure 224 McDougall House, 1900. 412 West Morton Street. Source: "Residence of J.B. McDougall." Robinson, Frank M., comp. Industrial Denison. [N.p.]: Means-Moore Co., [1901]. Page 59. Reprinted in Industrial Denison: A North Texas Town in 1900, by Mavis Anne Bryant (2017). The book is available at amazon.com.

McDougall's origins were murky; he told diverse stories about his origins (Scotland, Canada, New York State), his childhood (ran away at ten and was a sailor for seven years), his adventures (floating the Amazon; seeking gold in California; travels in Holland, England, Pike's Peak, all through the West; founding the town of Breckinridge, Colorado; fighting on both sides in the Civil War; enduring time in Andersonville Prison). By 1869 he was operating a "large, well regulated billiard saloon" in Pleasanton, Kansas. One rumor held that Cole Younger and Jesse James, the "James boys," had fought for the Confederacy under Colonel McDougall. As the colonel always was loyal to his "boys," when the Jameses would come to Denison, carefully disguised, McDougall would supply them with food and liquor while they hid out in a barn on East Main Street.

McDougall came to Denison in September 1872, at the age of fifty-three, and first worked as a teamster. By 1876, he was operating the Wine and Liquors Saloon at 227 West Main Street. Here Charles H. Moulton was employed as a bartender. By 1887, this site hosted McDougall's Bank Exchange Saloon. As we have seen above, the McDougall Opera House was a big threestory building at 221-223 West Main Street, providing some of the earliest entertainment in the young Gate City. The McDougall was in operation for a couple of decades before it closed in the early part of 1907. John then opened a movie house, the Palace Theater, at 227 West Main Street; it ran for only a year.

The fates of the Moultons and the McDougalls were intimately intertwined. The Moulton family's first home is believed to have been a tent set up in what is now the 400 block of West Morton Street. The family moved to Texas for the health of the father (who may have been Charles H. Moulton), but he died a few years later, in 1879. When John McDougall married Charles's widow, Margaret O'Connell Moulton (1844–1917), in 1882, John was perhaps sixtythree, and she was thirty-eight. She had three surviving children: Florence Ellen ("Flora") Moulton (born in 1868, death date unknown); George David Moulton (1869–1944); and Edward R. ("Eddie") Moulton (1870–1935). Florence joined the Order of the Sacred Heart, taking her final vows in Chicago in December 1889. The three stained-glass windows behind the altar at St. Patrick's Catholic Church were placed there by McDougall in memory of members of his family.

During the forty-eight years of McDougall's life that remained after he arrived in Denison, he helped to establish many key businesses in the new town. By 1887 he owned the McDougall Opera House and the Bank Exchange Saloon. John and partner Aulson S. Bouchard operated the popular McDougall Hotel at Union Station. Designed by Joseph Schott, it cost $30,000, opening in May 1883. Later the partners founded the McDougall Hotel Steam Laundry, at 224 West Woodard Street; and then, in 1898, Snow White Laundry, at 314 West Woodard Street. McDougall also was a founder of the Denison Bank and Trust, incorporated in 1905 at 229 West Main Street; the First National Bank, which later was known as the Citizens National Bank and eventually Bank One, at 231 West Main Street; the State National Bank, at 300 West Main Street; the Denison Power and Light Company, now TU Electric; and Southwestern Surety Insurance. McDougall joined Walter Hibbard in erecting the Denison Grocery Company at 112- 114 North Houston Avenue, close to the present MKT Depot.

As McDougall operated bars, hotels, and an opera house in Denison, he became friendly with dignitaries of the Native American tribes situated north of the Red River. As time passed, he acquired ranch land, a mercantile store, and shares in coal mining ventures, railways, and bridges in Indian Territory. He was made a citizen of the Chickasaw Nation by act of the tribal legislature.

Lelardoux stopped by the Sunday Gazetteer office in January 1900, to share his drawings of the new McDougall home. The house, occupying more than half a block, needed to accommodate a sizable family, servants, vehicles, and frequent social activities. Construction began on March 12, 1900. By the end of that year, the home was nearly completed, with "finish touches" being done on the interior.

The house had a steep pitched roof, an asymmetrical façade, a large wrap-around porch, and an abundance of decorative elements. Among the latter were a corner turret, lots of fretwork, numerous dormer windows, attractive spindle work on the porches, gable trim, and a protruding bay window on the east side. There were four bedrooms, with only one bath; four fireplaces burned coal.

On August 19, 1900, the Gazetteer wrote, "Col. McDougall will have underneath his palatial new home one of the largest and best cellars in the state. It is waterproof and will be cool in summer and warm in winter. It has a very large storage capacity." Legend has it that John had the house painted red and gave his wife the deed as a Christmas gift. According to researcher Helen Johnson, the house went onto Denison's tax rolls in 1901 at a cost of $5,000. Using the website measuringworth.com, that amount in 2012 dollars would be over $900,000.

The McDougall house still stands on Morton Street. It has long served as an elegant bed-and-breakfast inn that hosts all manner of events.

Figure 225 McDougall House, May 2010. Inn of Many Faces Bed and Breakfast, 412 West Morton Street. Photo by Brian C. Hander, May 2010. Many remember this Queen Anne Victorian mansion as the home of a longtime Denison teacher, Mrs. Eunyce A. Cooke.

Lelardoux's daughter Marie likely attended St. Xavier's Academy in Denison; she may have taught there, too, as the 1896 Denison City Directory listed her as a teacher living with her father at 515 West Elm Street. The 1900 Census says she was a widow (perhaps an error). Five years later, she was a "teacher of languages" in San Francisco, California. In another year, she had moved to Fresno. In July 1907, in San Francisco, she married a French immigrant, Joseph Louis Pettithomme. He was naturalized, a machinist living in Oakland. Pierre began to prepare for his own move to the West Coast.

Figure 226 Quinn Chapel African Methodist Episcopal Church was built in late 1901 at 201 West Walker Street. Photo by Walter Lebrecht, ca. 1930.

In August 1901, Lelardoux showed the Sunday Gazetteer his "plans of the African Methodist Episcopal Church to be erected this summer. It will be a beautiful frame structure, 40 x 75 feet, with ... provisions for church festivals and other sacred entertainments. It will be equal to any of our churches in the height of the steeple." The church at 201 West Walker Street, corner of North Austin Avenue, was expected to cost about $4,000. Located near Stevens Public School on Bond Street, the church was named Quinn Chapel A.M.E. after Paul Quinn (1788– 1873), a missionary and bishop of the African Methodist Episcopal Church, for whom Paul Quinn College in Waco, Texas, was also named. The cornerstone was laid on August 25, 1901. Ed Burton had been awarded the contract for the stone foundation.

Charles John O'Maley (1861–1923) was born in Rochester, New York, the fourth son of Owen E. O'Maley and Mary Elizabeth "Libby" Yawman; both O'Maley grandparents were natives of Ireland. By the time Charles was four years old, his family had moved to Chicago, Illinois, where his father was a clerk in the U.S. Court. By 1880, the large O'Maley clan had settled in Denison, where his father had joined the ranks of those employed by the railroad. Frank (age 21) and Charles (age 19) were also working as railroad clerks. On October 2, 1890, Charles married Flora Kaufman (1867–1958) in her home in Fort

Scott, Kansas. A few years later, on May 28, 1899, the Sunday Gazetteer reported that C. J. O'Maley had had a wart weighing one pound cut from his foot. The wart had "been preserved in alcohol and will be on exhibition in the front window at Kingston's" drug store.

Charles O'Maley proved an astute businessman. By the end of the nineteenth century, he owned several downtown buildings. At 120 West Main Street, he operated a kind of pawn shop, acting as a railroad and steamship broker; buying and selling diamonds, watches, and jewelry; and making loans. In May 1899, he paid $5,000 for 113 West Main, directly across the street from the Sunday Gazetteer offices at 112 West Main.

Sadly, on November 13, 1901, the 113 building was utterly destroyed in a major fire. Insured for $4,000, Charles immediately hired Pierre Lelardoux to design a replacement. The Gazetteer reported on November 24 that it would "conform in details to the present building" at 120 West Main. By January 5, 1902, the site at 113 West Main was being cleared, and by January 19, carpenters and stone masons were at work. On April 19, 1902, a "first-class" Mexican restaurant opened on the ground floor, operated in "elegant new quarters" by the Busi Brothers, recently arrived from Texarkana, and a "noted Mexican chef."

* * * * *

When the 1903 City Directory for San Francisco was published, it listed "Pierre Lelardoux, architect, residence 1449 Greenwich." According to his obituary in the Sunday Gazetteer, "He left here several years ago and cast his lot with San Francisco, where he was engaged in his profession when he died." It is not known if he found work in California. We do have two long letters he wrote to San Francisco newspapers concerning a new sewer system planned by the city. One was sent to the San Francisco Call and published in May 1905. He was concerned that dumping sewage into the San Francisco Bay would be detrimental in the long run. "Why should not San Francisco establish pumping stations and distribute its sewage on some cultivable land where it could be utilized the same as is done in other cities?" A second, similar letter was published in the San Francisco Chronicle on March 21, 1908.

Pierre Lelardoux passed away at his daughter's house in Oakland on December 3, 1910. When the news reached Denison, the Sunday Gazetteer remembered him on December 25: Lelardoux "was a prominent resident of Denison for many years. He was the leading architect, and many public buildings in this city stand as monuments to his genius.

He was a man of superior ability and finished education and pre-eminent as an architect, in fact he had no superior in the state.

His eminent ability was recognized in many sections outside of Denison, and he was always a busy man. He was the soul of honor. No man who has ever lived here was more trusted in his profession than the deceased. In every transaction in life, his record was without a stain."

Figure 227 This undated photo of 200 West Main Street provides a view of Lelardoux's design for Mrs. Chichet. Although altered at the storefront level, the building still maintained incredible detailing and cornice work.

JoAnn Perkins
by Donna Hord Hunt

JoAnn Perkins was born on October 30, 1942 in Memphis, Texas. She grew up on Tower Lane in Denison and credited Texoma Business and Professional Women, Pat Welch, Cora Bell, Lee Alyce McGrew and Donna Lorance for their leadership and encouragement to accomplish her achievements. She was voted Woman of the Year in 2014 by the Texoma B&PW Club.

From B&PW she became involved in the Region VI and Texas NAACP Unit 6352 and then in 2006 was elected president of that unit. She brought home the Torchbearer's Award from the state NAACP conference in 2007 "lighting the way for civil rights, justice and community service."

Her focus was on building bridges instead of walls in the community which, with her help, produced some lasting relationships.

She was most proud of the Sherman and Denison units of the NAACP being combined during her term as president and the name being changed to the Grayson County chapter of the National Association for the Advancement of Colored People to include all the county.

She first went to Washington, D. C. to march on Capitol Hill to preserve the Voting Rights Act, and then attended the inauguration of President Barack Obama, traveling 24 hours one way to stand about six hours to witness the historic inauguration. She said that was "one of the most exciting times in my life."

Figure 228 Ms. Jo Ann Perkins

Ms. Perkins was also very active in the Democratic Women of Grayson County organization and received the Ann Richards Award in 2012 for her work.

At the end of her life, she was still giving to her church, neighbors, grandchildren, adult children and community. Bring all those roles together and you'll find compassion and generosity inside each heart. Jo Ann passed away on July 18, 2013 at Texoma Medical Center in Denison following a lengthy illness. She is buried at Cedarlawn Memorial Park in Sherman, Texas.

At the time of her death, former Denison City Councilman Wilbert "Bill" Malvern Sr. said, "She's going to be missed, I guarantee you. She's been a pillar in the community and a very active person. She was somebody we could depend on for things. She belonged to so many organizations doing positive things and working in the community for the community. She was that kind of person. Everything I was involved in; I tried my best to get her involved in it too because you could depend on her."

Shortly after her passing, a scholarship fund was created to honor her legacy and to ensure the future generations would not only know, but also benefit from her advocacy of education. An initial $10,000 endowment was given by Roger D. Sanders of Sanders, O'Hanlon & Motley.

A concert celebrating the legacy of Ms. Perkins was held in 2015 to raise additional funds for the Jo Ann Perkins/NAACP Scholarship Fund at Grayson College. The concert was a joint partnership between Greater Coffey Memorial Church of God in Christ and Mount Vernon Baptist Church, both based in Denison, and Faith Church. The three churches came together to perform music alongside individual selections, asking for love offerings to help fund the scholarship program.

To honor the many contributions of Ms. Perkins, the City of Denison announced the renaming of North 7th Avenue to Jo Ann Perkins Avenue in 2019. "Jo Ann Perkins lived a life of service to God, to her family and to our community," Denison Mayor Janet Gott said. "If she was needed, she came. Where she could serve, she did. And always with grace and joy. She made her mark on our community and today we want to leave a permanent reminder to commemorate her life." Perkins' children were on hand to accept an official street sign as a gift.

Figure 229 The street sign for JoAnn Perkins Avenue as it appeared in 2022.

The Preacher's Daughter, the Princess, and the P.O.

By James K. Sears

This little story about Denison, Texas, begins more than a century ago and almost a thousand miles away, at Martha Washington College in Abingdon, Virginia. Constructed as a private home in 1832 and opened as a college in 1860, it was more of an elite girls' finishing school than a traditional college. "The Martha," as it has been known to locals since the Civil War, closed as a school in 1931 and reopened four years later as a hotel. It operates today as The Martha Washington Inn & Spa.

There were no young ladies from Denison at Martha Washington College in the fall of 1888, but twenty-year-old Fannie Piner of neighboring Fannin County was beginning her final year. She was the youngest of five children and the only daughter of Methodist minister John W. Piner and Mary J. Stephens. The Piners were a distinguished pioneer family in Fannin and Grayson counties. They came by covered wagon from Kentucky in 1859 and settled in Honey Grove. One of Fannie's brothers, Robert G. "Bob" Piner, grew up and moved to Sherman, where he became a civic leader and longtime school board member. Piner Middle School is named for him. Another brother, Howell Lake Piner, was a man of many accomplishments. He founded Grayson College in Whitewright in 1887 and Columbia College in Van Alstyne in 1889. He was elected principal of Sherman High School in 1898, and he served as superintendent of the State School for the Blind in Austin from 1900 to 1906. In later years he authored three books and published several stories and poems in national magazines.

Fannie's parents could have learned about Martha Washington College from advertisements placed in Texas newspapers of the period. Her mother may also have been familiar with the school through her family. Mary J. Piner's paternal grandparents were prominent Virginians. Many of Fannie's schoolmates also came from old Virginia families. Among them was Edith Bolling of Wytheville. She enrolled at age fifteen in September of 1888 but turned sixteen in October, the same month that Fannie turned twenty-one.

Despite the difference in their ages, the two girls struck up a friendship. Perhaps it was born of a shared feeling of being somehow out of place at the school. Fannie was from a small town in Texas, not far removed in time or distance from

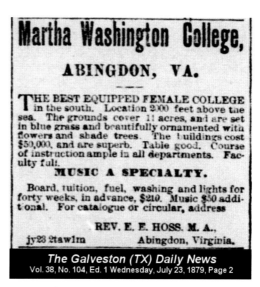

The Galveston (TX) Daily News
Vol. 38, No. 104, Ed. 1 Wednesday, July 23, 1879, Page 2

the American frontier. Edith, who was home-schooled prior to enrol-
ling, was unaccustomed to the discipline and regimentation at Abingdon. The accommodations were a bit too austere for a girl who claimed
to be the ninth great-granddaughter of Native American princess Po-
cahontas. She complained that her room was too cold, and the food
was not up to her standards. The curriculum was too rigorous and in-
timidating. Thoroughly miserable, she left after one semester, but she
would not forget her friend from Texas.

Edith Bolling in her youth
Library of Congress Catalog:
https://lccn.loc.gov/2011660893

Fannie graduated
the following
spring and went
home to Honey
Grove. About
four months later
she married
thirty-year-old
Samuel Price
King, a messen-
ger for the Pacific
Express Com-
pany in Denison.
He was living
with his widowed
mother at 916
West Sears Street.
Sam and Fannie
moved into the
house next door
at 920, where they
would remain for
the next two dec-
ades.

Around 1908 Sam
and his widowed
sister, Mollie Abernathy, took over a little grocery at 415 North Barrett
Avenue. That same year the wife of Fannie's brother Howell died of
tuberculosis in Plano. Howell himself, having resigned from the
School for the Blind two years earlier due to continued ill health, had
not been well enough to attend his wife's funeral. He soon relocated
to Denison and moved in with Fannie, Sam, their two young daughters, and Mary J. Piner, then the widowed mother of Fannie and Howell. Perhaps because the house on Sears Street was beginning to seem
cramped, the Kings and Piners moved to a two-story house at 931
West Bond Street, where they were listed in the 1909 Denison City Di-

rectory. Around that same time Sam and Mollie opened a second grocery at 800 West Morton Street. The city directory shows Mollie residing on the premises.

A few years later the term of Denison postmaster William J. Scott, who had overseen the construction of the city's new post office from 1910 to 1912, was set to expire on December 20, 1915. The names of several men were floated as possible successors. Foremost among them was Jesse Whitehurst, then a grocer but also a former postal employee. He supervised mail carriers at the Denison post office in the 1890s, and he held the position of chief clerk when he retired in 1906 to go into the grocery business.

That year Whitehurst bought the Tony Hill Grocery at 1220 West Gandy Street from Allen L. Jones in October. A little more than two years later, in January 1909, he sold it to A. Lincoln Knaur and W. Edgar Brown. In 1910 he purchased another grocery at 1101 West Woodard Street. He would remain in business there for the better part of that decade. In newspaper advertisements he distinguished himself from his competitors by claiming to be "The store that doesn't have flies."

FISH FLAKES

For fish balls, creamed fish, fish hash, etc. Extra quality fresh fish, boiled, slightly salted and put up within a few hours after taken from the ocean Ready for immediate use. Try a can.

JESSE WHITEHURST

BOTH PHONES 500

The store that doesn't have flies.

THE PURE FOOD GROCERY

The Denison (TX) Daily Herald
Vol. 25, No. 175, Monday, March 2, 1914, Page 5

Whitehurst was active in civic affairs, serving as city alderman and commissioner. Well-known and well-liked, he was considered by many to be the leading candidate to succeed Scott as postmaster.

Unbeknownst to Whitehurst and his supporters, the wife of fellow grocer Sam King had also taken an interest in the post office vacancy. Fannie did not want the job for herself. Rather she thought it would be a good opportunity for her brother, Howell, who was still living with her family. He was a capable, educated man with executive and managerial experience in the educational field. Because the job of postmaster, then as now, required no heavy lifting, his delicate health posed no impediment. Fannie shared her thoughts on the opportunity in a letter to Edith, her acquaintance from Martha Washington College some twenty-seven years earlier.

Edith had lived in Washington DC from 1896 to 1908 as the wife of a prominent jeweler, Norman Galt. After he died unexpectedly at the age of forty-three, she was left a wealthy widow. Seven years later she was introduced to a man in Washington whose own spouse had died about six months earlier. He took an instant liking to Edith and soon proposed. Edith accepted, but she insisted on postponing the wedding until the end of the official year of mourning for his deceased wife. The date was set for December 18, 1915, just two days before W. J. Scott's term as Denison postmaster would expire.

The end of Scott's term and the wedding in Washington were connected by more than mere temporal coincidence. Prior to 1936 postmasters in offices the size of Denison's were still appointed by the president. It happened that Edith Bolling Galt's fiancée was none other than Thomas Woodrow Wilson, twenty-eighth president of the United States from 1913 to 1921. We don't know whether Wilson gave any thought to refusing the favor that his bride-to-be asked of him in the days leading up to their marriage. We know only that, on the Monday before the Saturday wedding, H. L. Piner's name was announced as his choice to be the next Denison postmaster. Following the announcement, supporters of Whitehurst telegraphed the White House to request further consideration of the case, but on Thursday the White House sent Piner's name to the Senate for confirmation. Denison's representative in the House, Sam Rayburn, had found no reason to object, and the Senate confirmed Piner routinely. He was installed as the new Denison postmaster three weeks later, on January 7, 1916.

The appointment worked out well for the Piner and King families. Howell soon moved out of his sister's house. In his first year on the job he hired his twenty-year-old niece, Fannie's younger daughter, Mary. She went on to have a 26-year career with the post office. She was in charge of civil service examinations there when she resigned in 1942 to marry her second husband, an Oklahoma oil man. Howell got married again in 1917, the same year that Sam's and Fannie's older daughter, Marguerite, married Roy Geer of Fort Worth. Howell and his second wife, twenty-five years his junior, had a daughter in 1918. At the end of his term in June 1924, *The Dallas Morning News* reported that Piner "was considered one of the most popular postal officials Denison has ever had." He continued to write in his retirement and died in Sherman in 1935.

After their daughters and Howell moved out of the Kings' house on Bond Street, Fannie and Sam moved back to 920 West Sears Street for a while. In 1922 they purchased a historic home at 1200 West Morton Street, built in 1888 by Paul Waples, cofounder of the Waples-Platter Grocery Company. Fannie's mother, Mary Jane Piner, died in the house in 1925 at the age of 93. Sam King's funeral was held in the same house after he died there in 1929 at age 71. Fannie sold it in 1942 and moved to 1005 West Johnson Street, where she was living at the time of her death in 1949. She was 81.

Soon after Jesse Whitehurst lost out to Howell Piner for the postmaster job, the City of Denison acquired the block that included the little store on Barrett Avenue where Sam King had started out in the grocery business. Central Ward Elementary School was constructed on that block in 1917. Whitehurst's granddaughter and her future husband attended Central Ward in the 1920s and '30s, where they no doubt played at recess on the site of the Kings' former grocery.

Whitehurst retired from active business in 1937 at the age of 73. He died in June that year, after his wife passed away in February. Their granddaughter married in Denison eleven years later. She and her husband had a son and a daughter, great-grandchildren of the Whitehursts. In the 1950s and '60s the great-grandchildren attended Central Ward, where they, like their parents before them, played at recess on the site of the Kings' former grocery. Decades later, in 2009, the heroic great-grandson was invited to bring his family to meet the current occupants of the same White House where Woodrow Wilson had denied Jesse Whitehurst a job in 1915.

The Sullenbergers with President Barack and Michelle Obama.

Justin Raynal
Denison's Saintly Sinner
By Brian C. Hander

Justin Raynal, Denison's mysterious bachelor, was born March 15, 1814 in Bordeaux, France and made his way to the United States in 1846, along with his wife and two children. Initially Mr. Raynal was engaged in the jewelry business in New York. However, when the gold fever broke out, he disposed of his business and left for the Pacific Coast near Sacramento hoping to find gold. The story that Raynal had always told was that he had lost both his wife and daughter and had become estranged from his son due to his son's poor behavior. Afterward, Raynal moved around to various California towns, never staying in any one location for long.

He lived in Nevada, Nebraska, and several other states before finally settling down and opening a restaurant in Omaha that was hailed as second-to-none. His establishment was so popular that it was hailed as the best arranged and best kept restaurant in that section of the country.

Soon afterward, he ventured to Chicago due to a need for a different climate where he once again opened a restaurant. He proved to be incredibly successful until the Great Chicago Fire of 1871 destroyed everything he had worked so hard to build. All told, the fire would cause 4 billion dollars' worth of damage and take the lives of at least 300 people.

From Chicago, Raynal had hopes to move to Texas and make his claim in the mystical land below the Red River. However, he had little to no money so was forced to stop in Springfield, MO where he accepted a position as a cook at an academy. It's very possible that this position is what led Mr. Raynal to develop a love of education and all the opportunities it could offer an individual. He saved every penny and moved to the young town of Denison, Texas in January of 1873 with $100 in his pocket.

Raynal opened a restaurant near the corner of Main and Austin Ave and built a wood frame building in the summer of 1873 at this location with sleeping rooms upstairs and a saloon and restaurant downstairs. This was the site of his Grand Southern Restaurant and Saloon with John Wright and Alan Hornback operating the saloon on the lower floor.

This is where the Denison Gun Club and other civic organizations met regularly in the early days of the city. It has been said that Raynal kept a large jar labeled "For the School" in a prominent location on the bar, into which imbibing patrons were glad to deposit liberal amounts at Raynal's suggestion that the public school program desperately needed their support. Raynal's thorough knowledge of the saloon business, his agreeable manners, and his strict honesty secured him a large number of friends whom he never failed to call upon if he felt a need was going unmet in the community.

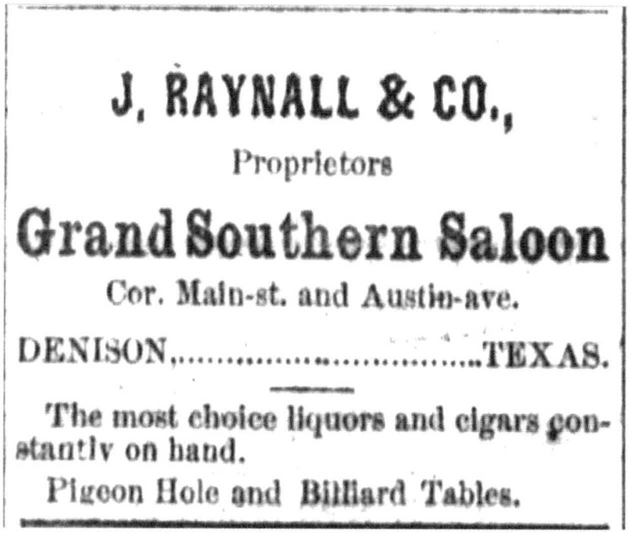

Figure 230 An advertisement that appeared in The Denison Daily Herald on October 11, 1877. Notice how Raynal is spelled incorrectly.

The greatest unmet need would prove to be that of public education. In Denison's earliest days a debate raged whether to use the city's funds to build a school or a jail with the populace fairly divided on the issue. Raynal was the ultimate catalyst and largest backer of the school movement, garnering the necessary votes to ensure the bond issue would pass. The school was built, and Raynal was hailed as a "knight in shining armor" for the Denison school system.

Figure 231 Denison's Educational Institute, the first free public graded school in the State of Texas. This structure was made possible by Justin Raynal's persistence and dedication to the educational needs of Denison's school children.

Most of Raynal's time was spent at his other saloon, known as the Raynal Saloon, at 101 West Main Street. The saloon proved so profitable that a new building was required in 1876 to accommodate the swelling crowds.

Raynal was elected to Denison's City Council in 1877 and re-elected in 1879. During this time his saloon and restaurant remained wildly successful, allowing him to purchase the land on which the building had been constructed.

On May 5, 1878, a contract for a new building for Mr. Raynal was awarded to Joseph Koehler, the same man responsible for construction of Denison's free public school. The stately new building was to be brick and would occupy a site 24 feet wide and 90 feet deep and was to occupy the site at 202 West Main, immediately west of his current saloon.

A small misfortune happened on September 12, 1878, when the only set of building plans blew off the roof of the new building while Koehler and Raynal were reviewing them. A reward was offered, and it is assumed the plans were found as construction was able to continue without delay.

Raynal operated businesses in his new building, but still kept his Grand Southern in its original location at the corner of Main and Austin. During this time Raynal was hailed as a very charitable man who frequently fed the poor. He also threw big parties and invited all to come, providing free food on his birthday.

On March 28, 1879, a letter was sent to Mr. Raynal from his 80 year old brother in France stating that the overseas family was doing well and that Raynal's nephew was serving in the French Assembly. It would appear that community service ranked high for members of this family, and it is said the Mr. Raynal often confessed his longing for his home country so it would appear a letter such as this would have brought him great comfort.

Figure 232 The Raynal building, seen here in the 1960's, still displays the Raynal name along the top left-hand corner of the structure.

Justin Raynal died on August 4, 1879, at 10:30 pm after complications associated with "inflammation of the bowels." He had been ill for ten days and while everything possible was done, it all proved in vain. Shortly before his death the nuns from St. Xavier's Catholic School visited Mr. Raynal to provide comfort and assistance throughout his illness. He passed away in his loft above his beloved Grand Southern at the corner of Main and Austin.

Raynal was buried in Oakwood Cemetery the day after his death with one of the largest funerals ever witnessed in Denison. The following was printed in *The Sunday Gazetteer* on August 6, 1879.

As he was a prominent member of the Masonic Lodge, he was buried by that noble order. The body was taken from the residence of the deceased to the public school building where a large concourse of people had assembled to witness the funeral ceremonies. The coffin was deposited in front of the entrance door, and the ceremonies were opened by Rev. Mr. Hall with an eloquent prayer, after which Rev. Mr. Parks delivered the funeral sermon.

Figure 233 The only known image of Justin Raynal, seen here, appeared in the local newspaper just months before his death.

Want of space forbids us from giving even a synopsis of the same, which was very highly commended. At its close the procession formed in the following order: First, the Maennerehor band, the Masons, the hearse, the pall bearers, who were members of the Masonic fraternity, the Gate City Guards, the Denison Cornet band, the different fire companies, the Denison Artillery company, the Mayor, members of the city council and city officers in carriages, and a long line of carriages with citizens. During the march of the procession, a section of the Artillery company, stationed in the park, fired salutes at stated intervals.

On arriving at the cemetery, at the place where the remains of Justin Raynal were to be interred, close alongside of the remains of his beloved friend, Judge W.D. Kirk, in accordance with a wish expressed shortly before his death, the Free Masons consigned him to Mother Earth with the beautiful and impressing ceremonies peculiar to the craft. The Gate City Guards then fired a military salute of three rounds over the grave of the departed, and the large concourse of people slowly and sadly returned to their homes.

The most pressing matter following Mr. Raynal's death was that of his property and possessions. As he had no family there had always been speculation as to what he would do with his accumulated wealth. Would it go to the Catholic church or St. Xavier's? Would it be used for Denison's schools? Or could it even have been left to some lucky individual? The answer would soon arrive and can be seen clearly spelled out in Raynal's final will and testament that he signed the day he died.

State of Texas, County of Grayson.

Know all men by these presents that I. Justin Raynal, of said County and State, being sound in mind and of disposing memory do make this my last will and testament, herby revoking all other wills by me heretofore made.

First. I do will and bequeath my two-story brick building and lot No. 2, in block No. 5 situated on South Main Street in the City of Denison in said State and County to the Denison Public Free School for the benefit of said school.

Second. After the payment of all my just debts, I will and bequeath to my brother Jean Raynal and my sister Maria Cherie Raynal equally to be divided between them, share and share alike, all the balance of my property, consisting of real estate and personal property, claims and so forth.

The property heretofore bequeathed to the Denison Public Free School shall be in charge of School Board of said City, to rent or dispose of the same as in their judgement shall be to the best interest of said school, my name to forever remain on the cornice.

Third. I constitute and appoint W.M. Peck, L. Eppstein, and J.B. Lalonde executors of this my last will and testament.

In witness whereof I have hereunto set my hand this, the 4th day of August A.D. 1879 in the presence of Ed. F. Radcliff and Adam Hornback, who attest the same at my request.

Justin Raynal

The above instrument was now here subscribed by Justin Raynal, the testator, in our presence and we at his request and in his presence sign our names hereto as attesting witnesses.

Ed. F. Ratcliff
Adam F. Hornbeck

Filed Sept. 22, 1879.

The will was filed for probate on September 22, 1879, by G.A. Dickerman, county clerk, and recorded in Book II of Grayson County Probate Records at pages 567-568. The executors filed an inventory listing four parcels of land in four different surveys totaling 292 acres, plus Lot 19 Block 60 in Denison. Lots 1 and 2 in Block 52 were not listed. At the time of his death Raynal had a worth of $2,000 in personal property and $8,000 in real estate with outstanding debts of $6,000.

This is when trouble began. For some reason, J. K. LaLonde requested new administrators be appointed to the estate and requested T.V. Cutler, John Gallegher, W. C. Chichet, J. M. Cook, F.B. Coleman and J.L. Jones as bondsmen.

By the end of September of 1879 Harrison Tone petitioned the court stating none of the other men were competent to serve in the capacity of administrator and he was officially appointed as acting administrator on October 1, 1879. At the time of his first reporting he stated Raynal was worth $8,700 in real estate and $1,300 in personal property.

Arthur H. Coffin was next to file an injunction, this time stating Tone was incompetent and could not serve, however, the judge denied this motion and Tone continued on. The will would not be fully probated until 1896.

On August 5, 1884 the original wood frame building that housed the Grand Southern Saloon burned and was a complete loss. The fire was so intense that it caused the east wall of the brick building built in 1878 to collapse, however it was repairable without causing serious damage to the brick Raynal structure. There were rumors that the fire was possibly arson because the building was in a legal dispute at the time.

Mystery really began to surround Raynal in 1886, when a letter was received by Mayor Peck of Denison from a woman claiming to be Raynal's estranged wife from France. The woman stated she had been alerted about her husband's death from a Frenchman in Denison.

The unnamed woman claimed she wanted part of Raynal's inheritance that she was due since they were married. She wanted his money but said the school district could keep his building as she had no use for anything other than liquid assets.

In 1891 a movement was made to remove Raynal's remains and rebury him in Fairview Cemetery as Oakwood had gone out of favor with the social elite. While Raynal had donated so much to schools and other organizations, he had not left enough funding available to provide for a headstone. A cheap wooden contraption was covered with canvas to resemble a headstone, and almost immediately the public began a campaign to pay for a proper stone for the benefactor. A headstone would finally be erected fifteen years after Raynal's death.

Figure 234 The headstone of Justin Raynal as it appears at present in Oakwood Cemetery.

Raynal Elementary School

Once fully probated, the portion of Raynal's estate that was left behind to the Denison School System amounted to nearly $15,000, roughly

$500,000 in 2022 figures. Because of this, leaders and citizens alike felt that some credit was due to Mr. Raynal for his philanthropy, his civic service, and his tireless efforts to garner support for public education.

To this end the Denison school board decided to name a new structure built at 500 E. Morton in 1891 as Raynal Elementary. Every May 1st was celebrated as Raynal Day with all children at the school walking to the nearby Oakwood Cemetery and depositing flowers on his grave – a tradition that would continue for nearly a century. This historic school would serve the east end of Denison

Figure 235 Raynal School as it appeared around the turn of the century.

for just a little over three decades before it was demolished to make way for a new structure.

After the 1923-1924 school year, a new Raynal Elementary was built on the site of the former school under the direction of School Board President W.B. Munson Jr. The new school was designed by noted Dallas architect Mark Lemmon who would go on to design many

Figure 236 The new Raynal Elementary School shortly after it was completed.

buildings throughout Texas, including the 1965 Waples Methodist Church campus.

Raynal Elementary was a thriving neighborhood school that had a PTA that provided curtains for the auditorium, a piano for musical lessons, and school lunches. A Dad's Club was also established and provided playground equipment, fans for classrooms, water coolers, and in 1957 they purchased a T.V. for the school-the first to appear in a Denison campus.

A cafeteria was added to the building in 1948 and eventually an annex was added several blocks away. This annex would be traded to the City of Denison in exchange for the land that Munson Stadium sits on today.

In 1979, following a tense city-wide debate, Raynal Elementary was formally closed alongside two other Denison campuses. Nearly 170 students were transferred to the newly rebuilt Lamar Elementary on the southeast side of Denison. The school building was traded to a Pentecostal congregation for property they owned near Denison High School.

Figure 237 One of the final photos of Raynal Elementary before it was closed. The school still stands on Denison's east end.

The Raynal Monument

In 1904, local newspapers begin printing articles decrying the need for a monument to Raynal. A Denison architect by the name of Shannon drafted the initial plans for the monument that called for construction using Texas granite with a height of twenty feet and six inches with a blue limestone foundation. The contract for this design was originally awarded to the Gate City Marble Company for $675.

L.H. Mitchell sent the first check in for the new monument in February of 1908. The amount was $25 and included a letter that stated, "Gentlemen; Enclosed please find my check for $25.00 to apply on a fund for erecting a suitable monument to the memory of Justin Raynal. Please deposit this amount with the proper person or bank as a starter, and I believe a fund can be raised among the boys and girls that are scattered throughout the United States who, like myself, obtained their education in Denison and therefore are greatly indebted to him for that education. It gives me great pleasure to be a subscriber to the fund. Yours very truly, Lon H. Mitchell."

A special committee was appointed in April of 1908 to help raise additionally funding for the monument. Mayor Acheson appointed the following ladies to the committee; Mrs. Bessie Leecraft Dumas, Mrs. Sallie Shallenberger Boyd, Mrs. Mary Fields Mathis, Mrs. Belle Porter Walker, and Miss Hortense Lingo. This committee also helped get permission from the City Council to construct a 20-foot roundabout at Woodard Street and Barrett Avenue for the monument to be placed in.

By 1909 the following contributions had been paid to the Raynal Monument Fund:

G.L. Blackford $5.00, James Boyd $5.00, Wm. Boone $4.00, Miss Abbie Cobb $4.00, H.N. L. Decker $2.00, Mrs. Bess L. Dumas $4.50, Mrs. R.L. Droulliet $1.00, Sidney Elkin $0.50, Mrs. E. Farley $2.50, Mrs. Thos. Fox $1.00, Mrs. Janet Fitzgerald $0.50, Joseph Gahent $5.00, Frank B. Hughes $5.00, MRs. Lulu Hudleson $0.50, Handy & Faires $2.00, Mr. Larkin $5.00, T.V. Munson $7.00, Lonne Mitchell, Los Angeles, Cal. $25.00, Chas. O'Maley $4.00, Same Shone $2.00, Mr. and Mrs. Frank Sproule $2.00, Dr. Wm. L. Smith $1.00, P.H. Tobin $5.00, Mrs. E.A. Williams $0.20, Henry T. Walker $5.00, F.W. Wilson $2.50, Waldron Drug Co. $5.00, Vorwaerts $10.00, Unknown funds $0.30.

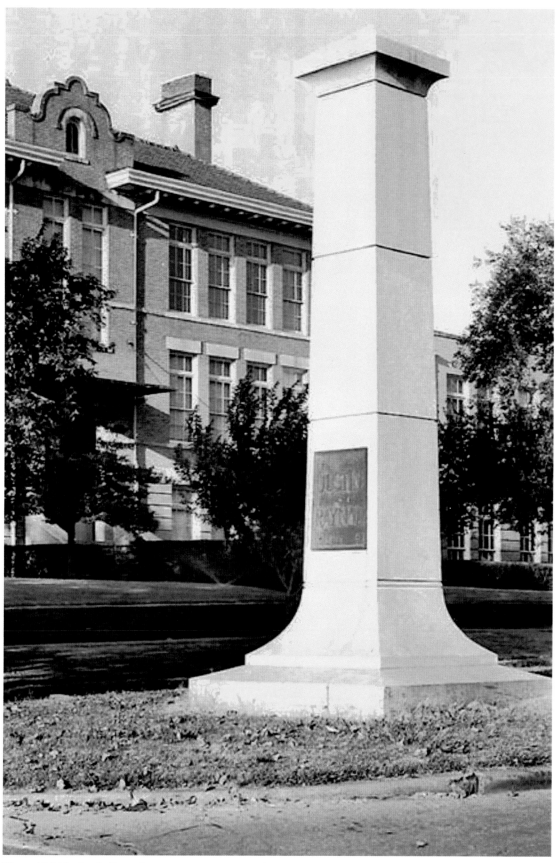

Figure 238 The Justin Raynal monument as it appeared in the 1940's in the median of Denison's Woodard Street.

Once funding was available the plan was changed, and the Denison School Board awarded a contract to Wells Bros. out of Ft. Worth to erect the monument. Cost was nearly $2,000 (around $52,000 in today's money) -all raised from those listed previously and penny and change drives held at local elementary schools. The obelisk was made of Barre granite with a 6x6 foot base and a height of 17.5 feet, and was completed at the end of 1909.

Erected in 1910, the Raynal Monument is believed to be the only monument in Texas erected in honor of a saloon owner. As vehicles became more prominent several near misses occurred at the site of the roundabout that caused city leaders to rethink the location. In 1922 the monument was moved to the Woodard Street median to allow the intersection to be paved and to prevent any further accidents. Incredibly, the monument was moved without any dismantling required. The move was made by placing timbers as tracks and the monument was jacked up on rollers and rolled onto its new home.

In 1958 *The Denison Press* recommended moving the monument to Forest Park due to the risk of it being hit by an automobile, however, no move was ever made and the monument remained in the Woodard Street median.

Figure 239 The damage inflicted upon the Raynal monument after being struck by an intoxicated motorist in 2007.

In 2007, a motorist struck the monument-essentially destroying it. Ironically, the motorist was intoxicated and hit a monument to a saloon owner. The granite pieces were collected by the City of Denison and stored in an unknown location. All looked lost until Denison Main Street Director, Donna Dow, began researching ways to resurrect the monument.

In 2017, funding from the Anice Read Fund and Denison Heritage Inc. made the marker restoration possible. The pieces that had been stored for so long were assessed and those that could be used were cleaned and reassembled in the median on Woodard Street. Although not as magnificent as it once was, the marker remains a testament to Justin Raynal and his benevolent spirit.

Figure 240 The Justin Raynal monument as it appears today in the median on Denison's Woodard Street.

Three More Denison Heroes Recognized
By Donna Hord Hunt

On June 6, 2009, Denison had a special day when we honored three of our city's heroes. A huge crowd turned out at the former railroad depot downtown and even the governor showed up to help pay recognition to T.V. Munson, who saved the grape orchards of France; former General and President Dwight D. Eisenhower who needs no further introduction; and our newest hero, Capt. Chesley Burnett "Sully" Sullenberger III, the pilot who saved 155 lives when his U.S. Airways Airbus ditched in the Hudson River outside New York City. All three were born in Denison.

Well, it turns out there are at least three other heroes. I found their brief biographies recently while going through a box of information as my friend, Mavis Bryant, and I have been reorganizing my little office at home. All three were not born in Denison, but they did get here as quickly as they could.

Randolph Bryant was born in 1893, a descendant of a pioneer jurist of Grayson County. He was first appointed by U.S. Attorney for the Eastern District of Texas by President Warren G. Harding in 1922 and again by President Calvin Coolidge in 1926.

He became the District Judge of the Eastern District of East Texas and served from 1931 until 1951. He occupied the bench once held by his father, David Ezekiel Bryant who was U.S. District Judge from 1890 to 1910. Randolph Bryant died in 1981.

His grandfather, Judge Anthony M. Bryant settled in Kentuckytown in 1832 and became a County Judge of Grayson County. His grandfather died as a result of a run-away team in 1889.

Figure 241 The Thompson home as it appears today at Frontier Village, Loy Lake Park, Denison, Texas

Judge James G. Thompson, Randolph's grandfather on his mother's side, moved from North Carolina in 1821 and located at Preston Bend. He too had a judicial appointment in Grayson County and was the county's first Chief Justice. His home is part of Grayson County Frontier Village at Loy Park in Denison.

I talked a little bit about George D. Moulton previously, but today I'll reveal a little more.

Moulton was known as "The father of the Denison Dam." He was a man of many interests and was regarded by some as a dreamer. He was born on March 14, 1869, in Chicago, then moved to Denison while the town still was a tent village. Their first home was a tent set up in the 400 block West Morton.

On Jan. 20, 1913, Moulton married Daisy Bryant McLynn, a granddaughter of the aforementioned Judge James G. Thompson. They lived their entire married lives in Denison, many of those years at 412 West Morton, now known as the Inn of Many Faces. After his father's death, his mother married John B. McDougall, who might also be called a hero of sorts for his many business interests in Denison.

The first thought of a dam on Red River was that of George Moulton after a visit to the Boulder Dam. In 1926 he wrote a letter to Congressman Charles D. Carter, presenting his plan for one.

His proposal did not cause excitement because most thought he was crazy. However, the U.S. Corps of Engineers, after years of study, adopted his plan to build the dam at Baer's ferry, four miles north of Denison. Construction of the dam was completed and dedicated in 1944.

About six months after completion of the dam, George Moulton died on Dec. 14, 1944. North Texas and Southern Oklahoma have cause to be grateful to this "dreamer" and his dedication to his biggest "dream."

The third hero of this most recent trio is one that perhaps many Denisonians will remember. A bronze bust of Judge Jake Jackson Loy stands at the entrance to the fair grounds at Loy Park that was named in his honor.

Figure 242 A 1935 photograph of George Moulton pointing to the location of where he believed a dam should be built near Denison.

At the time of his death on July 4, 1945, Judge Loy had become one of the best known county officials in the United States.

He was born March 2, 1888, in Tennessee and lived there until 1912 when he went to work for the Southern Railway Co., that brought him to Denison where he became an employee of the Missouri, Kansas & Texas Railroad, first as a brakeman, then as a passenger conductor.

In 1926 he was elected State Representative from Grayson County and was later elected a State Senator and served there with distinction, receiving many honors during his public career.

An energetic and productive lawmaker, Judge Loy took special pride in authoring and sponsoring the free bridge law that resulted in the now famous "Toll Bridge War" on Red River that eventually removed the toll from all bridges in Texas.

In 1932 he was elected County Judge of Grayson County and continued serving in that office until his death July 4, 1945.

During his active tenure as County Judge, Loy Park was created and developed between Sherman and Denison. Without his persistent and dedicated efforts, there would be no Loy Lake or Loy Park and possibly no Grayson County Frontier Village.

I'm sure Denison has other heroes, but it these three that stand out for their contributions not only to Denison but to all of Grayson County as well.

Figure 243 An aerial view of Loy Lake, ca. 1960.

Denison, Texas Chronology

September 23, 1872   Town of Denison is surveyed, and streets are named for officials and directors of the Katy Railroad. First lots are auctioned in Denison.

December 23, 1872   First Presbyterian Church organized.

December 24, 1872   A heavily loaded construction train piled high with rails and ties to test the solid strength of the newly built bridge over Red River, pulled out of Colbert and headed across the river, past Red River City and in to Denison. The train is driven by a young Pat Tobin.

December 25, 1872   First MKT train reaches Denison. Pat Tobin secured the whistle to Locomotive No. 15 and brought the first regular train screaming into Denison.

1872   A bucket brigade is formed to protect the community from the threat of fire.

March 6, 1873   Temporary policemen, including Richard Fossett and Charles Orton, are named and funds are collected for the erection of a calaboose.

March 10, 1873   Houston & Texas Central Railroad meets MKT Railroad at Denison, linking northern and southern borders of the United States.

March 13, 1873   City of Denison is incorporated, with L. S. Owings as first mayor. He has been appointed as mayor by the Governor of Texas.

April 4, 1873   The policemen of Denison sport gold stars and "look down with contempt on the silver marked fellows who parade the streets of Sherman."

April 11, 1873	First ad valorem tax rate approved: ¾ of one percent.
May 7, 1873	City Council designates site of first free, graded public school in Denison.
May 10, 1873	First child born in Denison, Texana Denison McElvaney.
July 8, 1873	Denison police are about to get uniforms. There are eight police officers plus the marshal.
November 1873	St. Luke's Episcopal Church founded.
1874	Lone Star Masonic Lodge #403 AF&AM chartered.
1874	Hopewell Baptist Church founded.
October 12, 1874	Formal opening of Denison Educational Institute (later called Washington School). It is the first free, graded public school in Texas. Nat Summerville is first superintendent.
November 21, 1874	Bell is installed at the Educational Institute. It weighs 1,480 pounds and measures 45 inches across the mouth. Professor Phillips raised money for bell from pupils and private donations.
October 22, 1875	Thirty men meet at Police Captain Kirk's home to organize a hook and ladder company. P. Ledrick is foreman and officers include M.B. Tallent, H. Mamlock, J.C. Montgomery, C.A. Cunningham, and W.S. Lowe.
March 25, 1875	First Baptist Church is formed by the merging of two earlier congregations.
1876	First ice factory in North Texas established at Denison.
1876	T. V. Munson establishes nurseries in Denison, soon gaining international fame through development of grapes and other fruit stock.

1876	The Denison Fire Department is officially established when the first horses are purchased to pull the fire wagons and hose carts. Bob Fisher is said to be the first chief.
January 21, 1876	First Firemen's Ball is held to help pay for the expenses of Denison's Fire Department.
January 24, 1876	Founding of Saint Xavier's Academy, a Catholic boarding school.
February 8, 1878	Ten balls and chains are received from St. Louis to be used on city prisoners.
1881	Leeper (Security) Building constructed at 331 West Main Street. When built, it is the tallest building in Texas.
June 1881	J. B. McDougall establishes the elaborate Denison Opera House on the second and third floors of 221–223 West Main Street in Denison.
1883	First Christian Church founded.
October 1883	State National Bank founded.
1885	Waples-Platter Building, 104 East Main Street, built in Denison.
1886	Denison's first separate white elementary school is opened and named for Sam Houston.
1886	Anderson School to serve the Black community is opened.
1886	Waterloo Lake is constructed as a water supply for Denison, decreasing the city's reliance on wells.
1886	Central Fire Station is constructed at 318 West Chestnut. The second-floor houses City Hall and the Police Department & Jail.

1887	Vinita, the home of T. V. Munson, is completed
1888	Munson Block is constructed in the 300 block of West Woodard Street.
1888	A street railway serves Denison. The first streetcars are lightly built wooden coaches behind Spanish mules.
1888	Mt. Olive Baptist Church is founded.
July 23, 1889	Denison Herald established.
November 15, 1889	Denison Light and Power Company is chartered by W. B. Munson Sr., John B. McDougall, and John Scullin.
1890	Denison Cotton Manufacturing Co. building erected.
1890	Exposition Hall opened at what today is 926 West Star at College Boulevard in the southwestern part of Denison.
June 22, 1890	Thirteen Denison Fire Fighters are elected from the volunteer department to be paid a rate of 75 cents per hour for work on fires.
October 14, 1890	Dwight D. Eisenhower born in Denison. He will be 34th President of the United States.
October 14, 1890	The XXI Club, second oldest women's literary club in Texas, is organized in Denison.
September 1, 1891	National Commercial College Opens at 500 West Main. The Board of Directors includes Samuel Hanna, T.V. Munson, T.W. Roach, and A.H. Coffin.
May 18, 1892	Denison's Night of Terror occurs. Several young women are murdered, and Denison's economic growth comes to a halt.

June 15, 1892	Elks Lodge No. 238 is established.
1893	First floor of Traveler's Hotel is constructed of stone quarried at the site.
1896	Denison's XXI Club builds the first women's clubhouse in the state of Texas.
1896	J. P. Crearer purchases an electric line in Sherman and begins construction of an electric railway between Sherman and Denison. To increase business, Crearer builds Woodlake Park, which will become the scene of pleasure-seeking Grayson County residents for many years.
1898	Snow White Laundry founded at 312-314 West Woodard by John B. McDougall and others.
1898	St. Patrick's Catholic Church is completed. Design is attributed to Nicholas J. Clayton.
April 1899	Methodist Episcopal Church, South is completed in the 800 block of West Main. Upon dedication it will be named Waples Memorial Methodist Church.
June-July 1899	Deemed "too tall to be safe" the fifth floor of the Security Building is removed and a new cornice is completed by Pettit & Waltz in June and July of 1899.
1899	Denison Mattress Factory is established by N. Marsico.
1900	Denison Merchants Association organized.
1900	St. Xavier's Academy constructs a four-story brick building.
May 1, 1901	First Texas Interurban, an electric railway, begins running over the 10.5 miles from Denison to Sherman, a trip of thirty minutes; fare, 25 cents.

October 1901	Denison Hotel Company is chartered following the closure of the National Commercial College. Charter members include E.H. Lingo, M.L. Eppstein, G.L. Blackford, and A.F. Platter.
September 22, 1902	Denison Hotel formally opens in what was the National Commercial College. Accommodations are hailed as the finest around and comparable to those of St. Louis and New York City.
1902	Denison Grocer Company Building erected at 112–114 North Houston Avenue by Walter, Fred, Charles, and H. A. Hibbard, four brothers.
December 5, 1902	The First Presbyterian Church, Denison's oldest house of worship, is destroyed by fire.
April 21, 1905	Annie P. steamboat lands at Denison. Named for W. M. Porter's wife and brought supplies for Hall-Leeper Hardware and groceries for Waples-Platter.
1905	First motion picture in Denison shown behind Madden's Store at 301 West Main Street, in a tent across alley on North Rusk Avenue.
August 3, 1905	Denison Cotton Mill is incorporated by William Benjamin Munson, Sr.
1907	Denison City Charter calls for election of first mayor.
1907	Ashburn's Ice Cream begins operation.
1907	First Baptist Church completed at Woodard and Mirick.
1908–10	Board of Trade leads movement to beautify Denison.
1909	S. H. Kress building built in Denison.

1909	Lake Randell is completed for additional water supply for Denison.
June 18, 1909	Katy Railroad car shops leveled by fire.
1911	First transcontinental airplane flight, sponsored by "Vin-Fiz," flies over Denison and surrounding communities.
1911	St. Patrick's Catholic Church is destroyed by a devastating fire.
1911	Third MKT Depot dedicated.
1912	United States Post Office completed at 231 West Woodard Street.
November 16, 1912	Dedication of Woodmen of the World Building, 201 West Woodard Street.
1913	Construction of Madden House at 1101 West Morton.
February 12, 1913	Denison City Council accepts A. O. Watson's plans for a much-needed new high school building.
April 1, 1913	Denison Fire Department becomes motorized with an American La France 750 G.P.M. Pumper truck.
June 4, 1913	Ninth annual graduation exercises of Denison's Anderson High School Class of 1913, held at Denison Opera House. Three girls and two boys graduate.
October 16, 1913	Southside Fire Station is opened and equipped with one fire wagon and two horses, Ted and Alex.
December 30, 1913	R. D. Beirne, a "retired merchant of Denison," will donate an eight-day E. Howard "town clock" that will toll the hours. The clock will be installed in tower of new 1914 DHS, necessitating modifications to plans for tower.
1913–14	Historic Denison High School constructed at 701 West Main Street.

February 1, 1914	Formal dedication of the new St. Patrick's Catholic Church constructed following the original Clayton design. Bishop Lynch of Dallas dedicates the church.
February 11, 1914	Denison City Hospital opens and marks the first period Denison has had a hospital since the 1870's.
April 4, 1914	Prohibition election is held. Sherman votes dry; Denison votes wet.
June 29, 1914	Construction completed on Mission Revival–style First Christian Church at 800 W. Woodard St. Architect, R. T. Forsythe of Denison; general contractor, W. S. Gannon of Denison.
1914	Old Denison High School and outbuildings demolished.
Fall 1914	Denison High School begins first year in new quarters.
1915	Liberty Bell exhibited at MKT Depot.
1915	Denison baseball player Rogers Hornsby signs with St. Louis Cardinals.
1916	Company K, Third Texas Volunteers ("Denison Rifles") serves in Spanish-American War.
1916	Denison Rotary Club launched.
April 1916	Denison Fire Department gets first hook and ladder truck. The truck had no pump and was solely used to transport ladders to and from the scene of a fire.
1917	Central Ward School built.
1917	Texas Electric Railway Terminal built at 100 West Woodard Street.
April 1917	United States enters World War I.

1918	Construction of Hopewell Baptist Church is complete.
1919	First Denison Boy Scouts troop organized.
January 24, 1920	Fire destroys Denison Commercial College (first Denison Hotel) Building at 500 West Main Street. One of Denison's greatest fires ever, with an estimated loss of $300,000.
August 4, 1920	Rialto Theatre is opened at 424-426 West Main by Boston Campbell and Babe Peebles.
1921	Denison's population estimated at 24,930
1921	Denison Lions Club organized.
November 1, 1921	Katy Hospital opens to serve Katy employees and family members.
1922	W.J. Smith Wood Preserving Plant begins operation to serve the MKT Railroad and related businesses.
July 1922	In Denison, Railroad Shopmen's Strike of 1922 focuses on MKT Railroad. Martial law is declared, effective July 26 at 5 A.M. Texas National Guards arrive July 25, camp in Forest Park. A total of 536 guardsmen would occupy Denison during the strike. As a result of strike, Katy's locomotive shops will move to Waco. Impact on Denison will be devastating with population decreasing from 17,000 to 13,500.
1924	Denison Rod & Gun Club building burns.
1924	New clubhouse for Elks Lodge is constructed at 301 West Gandy Street.
October 1, 1924	Hotel Simpson (later Hotel Denison) opens.

October 14, 1924	Harry Houdini is a guest at the Hotel Simpson, immediately following its opening.
1925	XXI Club abandons their clubhouse due to subsoil conditions that have made the structure unsafe.
1925	Mercy Hospital opens at 1030 W. Munson under the direction of Dr. Roscoe C. Riddle. Opened in response to the need to serve Black residents of Denison and surrounding communities.
1926	Southside Fire Station is closed once the new viaduct is built.
1926	Denison boasts 1,873 pounds of police force, claiming the heaviest police squad of any city in Texas. The heaviest policeman wis T.W. Price at 302 pounds and the lightest is Bruck Jay, desk sergeant, at 135 pounds.
March 1927	Terrell High School established. Named in honor of A. H. Terrell. W. R. Wims was first principal.
1929	Denison Jaycees chartered.
1929	Kraft-Phenix Cheese Company makes Denison headquarters for Southwestern Division.
1929	The first full-time band director is employed in Denison High School.
February 1929	Rialto Theater switches to sound.
1930	Denison's population estimated at 13,850.
1931	Red River free bridge opens.
1932	A Ford V-8 patrol car is purchased for the Denison Police Department.
1933	Denison Veterans of Foreign Wars chartered.

1933	Land purchase approved ($5,000) for construction of Loy Park.
November 22, 1935	Junior Alpha Delphi Club, with WPA help, opens first Denison public library. XXI Club donates its circulating library.
1936	Denison's population is 13,850 residents and there are 460 businesses in the city.
1936	Auditorium, mechanical arts shop, and classrooms added to Terrell High School.
1936	President Franklin D. Roosevelt visits Denison on his Texas Centennial tour. Accompanied by Eleanor Roosevelt, Governor and Mrs. James V. Allred, and U.S. Rep. Sam Rayburn.
August 1936	Denison City Hall constructed in the 100 block of West Main Street. City offices and Police Department relocate to the new building.
September 15, 1936	Citywide referendum approves Denison Public Library funding by City of Denison.
1937	B. McDaniel becomes superintendent of Denison schools.
1937	Denison teachers start receiving their wages on a twelve-month basis.
1938	Denison Dam on Red River authorized by Congress.
1938	Denison schools buy their first school bus.
1938	Architect Donald Mayes designs his first residence in Denison at 1103 W. Walker for Carl W. Wilson Sr. and Virginia Wilson.
January 12, 1938	The Denison Police Department becomes one of the first in the state to have two-way radio service.

1938-1939	Methodist Episcopal Church, North (known as First Methodist) merges with Methodist Episcopal Church, South (known as Waples Methodist).
1939	Historic Denison High School receives a big new auditorium, built by the Public Works Administration.
1939	WPA Federal Writers Project issues *The Denison Guide*.
1939	Funds allocated for construction of Denison Dam.
1941	R.D. Beirne Trust is created.
August 1941	Perrin Air Force Base Opens. First basic flying school put into operation following Japanese bombing at Pearl Harbor. More than 10,000 flying students received their training before it was deactivated in November, 1946.
1941	Denison schools employ first full-time nurse.
1942	Denison Dam closed; lake begins filling.
February 23, 1942	Perrin Field dedicated with fitting ceremonies. Named after Lt. Col. Elmer D. Perrin, a native of Boerne, Texas, who had been killed in a plane crash in Baltimore on June 21, 1941.
1943	First married women teachers in Denison are employed under Trustees' policies.
1943	W.B. Munson Foundation is created.
1944	Butane gas explosion claims thirteen lives in Denison.
July 1, 1944	Denison Dam formally dedicated.
September 1, 1945	Madonna Hospital opens after extensive remodeling.

April 20, 1946	Gen. Dwight D. Eisenhower makes first return trip to Denison, city of his birth. 50,000 attend his speech in Forest Park.
1947	Ballard Biscuits opens plant in Denison. Purchased by Pillsbury Mills March 25, 1951. Deed filed June 15, 1951.
1947	Mission Revival–style First Christian Church at 800 W. Woodard demolished.
1947	Twin City Drive-In Theater opened by C. D. Leon as county's first drive-in theater; located between Sherman and Denison.
May 30, 1947	A new 170-foot radio tower is completed behind the police station in the 100 block of West Main. All work is done by local man George Clark and for many years the tower is called Borum's Tower after Police Chief Borum.
September 1947	Celebration of 75th Birthday (Diamond Jubilee) of Denison.
1948	Architect Donald Mayes opens office in Denison.
1948	Bachelor's degree is required for all Denison teachers.
1948	Sherman-Denison Twins win Big State League baseball pennant.
February 1948	Hubbard Furniture Company, 130 West Main, founded.
August 25, 1948	Rialto site of world premiere of *Red River*.
November 1948	Star Theater remodeled and renamed the State Theater.
December 31, 1948	Last interurban rail service run in Texas, from Denison to Dallas.
1949	The first business manager is employed for the Denison school system.
January 21, 1949	Kraft Foods closes permanently.

February 22, 1949	Levi-Strauss plant begins Denison operation.
April 25, 1949	Public Library moves to basement of Barrett Building in preparation for construction of a new building.
October 17, 1949	Excavation work begins for new Denison Fire Station. Christening December 23.
August 7, 1949	Safeway purchases land at corner of Mirick and 500 West Chestnut for new supermarket. It was constructed in 1950-51. Formal opening June 4, 1951.
1950	Denison Public Library desegregated.
1950	Edgehill Addition, Denison, plat designed by architect Donald Mayes.
1950	Denison Public Library. The library opens in its new building in January 1950. The architects are Preston Geren Sr. and Preston Geren Jr.
1950	Nathan Crouch Appliance Store opens at 220 West Main, March 19, 1950. Moved to 331 West Main March 20, 1953.
1950	New Central Fire Station, clad in Austin Stone, is built at a cost of $38,142.17 at 700 West Chestnut.
March 26, 1950	New four-lane Highway 75 [Texoma Parkway] officially opens between Denison and Sherman.
May 1950	Denison Little League founded.
May 21, 1950	New Denison Public Library Opens with Sam Rayburn as speaker.
June 27, 1950	First major strike in the history of Denison Cotton Mill takes place. Ends May 9, 1951.
September 1950	St. Xavier's Academy celebrates its Diamond Jubilee.

October 1, 1950	Denison Mattress Company celebrates Golden Anniversary.
February 1, 1951	Denison votes 8 to 1 to separate schools from city government.
February 23, 1951	Southside Fire Station is reactivated with two firemen on duty.
September 5, 1951	Work nearing completion on expansion of both Katy and Madonna hospitals.
April 9, 1952	Denison gets first earthquake.
June 22, 1952	Gen. Dwight D. Eisenhower visits Denison.
July 1952	Perrin Field designated a permanent U.S. Air Force installation and its name changed to Perrin Air Force Base.
September 23, 1952	School bond election carries by more than 4 to 1.
November 5, 1952	Dwight D. Eisenhower elected U.S. President.
1953	Minnie M. Jones Trust created.
1953	Junior high school program is inaugurated in Denison.
June 19, 1953	Mr. and Mrs. Charles Logan buy the stock of Walter Jennings music department and open Logan's Music at 116 S. Barrett Avenue.
September 8, 1953	First junior high opens, in Historic Denison High School.
September 13, 1953	Citizens National Bank opens drive-in bank.
1954	Land purchased for new Senior High School on Mirick and clearing begun. School formally accepted May 23, 1954.

1954	Leeper/Security Building at 331 West Main Street, once the tallest building in North Texas, is condemned as a safety hazard and removed by the Interstate Wrecking Company of Dallas.
1954	The Denison Fire Department gains civil service status
May 23, 1954;	New DHS campus is officially accepted; occupied Sept. 1954.
November 26, 1954	Viaduct formally opens on Austin Avenue.
December 1, 1954	First dirt turned in dial telephone plant of Southwestern Bell, at corner of Mirick Avenue and Crawford Street.
December 12, 1954	New sewage treatment plan put in operation.
1955	Founding of Denison Service League.
May 24, 1955	First dial telephone installed in City Hall.
1956	Hyde Park Elementary is built.
1956	Denison changes its form of city government, employing a city manager for the first time (David Harner).
June 1956	B. McDaniel retires as superintendent of schools. H. W. Goodgion succeeds him as superintendent of Denison schools.
1957	DISD Central Administration Building is completed.
May 8, 1957	New Lilley-Linn [Lilley-Ayers] Department Store building, 331 West Main Street, formally opens.
1958	Layne, Cotton Mill, and Hyde Park additions are annexed to City of Denison.
February 1958	Eisenhower Birthplace reopens after extensive restoration program.

June 1958	Historic MKT Depot Plaza made into a parking lot for employees.
June 1958	Study launched to explore possibility of Grayson County Junior College.
June 1958	Denison Fire Department installs the first tornado siren in the city.
September 1958	City of Denison bond issue of $4 million for ten-year improvement program passes.
Fall 1958	New First Baptist Church opens at Woodard and Mirick.
October 1958	The Armory of the 36th Signal Company of the Texas National Guard is dedicated in Denison.
March 3, 1959	First scholastic "letter" awards in nation made at 1954 DHS. Life magazine and NBC Television report event. Terrell High School gives similar awards later in same month.
1959	New Citizens National Bank under construction. Ford Building/Citizens National Bank at 231 West Main Street, remodeled in 1950. Demolished in 1959 to make way for a new bank designed by architect Donald Mayes.
1960	Denison Industrial Foundation established by Chamber of Commerce.
1960	West End Fire Station is opened at 2720 West Morton and equipped with a new Ford 750 G.P.M. Pumper. This is originally known as the Layne Station.
May 1960	St. Patrick's Catholic Church purchases St. Xavier's Academy from the Sisters of St. Mary of Namur, for $120,000.

July 1960	City Council passes the first limited-purpose ordinance enacted by a city in the state of Texas, giving the city control over planning, zoning, sanitation, and health in an area extending a mile beyond the corporate limits.
July 1960	Denison votes to allow liquor sales. First liquor stores open.
September 4, 1960	New Citizens National Bank building erected, designed by architect Donald Mayes.
1962	Dr. Martin Luther King, Jr. Park is created.
1962	Denison voters pass a $1.5 million bond program to erect new school buildings.
1963	Dr. and Mrs. Paul Pearce Memorial Foundation created.
1963	A $2 million bond issue is voted for construction of Grayson County Junior College.
1963	New Eisenhower Auditorium and classroom wing are completed at the Denison Senior High School on Mirick Avenue.
Fall 1963	Stair-step racial integration plan begins with the first grade of Denison ISD.
1963-64	Construction of first buildings at Grayson County College. First students to occupy buildings in September 1965.
1964	Golden Rule School consolidates with the Denison ISD.
1964	New $200,000 Mayes-designed branch office building is formally opened is completed and is one of the first sub-courthouse structures in the state of Texas.

January 12, 1964	Formal dedication of new auditorium, eight classrooms, and other features at Denison Senior High School on Mirick Avenue. General contractor is Danielson Construction Company.
September 8, 1964	Hughes Junior High School is occupied for the first time. It was named after F. B. Hughes. When B. McDaniel Junior High School closed in the 1980s, the Hughes School's name was changed to honor B. McDaniel, former school superintendent. Formally dedicated October 4, 1964.
1965	New Memorial Hospital opens as a 144-bed institution; succeeds old Katy Hospital; to become Texoma Medical Center.
July 1, 1965	Last MKT passenger train, ending 93 years of passenger service to Denison. The Texas Special arrived from Kansas City 8:50 a.m. and left for Dallas and the end of the line at 9:22 a.m. Brakeman from Muskogee, Okla., to Denison was Tobin Williams, grandson of P. H. Tobin, who was engineer on the first train into Denison in 1872. Engineer from Denison to Dallas today was Tom Penn, who served as fireman on the first Texas Special run out of Waco in 1915. This was Penn's last run prior to retirement.
July 11, 1965	Policy of full racial integration of all Denison schools is adopted by Denison School Board, under a "Freedom of Choice Plan." All school boundaries are abolished.
September 1, 1965	U.S. President Dwight David Eisenhower makes last visit to Denison, for dedication of Eisenhower Auditorium at the Denison High School on South Mirick Avenue.

September 7, 1965	First day of school in Denison with racial integration under "Freedom of Choice Plan." 261 African American students enrolled in formerly all-white schools, compared with 25 on the first day of school the year before. Only one school (Raynal Elementary) had an entirely white enrollment. Previously all-black schools had no white enrollment: Terrell Senior High, Terrell Junior High, Terrell Elementary, and Wims Elementary.
Fall 1965	Classes begin at the new Grayson County Junior College designed by Donald Mayes.
1965	Waples Methodist Church builds new $1 million church plant. Design is attributed to Mark Lemmon.
1966	Denison's population is 26,000 and contains just under 600 businesses.
1966	Barrett's Drug Building, 523 West Main Street, Denison. Formerly a bus station with cafe. Donald Mayes created the current façade, with horizontal row of low concrete arches, high windows, and neon signage.
1966	Denison Public Library remodeling completed early in 1966. Donald Mayes designed the mezzanine addition.
December 1966	Founding of Downtown Denison Inc. Late December or early January 1967.
June 25, 1967	First Presbyterian Church, 400 West Gandy at North Burnett Avenue, Denison. Sanctuary, steeple, and education area were designed by Donald Mayes. The church's building chairman was W. E. Wilcox. The design for the stained-glass steeple was inspired by a chunky stained-glass candle holder the architect owned.

Formal dedication was held on June 25, 1967. This was Donald Mayes' last project.

1967	Main Street Serpentine Configuration, 200, 300 and 400 Blocks of West Main Street, Denison. General concept for the Serpentine was proposed publicly by Dallas urban consultant Marvin Springer in January 1966. A garden-like atmosphere was to be created through the use of curved sidewalks and routing for vehicular traffic, landscaped plots through each block, ornamented benches for rest stops, added crosswalks, and parking lots on Woodard and Chestnut streets behind Main Street businesses. January 1967 saw further public discussion of revisions of Marvin Springer's plans for Main Street Serpentine.
1968	Serpentine configuration installed in 200, 300, and 400 blocks of West Main Street.
1968	St. Xavier's Academy closes.
November 13, 1968	City Council adopts Resolution 707 adopting the newly rediscovered 1873 Denison Flag design.
October 16, 1968	*Denison Herald* special edition backs "Come Alive and Modernize" project which will add 500 parking spaces and eliminate "unsightly buildings."
1969	St. Xavier's Academy is demolished.
March 28, 1969	Death of President Dwight D. Eisenhower.
1970-71	Interfirst Bank demolishes the Beaux Arts–style State National Bank Building, constructed around 1893, replacing it with a large three-story white marble structure.
July 30, 1971	Perrin Air Force Base closes. This results in 2,000 military and civil service employees transferred from city.

1972	Woodmen of the World Building at 201 West Woodard destroyed by fire.
January 1, 1972	Denison Fire Department takes over ambulance services from local funeral homes. The first vehicle used is red van donated by Johnson-Moore Funeral Home.
June 26–July 1, 1972	Centennial Celebration, Denison, Texas (1872–1972)
1975	Major Denison Public Library expansion is completed. This addition was designed by Ralph Covington. At this time the Rusk Avenue entrance was closed, and the main entrance shifted to Gandy Street.
1975	Present Central Fire Station is constructed on the site of the 1950 structure.
1976	Citizens National Bank by architect Donald Mayes remodeled, facade altered.
1976	Memorial Hospital name changes to Texoma Medical Center.
1977	Denison Cotton Mill closes its doors after decades of declining business.
1978	Clara Blackford and Aubrey W. Smith Foundation is created.
1980s	Johns-Manville plant closes.
1980	Thelma Braun and Bocklett Family Foundation created.
1981	Denison Arts Council incorporated.
1981	Hotel-Motel Occupancy Tax imposed in Denison.
1981	Peter Phillips, an employee of the City of Denison, prepares survey of Downtown Denison's historic buildings.

October 19,1981	Denison Cotton Mill burns in spectacular fire.
May 31, 1983	MKT Depot and adjoining property is traded for Safeway Building in 500 block West Chestnut Street. MWM Investments (led by C. J. McManus, with his two sons Paul and C. J. Jr.; and Robert D. Wilson of Dallas) now owns land between Main and Woodard streets, and between Woodard and Gandy streets. This includes the Katy Depot, the parking lot in front, the old REA Express building, buildings north of the Depot to Gandy Street, and property east of the current Katy offices between Main and Chestnut. In the trade, MWM also acquired an option to lease property east of the depot between the first and second Katy tracks.
	On hand for the announcement were Mayor Ronnie Cole, David Bayless Sr., Pete Phillips, community development officer for the city; Larry Evans; and other city leaders.
	McManus said he hopes to restore the depot and the entrance parkway, which at one time included a fishpond; shops, offices, a restaurant, etc., may be added. A *Denison Herald* editorial lauded the plan, stating, "It can be a potential tourist attraction. Other Texas cities, notably Galveston, have turned these landmarks into drawing cards. There is no reason Denison cannot do the same."
June 9, 1983	Rialto is refurbished and dedicated.
September 1983	Denison Commercial Historic District application submitted to National Register of Historic Places, U.S. Department of the Interior. 51 percent of the buildings in the district are identified as "contributing" buildings. Identified as the "major historic buildings which characterize the district" are MKT Depot, Travelers Hotel, Historic Denison High School, Waples-Platter

Building at 104 East Main, and A. R. Collins Block at 511-513 West Main.

October 1983	C. J. McManus and architect Kenneth A. Siegel address Denison Rotary Club on plans for restoration and development of MKT Depot.
1983-84	Chamber of Commerce Historic Affairs Committee defines "Old Town" district, a larger area than that included in the Denison Commercial Historic District. Boundaries are Morton Street on the north, the railroad tracks on the east, Morgan Street on the south, and Scullin Avenue on the west. Chamber of Commerce offers prizes for most-improved residential and commercial properties in the area. Low-interest loan program begins. City Council initiates citywide Neighborhood Improvement Program and "Alley Rally" clean up and "Litter Critter" trash pickups. Unfortunately, participation in the "Old Town Project" is limited.
1984	Denison wins state football championship.
1984	Denison Public Library is remodeled.
April 19, 1984	C. J. McManus announces public auction of MKT Depot, to take place May 24. [Later the date was changed to June 12.] He says he is taking this step to secure partners (developers) for restoration and reuse of the depot as a shopping mall, since he could not do the project alone.
May 24, 1984	Depot sold without auction to Presley Gardner and Gerald R. Chester, Dallas businessmen. McManus remains a partner in the venture. The group plans renovation and development of restaurants, shops, offices, and a museum. Project architect is Brent Byers of Corgan Associates Architects of Dallas. Mayor Ronnie Cole on hand for the transfer.

June 26, 1984	Plans announced to create plaza in front of MKT Depot. Cost estimated at over $200,000. A committee from the Chamber is formed to develop master plan for the plaza, explore funding possibilities, and raise money for the park construction. Developers hope money could come from local foundations, City Hall, and private sources. Mayor sees no problems.
July 17, 1984	City of Denison assures local foundations that Depot Plaza Park will be maintained by the City, that the city would be dispersing agent for any funds collected, and that the project is tax-exempt.
August 28, 1984	City of Denison agrees to spend $81,000 on improvements to 100 block of West Main Street when citizens have raised $100,000 for renovation of Katy Plaza Park.
November 6, 1984	Frank Waltz, former Katy clerk, makes first private contribution to Katy Plaza Park project.
1985	Elias and Hannah Regensburger Foundation is created.
1985	Denison requests designation as a Texas Main Street city, but is turned down.
May 23, 1985	MKT Railroad is sold to Union Pacific.
July 23, 1985	City begins Main Street beautification "designed to give the [100] block a turn-of-the-century appearance to tie in with the renovated Katy Depot and Katy Plaza Park: new sidewalks, brick pavers, period lampposts, benches, trees, and brick pedestrian crossings at Austin and Houston avenues.
1986	Luella Kemper Trust is created.
May 24, 1986	Renovated Katy Plaza Park dedicated with much hoopla. Leasing of space in Depot continues.

May 30, 1986	Last day of classes for McDaniel Junior High School (Historic DHS).
December 14, 1986	In Katy Plaza Park, dedication of statue honoring 150th anniversary of Texas Independence.
1987	First Reba McEntire concert.
February 22, 1987	Announcement that three-block Main Street serpentine will be removed, and property owners will pay for it. Leaders include Charles Green, Herman Ringler, C. J. McManus, David Bayless Sr., and Norman Gordon. "The community sees the renovation project as a necessary tool for revitalizing the downtown shopping district," the *Denison Herald* reports. Controversy ensues.
Spring 1987	Job cuts announced by Union Pacific.
August 16, 1987	Katy Railroad Historical Museum will be housed at Katy Depot in Denison. Board: Allen Crenshaw, Pat Coughlin, Wally Decker, Chris Yoder, Jim O'Brien.
September 4, 1987	Union Pacific Railroad makes offer to City of Denison if latter will drop its opposition to UP's acquisition of MKT Railroad. UP offers, among other things, to give the City the old Safeway building on Chestnut Street; and incentives for economic development. A similar settlement has been reached with another Katy stronghold, the city of Parsons, Kansas.
November 10, 1987	Texas Main Street Program director, Anice Read of the Texas Historical Commission, visits Denison. Asked which was more important, industrial recruiting or downtown development, Read noted that a shabby downtown makes it hard to attract industry.
November 26, 1987	Terms of settlement between Union Pacific Railroad and City of Denison announced.

1988	Munson Center opens at Grayson County College. Contains the T.V. Munson Memorial Vineyard which boasts 3 acres of various grapes, including over 65 of the original varieties bred by T.V. Munson.
1988	Denison Main Street Program begun as a local initiative.
March 1988	Main Street Advisory Board created.
May 16, 1988	Sale of MKT Railroad to Union Pacific is approved by ICC. Over 600 jobs are relocated from the city with many MKT buildings remaining vacant.
October 1988	Texas Historical Commission (THC) names Denison a Main Street USA city.
1989	Denison's population is 24,234 with 427 businesses.
December 23, 1989	Disastrous fire in 300 block West Main takes life of a Denison fireman and destroys three buildings: Beall's Department Store, Denison Optical Center (owned by Dr. John Thomson), and the old Kingston Drug Store. Fire departments of Sherman, Pottsboro, Howe, Anna, Van Alstyne, Colbert, and Whitewright are called in to help fight the fire in freezing temperatures. An 18-year veteran of the Denison Fire Department, T. O. Fulce, is killed in the blaze. This is the first fireman killed in Denison since 1900. His family sues Beall's owners.
1990	Denison's population is 21,505.
May 14, 1990	Cole and Smithen, a Denison construction company, begins removal of Main Street serpentine. The work is paid for by property owners.
1991	W. J. Smith Wood Preserving Company closes.

1995	New Hopewell Baptist Church at 601 West Bond is dedicated.
July 1, 1996	Denison Heritage Inc. (DHI) is founded "to preserve the heritage and enhance the artistic and cultural life of Denison and Grayson County."
September 1997	DHI mounts exhibit at Denison Public Library commemorating Denison's 125th Birthday.
2000	Denison's population is 22,773.
2000	Former Terrell High School building demolished.
November 7, 2006	Election Day. Grayson County College bond issue passes by two votes.
January 30, 2007	Bids received for demolition of Historic DHS.
March 6, 2007	City Council awards bid for demolition of Historic DHS. Neighbors Demolition bid is $495,716, "subject to the Mayor and staff addressing the noise and dust control issues to their satisfaction." Wright Group is awarded $25,000 to monitor asbestos abatement and $10,000 for bid specs. Thus the total is $531,156. The demolition contractor is permitted to salvage and resell all portions of the building, including clock tower.
January 3, 2007	Universal Health Services completes acquisition of Texoma Medical Center
2007	Texoma Health Foundation is created.
2008	Old Hopewell Baptist Church is demolished after remaining empty for more than a decade. The site became the location of Terrell-Griggs-Marshall Legacy Park.

2009	New Texoma Medical Center is complete at a cost of $135 million
June 2009	Central Fire Station is remodeled with a new stucco exterior. Kitchen upgrades are also accomplished at this time.
2010	Denison's population is 22,682.
March 30, 2017	Holly Jenkins becomes the first female sergeant in the history of the Denison Police Department.
March 8, 2018	New TMC ER and $50 million expansion opens including new level 2 trauma center and neonatal ICU.
August 18, 2018	Texoma Health Foundation Park opens to the public. The park consists of 80 acres and cost $16 million to build.
September 4, 2018	Denison opens new City Hall at 300 West Main Street at cost of $3.5 million.
May 2019	New living quarters are constructed at the West Side Fire Station for $600,000. The former building is demolished.
October 9, 2019	300 block is damaged by fire.
December 18, 2019	Katy Trail groundbreaking.
2020	Denison's population is 24,479.
January 27, 2021	First phase of D3 project breaks ground. Anticipated cost is $16.4 million.
November 1, 2021	First phase of D3 is complete and portion of Chestnut and Houston is reopened.
December 31, 2021	A fireworks show lights up downtown Denison as the city officially kicked of the Sesquicentennial Celebration.

Figure 244 The Denison Herald building at the corner of Woodard Street and Burnett Avenue. The Herald printed many of the base material used for different topics in this publication. As Denison's oldest newspaper, the Herald had unparalleled access to our city's history and often displayed that rich history in special editions, extras, and news stories. Although no longer in Denison, the work completed by so many at the esteemed newspaper still shines and allows a new generation to learn about our history like never before.

Denison Service League
Charter Members

Dolores Banner	Mary Emma Marsico
Virginia Bauder	Ruth Marsico
Lois Bond	Angie Martin
Helen Blassingame	Blanche Martin
Lee Ann Bratteli	Mac Martyn
Mavis Bryant	Ann Massey
Lucille Campbell	Ruth McFarling
Rena Chesnutt	Jane McKinney
Laraine Clayton	Genie Miller
Kyra Clift	Werdna Morrison
Dorothy Conatser	Betsy Munson
Blanche Conn	Martha Munson
Roy Dossey	Verda Murray
Winston Crawford	Betty Otis
Louise Freeman	Carolyn Ozment
Gladys Gleckler	Annie Peterson
Helen Hewlett	Geraldine Prather
Marian Jones	Mabry Thomson
Nelle Jones	O'Tera Treece
Henri Leslie	Doll Watson
Mary Levin	Becky Wright
Hazel Loy	Donna Zink

VFW
Charter Members

J. Clayton Evans

Tom E. Flowers

H.B. Dodge

Joe D. May

J.W. Donald

Ralph Geisenhoner

George Whitney

Prue E. Compton

James M. Henderson

Will L. Hoket

Carl Akers

W.T. Lingo

Joe Newcomb

Gus Johnson

Jim C. May

Oscar Brown

John C. Thompson

Roy McDaniel

E. O. Davis

Earl A. Gary

Leo T. McMillan

Bennett Hogue

Ernest Kimbrell

Clifton C. Gaskill

VFW Ladies Auxiliary
Charter Members

Callie Akers

Lillian Bunn

Myrtle Casebolt

Genevieve Champion

H. C. Dodge

Eddie Mae Dotson

Viola Donald

Eva Mae Elms

Mildred Evans

Geneva Flowers

Bertha Gaskill

Rachel Henderson

Velma Hoket

Bertha Houlihan

Beatrice Johns

Athie May

Inez May

Georgia Monk

Iva Napier

Ruth Newcomb

Mayme Thomason

American Legion
Charter Members

Howard C. Baird
LeRoy Barton
C.C. Beasley
Oscar Brown
Walter T. Brown
J.A. Burrows
Frank B. Clark
Charles Cole
Eugene B. Cole
James S. Collet
Ralph Corbett
Francis W. Cowell
Ruben C. Davis
Lonnie Dumas
Lee T. Eastham
C.R. Eggleston
A.P. Elkert
C.M. Esler
A.L. Fleming
Floyd E. Ford
Ralph Geisenhoner
D.K. Glass
Sydney M. Goldman
Charles A. Harris
Oliver W. Hayes
R.D. Henderson
William Higginson
W.W. Hill
W.C. Bill Jackson
Gus Johnson
Clyde Jones
Daniel Kemper
Russell Lacy
R.K. LaLonde

F.H. Lane
Abner L. Lewis
Phillip Lingle
Lewis L. Loy
A.A. McCarty
Jesse O. Maxwell
F.R. Mock
W.J. Moffitt
W.L. Montgomery
Thomas A. Moodie
Lawrence A. Moss
John J. Murphy
Arthur W. Payton
Leo A. Pierce
Lingo Platter
Francis W. Powell
Charlie Reasonover
Farley Reasonover
Tull O. Richardson
E.C. Robinson
Oswell J. Sanders
Clarence Scott
Ira F. Sproule
Clyde Stewart
Lonnie Stewart
Ewell Stroach
Britton Swain
H.W. Torian
J.H. Upshaw
John W. Weaver
R.W. Wells
James P. White
Wilber J. Winkler
W.R. Woods

Lions Club
Charter Members

H. A. Newsom	Ben W. Grimmett
E. M. Beazley	E.V. Johnson
J.T. Scott	J.J. Loy
Dr. W.A. Lee	A.P. Linn
Rev R.E. Boykin	C.D. Kingston
S.E. Allen	B.F. Shepherd
Dr. R.E. Truly	W.J. Christian
Mayor W. F. Weaver	Roy B. Hotchkiss
W. D. Collins	Dr. J.T. Long
Burr Weaver	Rev. T.L. Hufstutler
H.H. Cummins	W.A. Badgett
Roy E. Kentz	Roy D. Henderson
S. Karchmer	O.R. Nicholson
W.G. Langston	Chas. C. Parrish
J.W. Weaver	W.A. Thompson
Dr. H.T. Walker	R.O. Simonson
R.W. Gillin	W.F. Jennings
Hugh B. Thompson	R.M. Gray

Rotary Club
Charter Members

H.C. Platter	J.E. Morris
P.A. Rogers	H.L. Piner
H.E. Ellis	R. M. Finley
F.B. Williford	P.H. Tobin
A.G. Pierce	F.B. Hughes
N.C. Calvert	J.G. Ellis Jr.
A.S. Johnson	A.R. Meador
Dewitt Jones	J.T. Owen
F.H. Kofeldt	F.S. Fisher
W.E. Brown	W.H. Halton
W.S. Hibbard	J.F. Tinsman
R.S. Legate	J.B. McLeod
J.E. Aubrey	R.H. Peter
H. Guy Alexander	P.R. Knickerbocker
W.B. Munson Sr.	J.L. Greer
W.B. Munson Jr.	W.M. Esler
F. A. Glackin	W.B. Balance
J.S. Knaur	J.R. Handy
C.B. Sullenberger	G.W. Pitman
H.W. Lingo	D.D. Crawford
W.N. King	R. B. Ellis
H.E. Pearce	J.M. Crumpton
J.W. Madden	Walter P. Lebrecht
Fred Marcus	
W.H. Hall	
G. O. Morgan	

City of Denison Mayors

Lewis S. Owings 1872-1873

S.A. Cook 1873

Major Frank Shrader 1873-1874

Edward Perry 1874-1875

W. H. Winn 1875-1876

Major Robert M. Grubbs 1877-1878

W.M. Peck 1879-1881

W.B. Boss 1881-1884

Dr. T.B. Hanna 1884-1885

Sam Hanna 1886-1887

Harrison Tone 1888-1893

Jesse D. Yocum 1893-1896

Louis Lebrecht 1896-1900

John S. Knaur 1900-1902

S.C. Kennedy 1902-1903

Alexander W. Acheson 1904-1906

S.C. Kennedy 1906-1907

Alexander W. Acheson 1907-1913

C.T. McElvaney 1913-1917

Fleming G. Coleman 1917-1921

William F. Weaver 1921-1923

Walter S. Hibbard 1923-1929

Clarence Scott 1929-1941

Dr. T. J. Long 1941-1943

W.L. "Bill" Ashburn 1943-1947

W.E. Marsico 1947-1949

Harry Glidden 1949-1951

A.C. Casey 1951-1953

Harry Glidden 1953-1956

Ernest J. Lilley 1956-1958

Albert Martin 1958-1960

Ralph Porter 1960-1961

Jack Atkins 1961-1962

John H. Anderson 1962-1963

W. Worth Campbell 1963-1966

Joe W. Gay 1966-1969

Robert L. Cherry 1969-1972

Jerdy Gary 1972-1976

Tobin Williams 1976-1977

Jack B. Lilley 1977-1978

Jerry Culpepper 1978-1982

Scott Smith 1982-1983

Ronnie Cole 1983-1988

William "Ben" Munson IV 1988-1994

Wayne Cabanasis 1994-1999

Bill Lindsay 1999-2006

Robert Brady 2006-2012

Jared Johnson 2012-2018

Janet Gott 2018-

Figure 245 The Denison Municipal building in the 100 block of West Main Street, 1968.

City of Denison
Fire Chiefs

Bob Fisher 1876-mid-1880's

Phil Ledrick 1876-1878

W.M. Yokum mid-1880's-1890

Vic Morefield 1890-1913 (Bill Linden served for two years during

Morefield's term)

C. Cooper April 1913-1932

O.L. Garvin 1932-1935

Pat Lowe 1935-July 1, 1955

George L. Cravens 1955-September 1985

Bill Taylor 1985-1986

Dave West June 1986-Spetmeber 1988

Bill Taylor December 1, 1988-April 1, 2005

Gordan Weger June 1, 2005-October 31, 2015

Gregg Lloyd April 1, 2016-September 20, 2021

Kenneth Jacks September 21, 2021-January 1, 2022 (Interim Chief)

Kenneth Jacks January 2, 2022-

Figure 246 Denison's Central Fire Station and equipment, ca. 1895.

City of Denison Police Chiefs

Sheriff Red Hall-1872

City Marshal J.C. McDowell-1873

Thomas D. Farmer 1873-1874

City Marshal G.L. Patrick 1875-1877

City Marshal William Hardwick-1877-1880

City Marshal Bud East 1880-1883

City Marshal Allen G. Hall 1883-1885

City Marshal Wyatt Thomas Cutler 1885-1888

City Marshal Ed James-1889-1894

City Marshal H. Hackney 1895-1896

City Marshal John James 1898-1905

Chief H.M. Wisdom-1908-April 1911

Richard "Dick" Wagner April 1911

W.H. Hughes April 1917

J.W. Russell 1921-April 1923

W.E. Bevers April 1923-February 1924

William Whittle February 1924-April 1925

J. Gordon Nix April 1925-September 1928

J.R. Dishner September 1928-April 1941

Paul S. Borum April 1941-May1949

William Leland Miller May 1949-September 1950

Louis Carlat September 1950-April 1951

Paul S. Borum April 1951-December 1974

Edwin E. Eubank January 1975-February 1985

Clyde W. Nave February 1985-May 31, 1991

Jimmy A. Lovell (Interim Chief) June 1991-July 1991

Jimmy Lovell July 1991-August 2011

Joe Clapp (Interim Chief) September 1, 2011-August 31, 2011

Johnnie (Jay) C. Burch September 2011-February 2019

Danny P. Neumann (Interim Chief) March 2019-July 2019

Michael Gudgel July 2019-

Figure 247 The Denison Police Department above, ca. 1895 and below, ca. 1934.

City of Denison
City Managers

David Harner January 1957-February 1962

W.L. "Bill" Somers 1963-1965

John C. Dodson 1966-1967

Everett M. Delashmutt 1967-1971

David Harner 1971-1976

C.J. Griggs 1977-1977

Voin R. Campbell 1978-1979

B.R. "Skipper" Wallace 1980-1982

Thomas "Tom" E. Hart 1982-1983

Jim Stiff 1983-1987

Larry Cruise May 1987-February 2011

Robert Hanna March 2011-October 2015

Judson Rex October 2015-December 2020

Bobby Atteberry (Interim) December 2020-September 2021

Greg Smith September 2021- February 2022

Bobby Atteberry February 2022-

Figure 248 The Hopewell Baptist Church's Men's Bible Class, 1923.

Denison Alumni Association
Distinguished Alumni

1998

Linus Wright, Class of 1944

1999

Brigadier General (Ret.) Larry D. Lessly, Class of 1960

2000

Dr. Doak Blassingame, M.D., Class of 1928

Ann Sproule Rowland, Class of 1947

Frank Darnell, Class of 1938

Lola Mae Hensley Stevens, Class of 1924

Buddy Wagner, NSN, Class of 1937

District Judge (Ret.) R.C. Vaughan, Class of 1931

2001

Claud Easterly, Class of 1925 (posthumously)

John Krattiger, Class of 1933 (posthumously)

Dr. Kendall Ray Phillips, Class of 1987

Dr. Dorothy Hawkins Rushing, Class of 1942

Noel D. Wall, Class of 1957

2002

Clora Bryant, Class of 1943, Terrell High School

Ray Clymer, Class of 1942

2003

Danna Burns Harvey, Class of 1960

Donald Mayes, Class of 1932 (posthumously)

Donna Hord Hunt, Class of 1953

Dr. Bill L. Jacobs, Class of 1947

Bob Cherry, Class of 1942

2004

Dr. Claud H. Organ Jr., MD, Class of 1944, Terrell High School

Dr. Judith Thomas, Ph.D., Class of 1956

Dr. Don Rice, Class of 1952

Dr. Jerome L. Duggan, Ph.D., Class of 1952

2005

David Bryant, Class of 1969

Jack Hicks, Class of 1947

Jack Lilley, Class of 1948

Gil A. "Sonny" Stricklin, Class of 1953

Dr. Gaylon Don Taylor Jr., Class of 1978

Dr. Frances Cornell Willis, Class of 1935

2006

Federal Judge Paul Brown, Class of 1943

Rev. Hulen L. Jackson, Class of 1931

William "Bill" Martin, Class of 1959

Dr. Robert Noe, Ph.D, Class of 1948

Dr. Phyllis Wright Shaw, Ph.D, Class of 1958

2007

Dr. C.J. Ransom, Ph.D, Class of 1958

Tom Murray, Class of 1957

John Hoover, Class of 1956

2008

Edmond Ellis, Class of 1957

County Judge (Ret.) Horace Groff, Class of 1958

Dr. Linda Chapman Medearis, Class of 1957

Judith Waldine Trim Nevil, Class of 1958

2009

Raymond Doak Bishop, Class of 1967

Gregory T. Davis, Class of 1975

Philip Hurley, Class of 1969

Don Lummus, Class of 1954

David M. Munson, Class of 1945

Dr. Don Russell, Class of 1966

2010

Carl E. Bilderback, Class of 1954

Joseph Duggan, Class of 1949 (posthumously)

Jim Hightower, Class of 1961

Emily C. Jones, Class of 1967 (posthumously)

Drewey D. McKnight Jr., Class of 1942, Terrell High School

2011

Robert S. Beckham Jr., Class of 1960

2012

Jeff B. Powell, Class of 1981

Dr. Rashona Thomas, Class of 1991

2013

Ross Stoddard III, Class of 1968

Bredette (B.C.) Thomas, Class of 1960

2014

Vernon Finis Beckham, Class of

2015

Tom Anderson, Class of 1959

David Burton, Class of 1969

Dr. Robert McCarley, Class of 1948

Vaughn Oliver, Class of 1959

2016

Keith W. Hubbard Sr., Class of 1937

Harold La Mont Epperson-Thompson, Class of 1995

2017

Dr. Martha Womack Haun, Class of 1960

Tim Murray, Class of 1959

Dr. Robert Christopher Cherry, Class of 1992

2018

Sharon Scott, Class of 1967

2019

John Mark Jennings, Class of 2019

2020

No awards due to COVID-19 pandemic

2021

Major Jewel Butler, Class of 1940, Terrell High School

(posthumously)

Figure 249 An aerial view of Denison High School on Mirick Avenue, ca. 1960.

Denison Alumni Association
Sports Hall of Fame

1998

Jim Freeman, Class of 1960

1999

Marvin J. Vincent, Class of 1949

2000

Kenneth Ellis Kinnamon, Class of 1951

Edwina Leuty Bates, Class of 1948

Phil Shaffer, Class of 1962

Charlie Jackson, Class of 1946

Bill Ashburn, Class of 1952

2001

Ralph Elliott, Class of 1969 (posthumously)

Glen Land, Class of 1948

Bob Leach, Class of 1952

Roy Jackson, Class of 1948

Fred Washington, Class of 1984 (posthumously)

2002

Mike Jordan, Class of 1963 (posthumously)

Howard Minor, Class of 1953

Oliver Jackson, Class of 1938

2003

Edward Butler, Class of 1949, Terrell High School

2004

Melvin Brown, Class of 1949

2005

Roy Butch Goodman Jr., Class of 1956

2006

Bill Lane, Class of 1951

Coach Les Cranfill, DHS Coach 1946-1967 (posthumously)

2007

Erick Harper, Class of 1984

Coach Marty Criswell, DHS Coach 1981-1991

Tony Brown. Class of 1984 (posthumously)

Elmar Perry, Class of 1986

2008

Natalie Polk Cobb, Class of 1978

Aaron Jackson, Class of 1986

Coach M. M. Marshal, DHS Teacher and Tennis Coach

2009

David Ray Smith, Class of1962 (posthumously)

2010

Dr. Jerome Duggan, Class of 1952

2011

Fred A. Taylor, Class of 1938

2012

Edward Hicks, Class of 1942

Raymond Hicks, Class of1944

2013

Scott Marr, Class of 1988

Gregg Watson, Class of1979

2014

1984 State Championship Football Team

2015

Lance Lindsay, Class of 1990

Reggie Perry, Class of 1989

Eddie Savage, Class of 1951

2016

Mike Miller, Class of 1989

Coach Corky Bowling and 1961-62 Track Relay Team

2017

Reggie L. Hunt, Class of 1996

2018

Elaine King Recer, Class of 1990

1989/1990 Volleyball Team

2019

Erik Brown, Class of 1992

2020

No awards due to COVID-19 pandemic

2021

Aaron Hunt, Class of 1998

Vinny Rhodes, Class of 2004

Tifney Kelly, Class of 1995

Paul Fulton, Class of 1987

Dr. Will Voelzke, Class of 1994

Tyrell Buckner, Class of 1993

Lakisha Gentry, Class of 2001

Figure 250 The Denison High School football team, ca. 1927.

Denison Alumni Association
Lifetime Achievement Award

2005

Billy Bird Jackson, Class of 1942

Figure 251 William Billy Bird Jackson was the first deaf person to graduate from Denison High School. He was awarded the Lifetime Achievement Award for serving as a shining example of the ability of the human spirit to overcome hardships, handicaps, and challenges to become a treasured and productive member of his community.

Distinguished Educator Award

2012

Dr. Henry Scott

2013

Dr. William "Bill" Blankenship, Class of 1944

John Terry, Class of 1961

Nancy Robinson Terry, Class of 1962

2015

Dr. Carole Linsteadt-Richards, Class of 1959

2016

Jeanne Groff, Class of 1958

2017

Kathy Blankenship Dophied, Class of 1961

2018

Keith McBrayer

Sylvia McBrayer

2019

John Parker

2020

No awards due to COVID-19 pandemic

2021

Rachel Ramer (posthumously)

Katie Palmer (posthumously)

Lyndol Irby (posthumously)

Denison Chamber of Commerce President/Chair of the Board

P.J. Brennan-1912

W.J. Mathis-1913

H. Regensberger-1914

_____-1915

G.W. Pitman-1916

H.C. Platter-1917

P.H. Tobin-1918

B.J. Lindsay-1919

L.L. Shackelford-1920

L.L. Shackelford-1921

H. E. Pearce-1922

W.B. Munson Jr.-1923

W.B. Munson Jr.-1924

J. Lee Greer-1925

J. Lee Greer-1926

Julian C. Field-1927

Julian C. Field-1928

G.C. Knaur-1929

R.W. Stoddard-1930

W. G. Langston-1931

W. L. Peterson-1932

Ford Seale-1933

Verne Murray-1934

Verne Murray-1935

W.L. Ashburn Jr.-1936

J. Tom Suggs-1937

W.J. Smith-1938

Dr. T.J. Long-1939

Dr. T.J. Long-1940

J. Lee Greer-1941

H.B. Perryman-1942

F.O. Babcock-1943

W.T. Loomis-1944

W.T. Loomis-1945

R.Leighton McKinney Jr.-1946

George Stratton-1947

B.V. Hammond Jr.-1948

F. J. Killey-1949

A.J. Martin-1950

Fred Conn-1951

Ralph Porter-1952

Roy Dossey-1953

Charles H. Gullett-1954

Ben Munson III-1955

E. H. Young-1956

L.F. Massey-1597

J.D. Bond-1958

J.C. Conatser-1959

Frank Banner-1960

Jack Hesse-1961

W.F. Wilcox-1962

Ed Cox-1963

Joe W. Gay-1964

Frank Darnell-1965

Cleo Crittenden-1966

Gil Eggleston-1967

W.E. Winter-1968

Coy Stanphill-1969

Worth Campbell-1970

Charles Myers-1971

Jack Harriss-1972

J. Bryce Wiginton-1973

Mike S. Burton Jr.-1974

W. David Bayless Sr.-1975

Walter Goodenough-Mike Mayes-1976

Mike Mayes-1977

E.E. "Gene" Meier-1978

Jerdy Gary-1979

Ben Munson IV-1980

Garland Thornton-1981

W.H. "Bill" Harrison-1982

Roy L. McKinney III-1983

Ken Lovell-1984

Larry Evans-1985

Herman Ringler-1986

Don Harper-1987

Charles Green-1988

Wayne Cabaniss-1989

Robert Crawley-1990

Bob Vincent-1991

David Bayless Jr.-1992

Coy Stanphill-1993

Robby Roberts-1994

Harry Kirshman-1995

Steve Voelzke-1996

Dale Bonner-1997

Larry Landrum-1998

Ronnie Cole-1999

Dennis Reeves-2000

Mike Broyles-2001

Diana Williams-2002

Jerry Chapman-2003

Mark Edwards-2004

David MacMullen-2005

James Green-2006

Deborah Magouirk-2007

Ty Sweeney-2008

Wes King-2009

Elaine Burkhalter-2010

Terry Tombaugh-2011

Shelle Cassell-2012

Bob Taylor-2013

Paul Kisel-2014

Aaron Quarles-2015

Jennifer Reed-2016

Elaine Burkhalter-2017

Jason Taylor-2018

Bob Dickson-2019

Shane Hill-2020

Joey Gunn-2021

Dr. Molly Harris-2022

Denison Chamber of Commerce Secretary/Manager/CEO

J.E.T. Peters February 1922-August 1925

Interim Myrtle M. Riley August 1925-November 1925

Interim Dr. J.E. Aubrey November 1925-April 1926

C.W. Graham Jr. April 1926-October 1927

Interim Myrtle Riley-Beggs October 1927-December 1927

R.R. Walker January 1928-August 1929

R.G. Gresham September 1929-May 1933

None due to Great Depression June 1933-December 1934

Grady Walker January 1935-May 1935

Elliott McClung December 1935 – January 1940

Interim R.L. McKinney Jr. January 1940-February 1940

A.W. Long March 1940-December 1941

W.O. Harwell January 1942-June 1946

Freeman H. Carney July 1946-December 1948

Paul D. Marable January 1949-March 1951

Freeman H. Carney April 1951-April 1957

Bill Henderson April 1957-December 1958

Harry Cowan January 1959-May 1963

Jim Hardy June 1963-1979

Bruce Barton1979-1982

Michael M. Lawson1982-1983

Duane O'Neill 1983-February 1991

Interim Charles Green March 1991-December 1991

Charles Page January 1992-December 1995

Anna McKinney December 1995-October 2016

Interim Shelle Cassell October 2016-October 2017

Kenneth Higdon October 2017-June 2018

Diana Theall August 2018-

Made in the USA
Columbia, SC
29 March 2024

f3709c20-93bb-4560-8746-c47ca1776a5cR03